# The Witness as Educator

# The Witness as Educator

Reading W. G. Sebald, Aimé Césaire,
and Walt Whitman

DAVID T. HANSEN

Cover art (detail) from *Three Women in Church*; painting by Wilhelm Leibl, Hamburg Kunsthalle, 1882.

Published by State University of New York Press, Albany

© 2025 State University of New York

All rights reserved

Printed in the United States of America

No part of this book may be used or reproduced in any manner whatsoever without written permission. No part of this book may be stored in a retrieval system or transmitted in any form or by any means including electronic, electrostatic, magnetic tape, mechanical, photocopying, recording, or otherwise without the prior permission in writing of the publisher.

Links to third-party websites are provided as a convenience and for informational purposes only. They do not constitute an endorsement or an approval of any of the products, services, or opinions of the organization, companies, or individuals. SUNY Press bears no responsibility for the accuracy, legality, or content of a URL, the external website, or for that of subsequent websites.

EU GPSR Authorised Representative:
Logos Europe, 9 rue Nicolas Poussin, 17000, La Rochelle, France
contact@logoseurope.eu

For information, contact State University of New York Press, Albany, NY
www.sunypress.edu

### Library of Congress Cataloging-in-Publication Data

Name: Hansen, David T., 1952– author.
Title: The witness as educator : reading W. G. Sebald, Aimé Césaire, and Walt Whitman / David T. Hansen.
Description: Albany : State University of New York Press, [2025] | Includes bibliographical references and index.
Identifiers: LCCN 2024057617 | ISBN 9798855803495 (hardcover : alk. paper) | ISBN 9798855803501 (ebook) | ISBN 9798855803488 (pbk. : alk. paper)
Subjects: LCSH: Witnessing—Philosophy. | Truthfulness and falsehood.
Classification: LCC BD171 .H36 2025 | DDC 248/.5—dc23/eng/20250128
LC record available at https://lccn.loc.gov/2024057617

For Elaine

*Because of the sound I always hear in your hello*

I cannot be grasped in the here and now. For I reside just as much with the dead as with the unborn. Somewhat closer to the heart of creation than usual. But not nearly close enough.

—Paul Klee (epitaph at Schosshalde Cemetery, Bern, Switzerland; composed for his one-person exhibition at the Hans Goltz Gallery, Munich, 1920)

# Contents

Foreword ix
    *Rachel Wahl*

Preface xiii

Chapter 1. A Perspective on Bearing Witness    1

Chapter 2. W. G. Sebald: Rightful Trespass into the Lives of Others    35

Chapter 3. Aimé Césaire: Witnessing Transformation in Self and World    73

Chapter 4. Walt Whitman: Democracy, Remembrance, and the Witness    111

Chapter 5. Bearing Witness and Education    153

Acknowledgments 181

Notes 183

References 205

Name Index 215

Subject Index 219

# Foreword

When I first began reading this book and preparing its Foreword, a friend asked what I was working on. When I explained, he suggested that it would be far more efficient to submit the manuscript to ChatGPT and ask the artificial intelligence program to write the Foreword. I could give the AI parameters, he suggested gamely, and specify the aims and style in which I would like it to be written. Caught off guard by his suggestion, I struggled to explain why doing so would feel not just like a significant compromise of professional ethics but would also miss the point of the entire enterprise. I quickly began to feel as if I were defending not only why this book, and this foreword, could not be written by a robot, but also as if my entire profession may be on trial. I felt a need to articulate why human writing matters at all.

Hansen's masterful book can be understood as a profound and original answer to this question. It could be provided as stand-alone evidence of why it matters for a person, and not a robot, to convey experience. Should such a trial occur, I know whom to call as an expert witness—however much Hansen would decry the very idea of expertise in this realm, as well as reject this form of the word *witness* in relation to his work.

Most fundamentally, Hansen places front and center the human call to attend to our lives: to the people we encounter, especially, and also to the texture of moments that do not announce their grandeur but arrive and pass away in seeming banality. His is a supremely democratic faith in witnessing, fittingly for the three exemplary witnesses on whom his book focuses: W. G. Sebald, Aimé Césaire, and Walt Whitman, who each in their own way expressed their commitment to a vision of justice through paying close attention to everyday life.

Such primary witnessing is only one form, though, and there would be no book (or books, in general) were it not for the act of what Hansen calls secondary witness, borne of the desire to communicate experience to others and the parallel need to move through the world accompanied by the interpretations of others. When a person like Whitman attends to the dying, he is moved not only to remain present but also to convey what this presence has meant to him. His readers become secondary witnesses, fed both by what Whitman saw and by Whitman's means of navigating it.

So when I write this Foreword, there is a larger meaning than might first meet the eye in my sharing my experience of having first read Hansen's book. My experience of Hansen's book is of value to others because it is written by a person who lives, dies, yearns, and laughs. It is because the reader knows this about me that what I've written here matters at all; my witness is of value because what we seek is to navigate the world accompanied by others. A Large Language Model mindlessly consolidating data into a similar format would lack this essential ingredient: the reader would fail to be accompanied in their experience (of this book, of the lives to which it refers, and by extension to the lives of the writer and the reader) by a mortal creature who says, tacitly: "You are not alone. I have been here too, and this is what I have seen."

Writing this Foreword is also good for me, the foreword-writer, as who I am deepens from the call to listen to Hansen and to those for which he serves as a secondary witness, and to then try to put something of the experience of listening into words. Witnessing, for Hansen, is good for the witness, and also for those whose own travels through this life will be accompanied by those who have gone before us.

In his undertaking, Hansen breaks with more than the trend to rely on robots for a more efficient product. For this book is not only about the value of generalized human experience. It is also specifically and groundbreakingly about a particular relationship of the personal to the political, and how this relationship is shaped by attending to injustice and the suffering it creates. In this, Hansen departs from two pervasive ways of thinking about this relationship in popular culture.

The first is the commonplace assumption that one should study closely the horrors of the world in order to be an informed citizen. Living responsibly in this view requires one to be a "news junkie" who does not look away from images and stories of wars across the globe. One must remain not only constantly aware of the details of how individual lives are torn asunder by conflict, natural disaster, and everyday greed and violence, but also must cast a critical gaze on the causes of these woes. One must not accept them as timeless tragedies, an interpretation that could allow one to live with this grief. Rather, one must understand one's own culpability in causing this suffering and therefore, by extension, one's duty to ameliorate these harms. One is aware, upset, and obligated to change the world. The pithy phrase that encapsulates this view is the often-heard axiom, If you are not upset, then you are not paying attention.

The most basic problem with this stance for Hansen is that it instrumentalizes experience. It takes the human complexity involved in suffering and its witness, and turns it into a useful ingredient for a predetermined outcome. To attend to other people in order to arrive at a political action precludes what it means to attend. For in order to attend, Hansen urges us, we must slow down. We are called on to be present with another without rushing to change what we encounter. Distinct from mere engineering, witnessing is slower, more ambivalent, and therefore, in some ways, more demanding of our ethics.

The other problem with this stance for Hansen is the way it disregards the subjectivity of the witness. The person acting as a witness is not simply an engine of political action. Her subjectivity matters as much as her potential readers, interlocutors, or the beneficiaries of her future action. To witness is to deepen one's own experience of living, to nuance and enrich the soul. One witnesses not to do violence to oneself to arrive at a politically responsible aim, but rather because it is a way to live more fully. The exemplary witnesses in Hansen's work write first of all for themselves, because they cannot help it. They feel the call to attend and to make legible what they find.

This fuller life has implications, Hansen argues, for politics. One becomes more attuned to suffering and the forms of injustice that cause it, and this is decidedly political. But one does not witness for this reason nor rush to this conclusion. Whitman, for example, in Hansen's careful study, does not attend to soldiers in order to whip himself into an antiwar frenzy. Nor does he write in order to engineer democratic outcomes. He is called to be present with the wounded, called further to write about it. The political implications, Hansen suggests, take care of themselves through how the very act of bearing witness works on the person.

At the same time, Hansen also departs from another tendency of contemporary life: the drive to believe that we can eliminate all discomfort through the right mind-set. For Hansen, not only can witnessing make us uncomfortable, it can be genuinely psychologically risky. Indeed, Hansen's is not an approach to life that sets one on a path of self-fulfillment that will surely lead to well-being, whether consumerist or contemplative. The narrator of Sebald's *Rings of Saturn*, Hansen reminds us as an example, had to be hospitalized because what he witnessed so thoroughly exhausted him. To live fully is a risk.

In all of these ways, Hansen's book is an act of resistance to the overwhelming tendency in contemporary life toward instrumental reason. We witness, and also move through the world accompanied by other witnesses, not because we will arrive at a particular place, whether that be political rectitude or personal well-being. We remain attentive to the people around us, in all of their beauty, despair, and banality, because to do so is to live a richer life. And there is something about this richness, Hansen seems to suggest, that is not measurable on the metrics of success, action or even happiness. We get to be more fully here, with ourselves and crucially, with each other—and this, Hansen wants us to understand, may be the whole point.

Rachel Wahl<br>
University of Virginia

# Preface

This book is a study of the nature and educational ramifications of bearing witness to human events. I engage the work of three exemplary witnesses: W. G. Sebald (1944 to 2001), Aimé Césaire (1913 to 2008), and Walt Whitman (1819 to 1892). Sebald stunned the reading world some years ago with a series of unclassifiable texts that powerfully evoke the human costs of the violence of the 19th and 20th centuries. Césaire deployed the term *negritude* to denote a creative black consciousness emerging from under the heel of European colonialism, and he attests to both its joyous and painful development in his extraordinary prose poem, *Cahier d'un retour au pays natal* (Journal of a Homecoming). Whitman's witness to American life in his epic poem, *Song of Myself*, alongside his extended testimony about caring for wounded Union soldiers during the American Civil War, speak to a hope deeper than hope for the prospects of democracy.

The writing of all three of these individuals constitutes an enactment of bearing witness. They did not "choose" to write about their respective themes. They had to. The circumstances of their lives and the events of their time summoned them to their respective tasks. I will address how their efforts, supplemented by those of other witnesses whose testimony I touch on, hold considerable educational promise in a world marked by continued polarization, misunderstanding, and violence.

The first chapter in what follows examines the elements of bearing witness as an orientation toward human lives and affairs. Chapter 2 focuses on what Sebald calls "wrongful trespass" into the lives of other people. As we will see, he wrestles in an intensely purposive and poignant way with the challenge of doing justice to the dignity of others in writing of them. Chapter 3 attends to Césaire's witness as he returns home to Martinique after a lengthy sojourn in Paris in the 1930s, studying French letters and discovering for the first time his African heritage. His quasi-Homeric poem recounts his severe alienation from his people upon his return and the sometimes soul-wracking experience he undergoes to see them truly. Chapter 4 features a deep dive into Whitman's extended commentary on American life as he witnessed it in his domestic travels and encounters, and as he experienced it in the sustained support he provided wounded Union soldiers in military hospitals. Whitman raises challenging questions about the character of the individual American as well as of the larger society. The concluding chapter portrays educational possibilities that emerge through studying witnesses while at the same time reviewing the very nature of bearing witness.

It is not a prerequisite for what follows to have read the featured texts by Césaire, Sebald, and Whitman, though I certainly commend them to any reader for whom they are new. I have composed the chapters ahead such that the reader can follow the three witnesses' testimony and perceive what is at stake in it. This approach constitutes a fusion of the philosophical and the poetical. It is philosophical in that I endeavor to be clear and argumentatively grounded in elucidating terms and in rendering interpretations, while keeping in view alternative perspectives. The study is poetical in acknowledging truths of human experience that cannot be rendered in argumentative or propositional form. Poetry and other arts do not formalize truths in the manner that philosophers and scientists do. Rather, they respond to the reality of ethical truths that people live and sometimes die by in their quest for meaningful, just lives. Artists and poets aspire to fashion images that heed such truths, whether through words, music, sculpture, painting, dance, film, or other arts. A central claim in this book is that witnesses do the same. They do not provide arguments or theories. Instead, they show, they enact, they shine a light, they reveal, such that readers find themselves examining the contours of their own lives and commitments. Like numerous other witnesses, Sebald, Césaire, and Whitman educate: not through precept or direct instruction, but through the power of their intense, persistent attempts to respond to the pressure of experience.

I write in what follows as a witness of their witnessing. I invite readers to adopt a similar outlook: that is, to read both philosophically and poetically. The latter is especially important in order to discern the moral frequency, so to speak, of the three witnesses' testimony. To heed that frequency requires responding with a hard-to-define merger of feeling, self-awareness, and reflection. Without feeling, the reader may as well be reading instructions for how to operate a vacuum cleaner. Without self-awareness and reflection, the reader may assimilate the witnesses' testimony into their preferred way of thinking rather than permitting the latter to be challenged. Fortunately, in my experience and in that of many other readers, the three witnesses are such extraordinary wordsmiths that they help the reader, if not in so many words, learn how to read them precisely in what I've called a philosophical and poetical manner. I do not mean that the three figures make the readers' experience easy. On the contrary, it is startling to discover the layers of meaning, questioning, and often confusion they express. In effect, these witnesses say to us: "We can help you see the ethical power in bearing witness, but you must want the help." I believe that help is worth wanting.

When does a book begin? For many scholars and writers, the process is familiar and relatively straightforward. They conceive a project, undertake research, and write the book. In some circumstances, however, the question of beginnings is elusive. Figuratively speaking, the question points to something other than the day when the author sits down and composes the first sentence. The matter becomes instead: what is the existential "moment"—which may be of long duration—when an idea, a theme, an image, a stirring, takes hold of the person? Put another way, when does a particular feeling take conscious form in a person's life such that they are compelled to write?

Let me touch on two experiences that, for me, reflect such an existential moment. They are the beginnings, of a sort, of this book. In retrospect, I would deign to call them enactments of bearing witness. But I will be arguing in the chapters ahead that only the recipients of a witness can determine whether such a designation is warranted.

*Soldiers in war*. When I was a boy, I used to listen to my father Lyle talking with two of his colleagues. Over time, they had become close friends. They would gather on a Sunday afternoon at our home and reminisce about their experiences during World War II. My father served in the Pacific theater as part of an anti-aircraft unit on a naval warship. His colleague John was in the British army and was part of the first wave that landed on Sword Beach in Normandy on June 6, 1944, as part of what is called D-Day. Their mutual friend Wolfgang was an officer in the German Afrika Korps. He fought against the British and Americans for two years until captured in 1943. I would stand nearby (never sit, as I recall) and absorb their stories, which seemed like graphic tales from some long ago epic, such as my father's recounting of a massive airborne assault on his naval flotilla in the summer of 1945. He and his gun crew were ordered to fire at a particular point in the sky rather than track individual Japanese planes. I could not (and cannot) imagine how harrowing it must have been for my then 19-year-old father to have planes roaring overhead, amid an utterly thunderous racket as the whole flotilla was under attack, and not be permitted to shoot at them. The battle plan was to try to fill the sky itself so full of fire that none could get through to bomb the ships (several were nonetheless sunk and many damaged).

John and Wolf shared comparable memories. Though I lacked the vocabulary at the time, I can say now that these men were not saber rattlers or jingoists. I recall their laughter which, in hindsight, must have been about some mess-up in the army or about some wayward comrade. But I also recall, though did not understand at the time, tones of sadness, of sobered voices, and of moments of silent stillness. From the time of those Sunday hours through the present, war has been a "mystery of life for me," to quote Svetlana Alexievich's (2018) terms from her witness to women soldiers in World War II.

One upshot of this absorption was a steady diet, beginning in adolescence, of reading about war, including a plunge into novels, poetry, and films about war. I focused particularly on the world wars of the 20th century, as well as on the Holocaust, where the scholarship, literature, and poetry are searing. As an undergraduate at university, I read intensively about war and peace, fueled then by conflicting feelings about the Vietnam War, which at the time was coming to an end. I had received a high number in the lottery of the military draft when I was 19 and eligible to serve. My mother was thrilled by that fact (I do not remember my father's reaction). I was thrown into confusion. Even though the military was in fact closing down the draft, I still found myself asking why I was spared duty, when so many others were not. By then I had metabolized a deep sense of solidarity with people who, whether by choice or not, found themselves in uniform and thrown into the unimaginable (for a noncombatant) experience of battle. I did not envy them. I have never had an interest in fighting anyone. It was more an unfathomable sense of awe and emotional constriction in contemplating fellow humans placed in circumstances that tested, and sometimes shattered, everything they knew and felt about being human.

For our required senior year thesis at university, I researched and wrote about the Stockholm Conference of 1917, an attempt in the very midst of World War I by labor and socialist parties on both sides of the struggle to create a peace conference. It was a strangely gripping experience to spend countless hours in the library reading parliamentary records, speeches, and writings by labor and socialist leaders, and others involved with the proposed conference. While taking in their words, I had in my mind's eye the devastating suffering of soldiers on both sides, about which I had read so much, trying to survive the brutal conditions of trench warfare. (The conference never materialized because the respective governments would not grant travel permits.)

The feelings and ruminations over the years touched on here came to a head in composing this senior year thesis. The outcome was what I describe in the chapters ahead as a summons to bear witness. I devoted six weeks the summer after university to walking, hitchhiking, and taking trains and buses down the entire Western Front of World War I, from the Belgian coast to the border of Switzerland. I visited countless battlefields, military cemeteries and memorials—whose number is legion in northeastern France—and museums in towns large and small. With an audacity I'm not sure I could muster today, I approached older people I would meet on the road, at hostels or campgrounds, and at outdoor marketplaces to ask about their parents' experience during the war. The young men my age who fought and died along that route did not choose their fate, and nor did I "choose" to make this journey. It was a summons whose echo reverberates through the pages of this book.

*Teachers in the classroom.* My scholarly career has pivoted, to a great extent, around studying the practice of teaching and considering the lives of individuals who dedicate themselves to it. I have written extensively about teaching as a calling, or vocation, and have listened to many teachers describe their sense of purpose. I have observed dozens of secondary school teacher candidates undertaking their very first classroom teaching, and have sought ways to provide them meaningful feedback. I have devoted hundreds of hours to sitting in the back of classrooms of experienced teachers, waiting for signs of what can be summarized as the moral dimensions of teaching—that is, the usually subtle ways in which the persons in the role of teacher, and the persons in the role of student, can exert a formative influence on one another. Quite literally, they help form the persons they are always in the process of becoming.

Some years ago, I initiated a field-based endeavor that included sixteen big-city teachers from a number of public schools, along with two doctoral research assistants (Ana Cecilia Diego Galindo, currently teaching in Mexico City, and Jason Wozniak, on the faculty of West Chester University). The teachers represented many grades, from kindergarten through grade 12, as well as subjects ranging from science to art to social studies. My previous work on the idea of cosmopolitanism as a mode of education triggered the project, which took its point of departure from two related questions: What does it mean to be a person in the world today? And what does it mean to be a person in the role of teacher? For two years, Ana Cecilia, Jason, and I met regularly with the teachers to discuss these questions. I also devoted nearly 200 hours to sitting in on their classrooms. (For a detailed account of this endeavor and its many educational, aesthetic, and ethical aspects, see my book *Reimagining the Call to Teach: A Witness to Teachers and Teaching* [Teachers College Press, 2021].)

In short order, what began as a formal research project devolved into what, for me, was a movement of bearing witness. Put another way, my abiding interest in teaching and teachers, and in their place in the world, became more than an interest. Through my classroom visits and the voices of the teachers, I began to discern aspects of what Rebecca Sullivan (2023), in her extensive witness of educators, calls "the personal core" of teaching. This term of art denotes how influential the person in the role can be, since it is the person, not the role, who teaches (or fails to teach, as the case may be). I found myself caught up in an extended experience that was at once familiar, having spent so much time previously in classrooms, and new in the sense of witnessing what I slowly began to perceive as *embodied dignity*. The teachers' quiet dedication, manifested as much in their most fleeting of gestures and actions as in their formal pedagogy, came alive in ways I had not seen in the same way or to the same degree before. My visits and participation in our meetings no longer constituted "a research project" in the conventional sense of that term. The vivid reality of the teachers' and their students' humanity, as they engaged one another in educational work, summoned me to attend to the truth of their experience. The lingering effects of that beckoning also run through the chapters that follow.

In this book, I respond to another summons: to heed the testimony of three exemplary witnesses who, in consequence if not through intent, are educators for any person aspiring to comprehend and deepen their ethical orientation toward the world. There are numerous other compelling witnesses who merit spotlighting, some of whom I will refer to in the pages ahead. My compulsion to follow the paths that Sebald, Césaire, and Whitman tread derives from (a) a long-standing absorption in what they focus on, and (b) from the fact their witnesses complement one another in highly significant ways, as I hope this book makes plain.

The issues they foreground include:

1. As touched on here, the nature of war and why it persists as part of the human condition. In what follows, we will encounter unsettling aspects of the American Civil War and of World Wars I and II, and how these traumas create distinctive moral and ethical challenges for the witness to heed them justly. (Sebald and Whitman)

2. A second concern is how to understand and retain moral balance in confronting the overwhelming historical realities of transatlantic slavery and the Holocaust, dimensions of which will also appear in the pages ahead. To face such events means grasping the difficulty, if not impossibility at times, of comprehension. It is to appreciate the dialectic of provisional insight and beginning again and again that is inherent in the quest for such understanding. To retain moral balance means to steer clear of resignation, on the one hand, and moralizing, on the other hand, both of which undermine efficacious thought and action in the name of justice. (Césaire and Sebald)

3. A third issue has to do with the history and meanings of democracy in the United States, which from its inception in the late 18th century has been at once fragile and sturdy, a failure in some ways and a success in others. The experimental nature of this democracy has been both inspiring and maddening. To echo terms from President Abraham Lincoln, it has allowed the "worst devils" and "better angels" of our nature to compete relentlessly and sometimes violently for what Lincoln called the soul of the nation. (Whitman)

There is no definitive answer, at least given contemporary human limitations, to the question of how such things as war, genocide, and antidemocratic oppression keep recurring. There is no final explanation forthcoming that would yield just the right strategy to eliminate such events from the human scene. There is only responsibility and action informed by responsibility: a personal and community reckoning rooted in a dynamic, agentive spirit of remembrance. As I hope to show, the latter is a practical posture whose value and importance have no measure. Sebald, Césaire, and Whitman shed crystalline light on this orientation, and the fact that they do so informs why this book focuses on their testimony.

Another decisive reason for featuring these particular wordsmiths is that they are, as mentioned, exemplary along the lines of the framework for bearing witness I will be elucidating. Indeed, that framework has its very origins, in part, in reading deeply into their oeuvre rather than in studying the secondary literature on bearing witness. I have since examined the latter in depth as well as the fascinating secondary literature by philosophers, scholars of religion, literary critics, historians, and others on the specific texts I take in hand. The reader will find numerous references to this literature in the chapters that follow, which I include for purposes of both greater insight and for further reading as interests dictate. My point here is that composing this book has not been the playing out of a preformed template. The writing itself has been a process of continued discovery, reflective clarification, and working resolution of epistemic and ethical challenges in enacting the role of reader qua witness—the witness of a witness.

Chapter 1

# A Perspective on Bearing Witness

> In city apartments and village cottages, in the street and on the train . . . I listen . . . I turn more and more into a big ear, listening all the time to another person. I "read" voices.
>
> —Svetlana Alexievich, *The Unwomanly Face of War*

To listen and to heed . . .

Etty Hillesum (1914 to 1943) was a Dutch woman studying at university in Amsterdam and teaching Russian when World War II broke out. She was also Jewish, and for that fact alone was eventually put to death by the Nazis at Auschwitz. The diary and letters she left behind (Hillesum, 1996) attest to her deepening moral and aesthetic sensibility under the pressure of wartime conditions. She traverses these circumstances through her poignantly rendered transformation from a self-absorbed posture to one of abiding social concern. She learns to see the existential significance in the most ordinary, everyday doings in her life: reading, writing, speaking with others, working, and contemplating. Inspired in part by her passion for the poetry of Rainer Maria Rilke—a poet acutely attentive to the affairs of everyday life—Hillesum discovers a world of human plenitude when one might most expect it to be vanishing. In the face of a reign of terror, she describes the smallest, most fleeting human actions as if they were miracles of being, and as if they attested to why what is *good and just* is inextinguishable despite how menaced it always seems to be.

Hillesum eventually finds herself working in an official capacity, side-by-side with others in her hard-pressed community. At one point in her diary, she seems to find just the right words to express her new outlook.

> I often used to think to myself as I walked about in Westerbork among the noisily bickering, all too energetic members of the Jewish Council: if only I could enter a small piece of their soul. If only I could be the receptacle of their better nature, which is sure to be present in all of them. Let me be rather than do. Let me be the soul in that body. And I would now and then discover in each one of them a gesture or a glance that took them out of themselves and of which they seemed barely aware. And I felt I was the guardian of that gesture or glance. (1996, p. 202)

Hillesum's outlook is not resigned or defeatist in the face of cruel pressure. On the contrary, she bears witness within an aura of radical love, a love that does not seek itself but rather recognizes the precarity and pricelessness of life.

To listen and to heed: readers who accompany Hillesum in her witness will invariably find themselves examining their own way of life. Indeed, they may be "pulled up short," as the hermeneutist Deborah Kerdeman (2003) puts the matter, wondering about the adequacy of their vision of other people and of the world writ large. They may also find themselves contemplating how they would have responded to the dire situation in which Hillesum and her contemporaries were forced to dwell. Her testimony invites readers to attend to reality in all its starkness: both the horrific and the sublime. Put another way, she educates readers—albeit indirectly rather than through precept—in how to enhance their moral regard for others, and indeed for all entities in the world. Her endeavor informs the title and the theme of this book.

## Layers of Witnessing

In formal terms, Hillesum's testimony can be seen as that of a first-order witness: an individual attesting directly to personal experience. The individual's witness is frank and sometimes immediate. At other times, it emerges long after the fact. It can vary widely in its expressivity, from straightforward, no-nonsense utterances to the poetic prose Hillesum achieves through her disciplined, contemplative effort (her diary is far more elaborate than what that term usually connotes, a mirror to her hope that it would survive her). The literature on historical and contemporary trauma is replete with first-order witnesses attesting to their personal experience within a context of war, genocide, persecution, or exploitation.

A second-order witness typically lacks the direct experience of the people to whom they are bearing witness. However, the second-order witness can provide invaluable insight into these people's situations to those who will never know or encounter them. The witness can do so through sustained listening, looking, accompanying, studying, and, finally, writing or speaking. The second-order witness becomes especially crucial when the people in question lack the resources or circumstances to speak directly to the world themselves. Though Hillesum did not live to see the outcome of her writing, she testifies both to her own experience as a human being under permanent wartime threat and to that of her fellow Dutch Jews too preoccupied or unprepared to attempt a witness like hers. She fuses the viewpoints of a first- and second-order witness.[1]

In this book, I portray in depth the efforts of three remarkable witnesses: W. G. Sebald, Aimé Césaire, and Walt Whitman. All three move in and out of first- and second-order positions. They attest graphically to the sometimes harrowing experience of people who in many cases lack a public soundboard for their own voices. The three figures heed these people's experience closely. Sebald renders his witness in highly affecting prose. Césaire and Whitman do so through their evocative poetry, though both have important things to say in prose, as we will see. The three confront how challenging it can be to bear witness. They show how much effort the endeavor demands, and why in peculiar, unexpected ways it can become more and more complex—if not downright elusive—the further one goes. Together, they make plain the difficulties, tensions, conundrums, and limitations in attempting to bear witness to others' lives. At the same time, however, and in a manner that echoes Hillesum's accomplishment, they reveal powerfully why a witness can be an educator of others, provoking them to deepen their moral sensibilities and to widen their circles of moral concern.

In the next section of this introductory chapter, I elucidate what is distinctive about bearing witness compared with the work of historians, journalists, documentarians, and other observers who attend to the very same issues and events. I describe the aesthetic, ethical, moral, and intellectual orientation of a witness (by which, from here on out, I will largely have in mind a second-order witness). I then turn to an account of how persons who are neither first- nor second-order witnesses might come to grips with the striking texts by Sebald, Césaire, and Whitman.

I will suggest that the reader of their work can become a kind of third-order witness who approaches their work as if it were an address directed personally to them.

## Contours of Bearing Witness

Bearing witness is a familiar if diversely employed term. At one end of its spectrum of meaning, witnessing conjures a detached, neutral standpoint. At the other end, it evokes images of passionate moral solidarity with others. The witness may inhabit the role for no more than minutes. Alternatively, the witness's experience may transform their life, as well as the lives of others. Witnessing takes its form and substance in response to that which calls it forth in the first place. The term has its vernacular, functional uses, as can be seen in everyday discourse. But it can also become a term of art for an important ethical orientation toward the world, as I seek to illuminate in this book.

The concept's association with religion and the law reaches back millennia. The Bible, for example, contains numerous references to the first-order witness who attests to a religious revelation or insight. It also refers to the second-order witness who spotlights others. In addition, the text associates the witness with the idea of a martyr (from the original Greek *martis*, to witness). The latter denotes a person who suffers a serious loss or even death as the cost of witnessing to an unshakable belief, value, principle, or practice.

Since the emergence of law in human culture, people have been summoned as witnesses to events. The witness in court, for example, attests to the facts of a case, and ideally does so with the reliability and impartiality of a machine. The expert witness brings to bear in-depth knowledge combined with professional judgment. The expert is counted on to offer interpretive rather than solely factual remarks. In contrast, the witness at a wedding, a bank, or a law office signs a formal document and, through this bare act alone, attests to the validity of what has transpired.

What we can think of as a first-order moral witness attests to their personal experience under conditions of violence. Unjustly imprisoned people, soldiers, refugees, abused migrants, and others can put forward direct testimony. For example, Frederick Douglass, Harriet Jacobs, Sojourner Truth, and others testify to the brutal injustices built into the institution of American slavery. Jean Améry, Tadeusz Borowski, Primo

Levi, and others write of their terrifying days in Nazi camps and prisons. Countless survivors of battlefields, including wordsmiths such as James Jones, Siegfried Sassoon, and Theodor Plievier, speak to the nightmarish circumstances forced on them.

Second-order moral witnesses, such as Sebald, Césaire, and Whitman, bear witness to suffering others as well as to their testimony. They evoke notions of justice, of a moral awakening, of remembrance, even while heeding the facts of the situation. They do not speak *for* others. Rather, they constitute a morally charged conduit or vehicle for helping others become *present* to a world that may all too easily overlook or ignore them. As I will touch on below, it bears adding that a first- or second-order moral witness can attest to goodness and beauty rather than solely to pain.[2]

There is no blueprint to follow with respect to the second-order moral witness. Every such witness ultimately charts a distinctive path. Moreover, while the analytic terms deployed here have heuristic value, they do not apply neatly or directly to Sebald, Césaire, and Whitman. For one thing, their modes of writing are unique and cannot be reduced the one to another. They defy easy categorization even with respect to familiar sorters such as "poetry" or "literature." For another thing, the three writers played many roles aside from that of witness. All three, for example, worked as teachers for varied lengths of time: Sebald spent his career as a university professor of literature, while Césaire and Whitman taught in primary or secondary schools for several years. Sebald published numerous academic articles that differ constitutionally from the witness he enacts in the texts I portray in chapter 2. Césaire became mayor of Fort de France, the capital of Martinique, and then served for decades as an elected delegate in the French parliament. In these capacities he undertook extensive correspondence as well as administrative writing. As I will touch on in chapter 3, he was also an outspoken critic of colonialism. Whitman held numerous jobs in journalism and printing, as well as in other lines of work, and penned an astounding number of essays, commentaries, and other writings even while composing voluminous poetry. Chapter 4 will address his singular blend of first- and second-order witnesses.

Despite their different circumstances, however, in their efforts *as* witnesses these three figures share common ground that points to the nature of bearing witness as framed in this book:

- They are summoned or called to their tasks, rather than choosing them as if there were alternatives.

- They are committed to truth, which entails continuous ethical self-cultivation as witnesses including ever-deepening attentiveness to people and the world.
- They are motivated by distinctive, dynamic fusions of wonder and concern.
- They confront the limits of language, while enjoying its many affordances within those limits, in finding ways to express their witnesses.

None of these elements, taken in themselves, are unique to bearing witness. For example, acute attentiveness to the most (apparently) mundane aspects of human lives is a feature of numerous moral and aesthetic theories. But attentiveness takes on a distinctive character within the constellation of elements that constitutes bearing witness. In other words, it is the fusion of these elements, their inter- and intrarelations, that marks the orientation. Let me touch on each of these dimensions in turn.

*Summoned to Bear Witness*

Sebald chose to become a professor. He did not choose to become a witness. This task has its roots in his being born a German in 1944, at the tail end of the Third Reich. As he came of age, he found himself horrified, if not at times outraged, by the oft-cited silence that descended on his country after its shattering defeat. He felt his fellow citizens were burying their heads in the sand, desperately seeking to forget and to move on. He could not move on. The many crimes of the Nazi period appalled him as he learned of them, and he eventually left Germany for good in his 20s, soon to settle into a position of professor of German literature at the University of East Anglia in Britain. In time, he found himself experimenting with prose in an attempt to come to grips with a deeply felt sense that he must *respond* to the history he inherited. Neither academic writing nor journalistic commentary would do the job for him. He felt they were too abstract, too formal, and too familiar. His arrival at a workable form, which we will encounter in chapter 2, instantiates his witness.

Césaire aspired at a young age to become a poet. This aim took hold of him before his political awakening to the realities of colonialism and its negative effects on his fellow islanders in Martinique, as well as on black people in Africa and in the larger black diaspora. Beginning in his 20s, as he comes to grips with how far back in history his cultural inheritances run, both his poetry and his prose feature searing critiques of colonialism. At the same time, he immersed himself in an extraordinarily rich manner in the long lineage of French poetry and of the French language itself, which he encountered firsthand during an eight-year-long sojourn in Paris in his youth (where he also mastered Latin). He discovered that the voice of Martinique—his voice as a native of the island—differed from the voice of France—also, in a very real sense, his voice. Upon his return to the island after his Paris education, he finds himself pushed, pulled, and torn between these voices and their quite distinctive registers and backgrounds. He finds himself summoned to resolve this internal struggle, familiar enough in some respects to the experience of other Western-educated colonial subjects, yet singular given Césaire's unusually deep literary knowledge and sensibility. In a wholly unanticipated manner, he finds himself bearing witness, in a long, magisterial poem at the center of chapter 3, both to his fellow islanders and to what it can mean to inherit and *live* multiple traditions of thought and practice while also being true to one's natal roots.

Whitman was a proverbial jack of all trades and lived in many respects like a nomad, not settling down until his 50s when a stroke seriously hampered his movements. But one consistent thread in his life was his engagement with the written and spoken word. The Walt Whitman Archive (www.whitmanarchive.org), among other sources, reveals the massive quantity of writing and poetry he undertook, as if he walked about and slept with a pen in hand. Walk and talk he did, for he relished conversation with fellow Americans from all domains of life and clearly had a highly responsive social touch. It seems everyone he met came to remember him. But he remembered them, in turn, and was moved by them. Person by person, voice by voice, he found himself called to evoke what he felt was their spirit as a people, alongside what he regarded as the dramatic experiment in democracy personified in the United States itself. What many regard as his greatest poem, *Song of Myself*—which I take up in chapter 4—constitutes an attempt, among other things, to bear witness to what he sees and hears in the nation.

But Whitman's convictions about the US and its people were severely tested by the outbreak of the American Civil War (1861 to 1865), which to many contemporaries signaled the possible termination of the democratic experiment. As if to confront this very challenge to his beliefs and hopes, Whitman devoted several years to tending wounded and ill Union soldiers in the many hospitals that sprang up in and around Washington, DC. In a way he never anticipated, he finds himself bearing witness, heeding the hurt bodies and spirits of countless soldiers, wondering all the while what to make of the manifold events of his time. I will consider, also in chapter 4, his witness as embodied in his memoir-like text, *Memoranda During the War*.

In sum, unlike the witness in court, Sebald, Césaire, and Whitman were not called to testify by an external, institutional source. They did not receive a summons in the mail but, figuratively speaking, from the world itself. Moreover, unlike the witness in court, who in many cases need not prepare at all, the three figures realize they must cultivate their aesthetic, moral, and reflective responsiveness to what is compelling them forward. Finally, unlike the expert witness, whose stance is necessarily clinical and detached, the three witnesses are personally implicated in their endeavors. They are compelled by a felt moral responsibility toward what confronts them in their witness.

The next sections further elaborate these points. Before proceeding, however, it is worth emphasizing that the concept of bearing witness at issue here reaches beyond its usual association with trauma. It also parts company with instrumental uses of the term, ranging from the all-too-familiar "Eyewitness News" to everyday expressions where the term could be replaced, without loss of meaning, by verbs such as *notice, see, attend to*, and so on.[3] With respect to the full horizon of human experience and what a moral witness can tell us about it, the summons that motivates people could pertain to something so beautiful in the world that they are called to attest to it: to put it in front of others in the hope they may see the beauty, too, and perhaps reorganize their ways of life accordingly. As we saw in the quote from Hillesum that opens this chapter, what the witness heeds could be a seemingly simple gesture, a tone of voice, a look in the eye, the movement or the stillness of a hand. Or it could be the apparently ordinary doings of a nurse in the ward, a teacher in the classroom, a coach on the sports field, a driver of a bus, a chef in the kitchen. In short, the person may feel summoned to bear witness to aspects of human life that are hidden in plain sight and which, when actually noticed, can speak volumes about fundamental aspects of the human condition.

For example, the poet-witness Rainer Maria Rilke, in his extensive oeuvre including his famed *Duino Elegies*, shows how everyday life can express "quiet testimony," to cite a term of art from the literary critic Shari Goldberg (2013), about the poignancy, yearnings, trials, and depths that supposedly "ordinary" life can hold. The writer John Berger and the photographer Jean Mohr collaborated on a witness to the life of a country doctor in England, which they entitled *A Fortunate Man: The Story of a Country Doctor* (1967). Through Berger's lyrical prose and Mohr's captionless, sometimes haunting photographs, they render the pathos and the beauty in the man's day-by-day encounters with his patients. The Nobel laureate Svetlana Alexievich bears witness to the devastations of World War II in works such as *Last Witnesses* (2019), about children caught up in the maelstrom, and *The Unwomanly Face of War* (2018), about women who fought and sometimes died in the ranks. The testimony she heeds illuminates in visceral terms the barbarism of war and, in effect, compels the reader to question any foreign policy that makes war-making an instrument of national self-interest. At the same time, however, her acute, patient attentiveness to the most seemingly trivial matters in children's and women's lives becomes an encomium to a human grace that violence can never sunder. Sebald, Césaire, and Whitman also, in their singular ways, attend keenly to people's everyday experience. In so doing, they discern phases of joy and beauty intermixed with those of despair and moral ugliness.

*The Necessity of Ethical Self-Cultivation as Witness*

A common element in the capsule overviews that appear earlier is the appearance of the verb *finds*. This verb wonderfully captures the nature of the summons to which the three figures respond. They do not set out to bear witness—a term that rarely occurs in their writing, although it is noteworthy when it does. Rather, this task ultimately "finds them," even as they find themselves *in* it. This claim is not to suggest that their habitation of the role is merely passive. It is *actively* passive. They put themselves under the sway of what is drawing them forward; they give themselves over to it.[4] Unawares, they had been readying themselves for it longer than they realized. Once engaged in it, as they compose the works featured in this book, they deepen their ongoing readiness. They discover that the close attentiveness on which bearing witness depends must be reignited if not rebuilt every day. This process constitutes ethical self-cultivation.

The term *ethics* here denotes something other than professional codes of ethics with their focus on right and wrong. Rather, ethics constitutes a highly personalized concept that incorporates an individual's aesthetic and moral sensibility. The term points to the ethos of the person. This notion of ethics is not new. It is rooted in ancient sources as diverse as the writings of Plato, Confucius, and so-called Stoic thinkers such as Seneca, Epictetus, and Marcus Aurelius. The idea also emerges, both directly and indirectly, from more recent writers—all of whom were familiar with ancient texts—such as Michel de Montaigne, Marie de Gournay, Sor Juana Inés de la Cruz, Ralph Waldo Emerson, and Friedrich Nietzsche. In this dynamic tradition of thought and action, ethics conjures a form of contemplative self-formation watered by feeling. "Feeling" is a mind- and heart-set more encompassing than emotion and reason taken in themselves, and it will play a large role in what follows. Feeling embodies emotional, attuned, and aesthetic responsiveness to people, events, and situations. It is not simply the triggering moment of response, but runs right through an encounter. In this light, ethics names an ongoing endeavor to cultivate as richly as possible one's aesthetic and moral orientation toward the affairs of life, an orientation that incorporates sustained feeling. This effort positions the person to wed the proximity to others, and yet also the reflective distance from their circumstances, built into the act of bearing witness.

The concept of "orientation," as deployed here connotes embeddedness in the world. On the one hand, it points to how a person turns or orients themself in order to see and hear others as best as possible. On the other hand, the concept spotlights how a person takes in or receives what is seen and heard. This "turn" toward the world, implied in the idea of an orientation, is another way to express the notion of ethics as encompassing aesthetic and moral considerations. As we will see in this book, bearing witness constitutes a distinctive orientation. It is neither a method that can be formulated, though it has its methodical aspects, nor is it a means to a predetermined end.

With respect to bearing witness, the aesthetic pertains to a person's responsiveness to the ethos or aura of persons and situations. It marks a mode of sensitivity to aspects of life that at first glance may appear ordinary and routine, yet at second glance—when responsiveness has transformed into awareness—can come alive with meaning and significance. Readers can discern this aesthetic sensitivity in virtually every line of Hillesum's testimony. The witness seeks to hold in view these moments of meaning that otherwise may come and go like a puff of wind. They keep them in sight long enough to render an account of them that they can pass on to others.

The concept moral, in this context, differs from the ethical in that the former pertains to how the witness regards and treats other people and other entities in the world. The concept spotlights modes of fairness, respect, and responsibility the witness brings to bear. The witness does not seek to agree with or to endorse what is witnessed. Their aim is not approval or disapproval, as such, as if they were themselves the arbiters of justice. Prior to any sort of judgment, on their part, is moral attunement. The witness aspires to heed the reality before them, to take the people caught up in it as seriously as possible. "Serious" does not imply being heavy-handed or ponderous. Rather, the seriousness of the witness is another name for their perseverance, in the conviction that they must attend, through thick and thin, to what is beckoning them on. Here the lovely English word *heed* comes into its own. To heed is not just to attend to or to note. It also means to respect and take to heart that which has called out for attentiveness. Thus, to heed is to act—that is, not simply note, but respond. Heeding can open the way to a deeper involvement with human concerns and aspirations.

From a moral point of view, the proximity to which I referred a moment ago does not necessarily imply physical closeness. The witness can move "near" to persons who dwelled long ago. Indeed, they can be much closer to them, spiritually and emotionally speaking, than to their contemporaries. Correspondingly, distance does not imply physical separation. No doubt every reader has had the experience of sitting right next to a person they know who they feel is miles and miles away, as unreachable as the planet Pluto. There is a dialectic of moral proximity and distance that every witness charts as sensitively as possible.

Meanwhile, ethics captures how the witness regards and treats themselves, not in an egoistic or narcissistic sense, but in the understanding that precisely *as* a witness I must literally work on myself if I am to cultivate my aesthetic and moral sensibility. I must engage in such work if I am to ready myself to bear witness as well as to sustain this witness.

*Ethical Self-Cultivation and Respect for Truth*

Like every good journalist and historian, the witness aspires to truth and disciplines themselves accordingly. Sebald, Césaire, and Whitman were all relentless note-takers as they moved to craft their respective texts. They were inquirers. They spoke with countless people. They read quite varied material intensely and sometimes obsessively in their quest to do justice to what they were witnessing. They questioned constantly their evolving viewpoints.

Yet their orientation differs from other truth-seekers. For example, journalists and historians, in their quest for reliability, enact well-known tenets in their respective fields for the gathering and interpretation of facts. As part of this endeavor, they often enunciate directly their assumptions and predilections so that readers can judge their work accordingly. They compare their descriptions and interpretations of events with those of others in their respective professions. They hope to contribute substantively to the knowledge base surrounding particular issues.

In contrast, the witness responds to a summons, felt deeply and intimately, which demands a personal reckoning. The response is not scholarly or journalistic, as such. As witnesses, Sebald, Césaire, and Whitman are not trying to add directly to a knowledge base, though they respect and draw widely on available knowledge about what concerns them. Their works addressed here are not arguments. They are not summaries, overviews, or lectures. Their judgments and conclusions, such as they are, are part of a reckoning with that which has summoned them, and thus differ in origin from the findings of scholarship and journalism.

In short, while dedicated to truth, witnesses do not seek the same truth as the journalist or historian. As we saw with Hillesum, their posture does not mean they stumble into fantasy, caprice, or pure fiction. But the truth that compels them is not propositional. It does not take the logical form of the assertoric, problematic, or apodictic. Its contrast is not that which is false but rather that which is not recognized and acknowledged. Put another way, the contrast is not epistemic considered in isolation from the moral and ethical. The truth they seek is moral, first and last, and requires ethical self-cultivation to discern.

This notion of truth is commonplace, and for good reasons. The truth of a friendship, the truth of a marriage, the truth in being a parent, a teacher, a social worker: many people appreciate that to perceive such truth requires something other than propositional logic, and that it cannot be grasped through formal argumentation alone. Rather, it requires feeling. John Dewey calls this quality sympathy, or sometimes "intelligent sympathy" (1985, pp. 127–128), where intelligence denotes not mental status but the ability and commitment, infused with feeling, to establish connections between people, especially in the face of differences and conflict. In Dewey's view, sympathy incorporates attentiveness, reflection, a measure of humility, and sometimes serious self-examination. As he remarks about the nature of friendship: "Friendship and intimate affection are not the result of information about another person even though knowledge may further their formation. But it does so only as it becomes an integral part of sympathy through the imagination. It is when the desires and aims, the interests and modes of response of another become an expansion of our own being that we understand him" (Dewey, 1989, p. 339). Dewey points here to people's capacity to intuit or see into the truth *of* things as well as the truth *in* things.

Patience and intelligent sympathy, for example, are essential in practices such as teaching and nursing. We require no formal proof of their value, though we may need to argue for it from time to time. We *learn* it organically as students and as patients. We *live* by such truth. Teaching and nursing as we know them would fall apart in its absence. This truth is not solely epistemic but is fused with moral and ethical meaning. As implied above, a person who fails to see such truth is not "wrong." Rather, the person is inexperienced with the aspect of reality in question, or lacks perspicuous grounds for adequate response and judgment, or may be locked at present in a dogmatic orbit.

The witness's endeavor is neither objective nor subjective in the familiar senses of those terms. As we will see, Sebald, Césaire, and Whitman do not compose from the standpoint of the persons they are. Rather, they operate on the basis of what they hope to become if their witness can bear fruit—that is, if they can resolve what is leading them onward, however incomplete that resolution may be. To recall a term of art from many forms of field-based research, the witness is not themselves "the best instrument" in inquiry. Rather, it is what they are not, or not yet, that opens the way. They testify through what they are *becoming*, through what they are receiving, not through what they are as if locked in a fixed identity that predetermines what they can see and say. Put another way, their "I" is not what can become deep with respect to bearing witness. It is their openness that can become deep—*what they are not yet in their engagement with the world*—and this possibility necessitates ethical self-cultivation. I will return to this complex issue later in the chapter in discussing how readers might approach the three figures' works.

*Waiting but not Awaiting*

Moral witnessing has a rich tradition associated with the natural world. From ancient times to the present, poets, philosophers, and occupants of other roles who are devoted to being in nature—whether walking in forests and along seashores, or swimming, or climbing, or simply sitting in a glade—have attested to how nature speaks if people learn to listen to its rhythms, rather than approach nature as merely a collection of objects to utilize. Many walkers in nature have put forward testimony about what it means to cultivate an ethical relation with it, in which their self-understanding and their fundamental regard for the world comes into question. For example, the painter André Marchand writes: "In a forest, I have felt many times over that it was not I who looked at the forest. Some days I felt that the trees were looking at me, were speaking to me. . . . I was there, listening. . . . I think that the painter must be penetrated by the universe and not want to penetrate it. . . . I expect to be inwardly submerged, buried. Perhaps I paint to break out" (quoted in Merleau-Ponty, 1964, p. 167). There is nothing sentimental or romantic in Marchand's deeply felt testimony. He attests, as does Hillesum and the poet Rilke, to the fact that human beings are immersed in the world, a world that figuratively speaking is always "looking" at them, "addressing" them, provoking them to respond.

Christopher Dustin and Joanna Ziegler (2007) provide a comparable image of persons in nature that further illuminates the orientation of the witness. The authors compare a botanist who enters a forest seeking a particular plant in order to study its morphology and medical potentialities, with a lover of forests who is not seeking any particular knowledge but rather a certain kind of reflective understanding. The botanist strides over countless species of flora and fauna in the quest to find the right plant. Put another way, the deeper the botanist penetrates the forest, the less he sees (p. 40). In contrast, the walker is not awaiting something: namely, the sighting of a specific plant. Rather she is waiting, *actively*, for meaning to come to her (cf. Heidegger, 2010, pp. 75, 76, passim). She is in no hurry. She takes things as they come. She notes the varied colors and textures of the life forms she encounters, the play of light and shadow as the sun's rays filter through the canopy above, and the sounds of birds, insects, and the wind through the trees. The walker also notes her responses to all this: to what Dewey (1988, pp. 15–16) calls "the immediate quality" of her experience, or her "primary experience," as he also puts it, which is precognitive and saturated with aesthetic, emotional, and somatic elements. "Secondary experience," according to Dewey, denotes those phases in the walker's activity in which she attempts to interpret and explicate consciously her primary experience.

The person's walk in the forest is a carefully undertaken endeavor. Put another way, the walker, like the botanist, brings to bear a critical mind respectful of the reality she seeks to engage. The walker has a profound sense of purpose and well-wrought self-discipline. There is nothing casual or one-off about her walk, as if she were a tourist looking for novelty. The walker aspires, for example, to a deeper sense of what a forest is and what it means, both as an astonishing expression of life and as an educator of the human being who seeks to grasp something about the ontology of existence, the *why* she and the forest are here rather than solely how they are or what they are. The walker moves as if called by the forest. She follows its lead in her walk; she follows what it shows her while she is underway. She may not cling to a map or preset route; she may not try to control her steps in that manner. Instead, she practices—step by step by step—self-control, self-awareness, and attunement. She is both an eyewitness, attending to minute details, and an engaged I-witness, readying herself continuously to be receptive to the lessons of the forest.

For the botanist, as for the journalist and the historian, it can be essential to block things out in order to focus squarely on a particular issue. Seeing less can sometimes imply seeing something well. It is not hard to imagine the botanist and walker having a productive discussion along these lines. Indeed, the very same person, presuming they embody the ecumenical epistemic and ethical outlook, can be both botanist and walker. They can experience the joy—which is deeper in meaning than typical notions of pleasure or happiness—that can accompany both botany and being in nature, with their two very distinct forms of discovery and truth. Sebald, Césaire, and Whitman take the path of a walker in the sense of not prescribing in advance what they will see and what they will find important. They *wait* for insight, however intermittently and unexpectedly it may arrive (as we will see, sometimes it does not). They do not *await*. Unlike the journalist, historian, or botanist, they are not guided by a preset question, at least in formal terms.

A close cousin of the idea of waiting, rather than awaiting, is the concept "lingering" (cf. Schweizer, 2021). To linger is to make time for close attention. It is an active, attuned quality that accompanies the patience of a witness. Consider for a moment the filmmaker Terrence Malick, who bears witness in a powerful manner to the existential realities of soldiers in battle in his acclaimed World War II film, *The Thin Red Line* (1998). Malick eschews the standard narrative of war films, preferring to focus slowly on moments in time. The film comprises scenes that come together not into a typical, linear story but into a collective portrait of both soldiers and the lush natural environment (the island of Guadalcanal in the South Pacific) into which they have been thrown. As Robert Pippin (2013) notes, a key effect of Malick's lingering, or waiting, is that we see not only objects—people, plants, birds, animals, reptiles, clouds, and much more—but also "the *objects in the light of such attention*, photographed as if *seen* in a mode of interrogative attention that, by its very intensity and independence from the plot, detaches the objects from any normal intercourse with viewers and allows some other dimension of meaningfulness (or some different sort of question about life) to emerge" (p. 269). As witnesses, Césaire, Sebald, and Whitman see more than objects. Through their capacity to wait and to linger, they see them in the light of care and concern. They position readers to do the same.[5]

As argued previously, and as I hope to illuminate in the chapters ahead, the three figures are guided by a summons. In this respect, they cede control to their actual experience. They follow where it leads them. They do not do so blindly or randomly. They commit themselves to working toward the truth of what has summoned them: a truth not of fact alone, but of what it is to have *experienced* the pattern of violence across the 19th and 20th centuries (Sebald), the violence of colonialism and the necessity of reconstituting self and community in its wake (Césaire), and the lived reality of an unwieldy, often chaotic and violent, yet sometimes inspiring democratic experiment (Whitman). The three walk and wait as if they were travelers on a quest. Sebald's narrator bears the marks of a moral pilgrim searching for restitution in what he sees as a blighted world. Césaire's narrator embarks on an inner and outer moral odyssey as he works his way, as witness, "back home" to his community and to the self he most longs to be. Whitman's narrator-witness is a wanderer, a nomad, yet wherever he goes—both literally and metaphorically—he remains deeply rooted in his love and hope for democracy.

## Trust and the Challenges of Composition

The witness faces a peculiar predicament compared with the journalist or historian who may be addressing the very same topic, such as colonialism, democracy, or war. Journalists and historians have many clear-cut precedents and methodologies to follow. Their precursors and contemporaries have established successful ways to frame inquiries, to determine the right methods of data collection, and to decide on the appropriate descriptive or argumentative discourse to deploy. Natural and social scientists perhaps have an even more straightforward trajectory for their work, given the central role of established method in their given fields. This point is not to suggest there is anything simple, much less simplistic, about their undertakings. The development of good judgment is a sine qua non for all who seek to inquire into the world, and it is an ongoing challenge for every inquirer.

However, and in contrast with inquirers named above, the uniqueness of every witness means they have no obvious models to follow. For one thing, their contexts and what is compelling them can differ markedly, as can be seen in Hillesum and in what I have said thus far about Sebald, Césaire, and Whitman. None of these figures can straightforwardly mimic one another or other witnesses whose voices they encounter. They can take note of the fact that other witnesses *have* heeded what is summoning them, whatever it may be. In other words, they can take heart to follow what is compelling them rather than conclude in advance that the effort will be futile. But this benefit, such as it is, tells them nothing about how to go about actually responding and then putting into composed form their witness. Again, no witness can simply mimic another's expressive bent because no other witness is responding to the same summons. To be sure, many Germans, for example, have felt compelled to address the grievous harm their nation inflicted on the world in the mid-20th century. They have much to say to one another about their shared motivation. But no two individuals will feel, grasp, enact, or formulate their witness, presuming they give themselves over to this task, in identical fashion. An entire life experience, which is never the same between one person and the next, informs every summons for every moral witness. I gestured toward this idea in the Preface.

These remarks attest to why the witness's compositional endeavor is, in some respects, closer to the practice of novelists and poets than it is to the work of journalists, historians, and scientists. Novelists and poets have countless precursors, but to convert a precursor into a model to mimic invariably leads to muting if not distorting one's own voice. Moreover, like the witness, many novelists and poets care deeply about reality and truth—even when, or sometimes especially when, they deploy magical, irrational, and irreverent elements in their work. They may feel deeply compelled to express truths of human experience. Though their images and stories are "made up," their moral concern is not, and it can be palpably felt in and between the lines of their writing. Every thoughtful reader of such work can attest to how a novel or poem can take them out of themselves, and then "return" them as persons who have been moved, if not shaken, by truths that will endure in mind. They will find themselves thinking again and again of that novel or poem, and will also find themselves recommending it to others, perhaps for years to come.

Correspondingly, the trustworthiness of a witness mirrors the trust readers put in a compelling novel or poem. As mentioned, readers may willingly give themselves over to the voice of the work. They will allow that voice to penetrate their being, so to speak, and to influence them. They will not read as if they were a spectator, but rather as a participant in the aura or ethos of the work as they live with it, in an almost literal sense of the term. It is not that the reader agrees with the writer or approves of the writer. The reader is not naive, and recognizes that a writer can misspeak and distort, however unintentionally. The point is that the reader takes them seriously, reading their lines almost as if they were a personal address to them and one that it is important to heed. It is not easy to capture this trust in words. But there is something about the verisimilitude in the novel or poem, something about how manifestly true it is lived experience, that positions the reader to be trustful rather than cynical, jaded, skeptical, or unmoved. At the same time, there are countless novels and poems that this same reader will never get close enough to with respect to establishing a relation of trust.

So things stand with the testimony from the witnesses featured here. They establish trustworthiness through the steps touched on above: a scrupulous attention to reality, ever-deepening knowledge of the concern at hand, a commitment of whatever time it takes to bring the witness to some sort of resolution (more on this point to follow), and above all a tenacious staying on the path, in which they are in fact *not* worried about the trust of others, at least at the time, but about getting things as right as possible in their witness.[6] In other words, witnesses must be accountable, first and last, to the summons itself that has propelled them forward. Not all readers will respond to their witness, but it will not be because the writer took easy or cheaply won routes. In my experience teaching the texts, readers of Hillesum, Sebald, Césaire, and Whitman more often than not find themselves in a relationship of trust with them. Again, this relationship is not a matter of approval or agreement with the particular propositions, as such, that the witness puts forth. It constitutes more a mode of respect, in which the reader says, in effect: "I see the sincerity and the moral depth at work here. I see the witness's quest for truth, I see how it has them in its grip. I know that what they're addressing is significant—let me walk and think with them before I judge."

The criteria sketched above for judging the trustworthiness of the witness are not identical with those used to assess the work of historians and journalists. Sebald, Césaire, and Whitman are keenly aware of the difference, just as they are aware of historical realities. They acknowledge the place of historians and journalists in addressing events. They value accuracy for how it can counter fantasy and downright false readings of the past. They do not aspire to replace historians or journalists, an act that would instantly problematize their trustworthiness. As discussed above, their purposes differ and what they bring to readers differs.

In this respect, readers will not be encountering in the pages to come a formal history of the events that so preoccupy Sebald, Césaire, and Whitman. They will encounter these writers' responses to the events: that is, *their witness*. These figures respond not as bystanders, but as human beings profoundly marked, in body and soul, by such events. They are compelled to come to close quarters with the human effects of such doings. To do so, they realize that the events demand a personal engagement, with all its vicissitudes and vulnerabilities, rather than a clinical stance.

I turn now to four final, related dimensions of bearing witness that we will see play out in the chapters ahead.

*Time and Bearing Witness*

As suggested previously, the witness earns trust by investing themselves in a long-term manner to nearing truth. They do not cut corners. Put another way, bearing witness does not follow clocks and calendars. It cannot be forced. Nobody can wake up one day and decide to bear witness. The summons that compels a witness typically emerges over a period of time, sometimes years. It may take further time to identify the summons. Indeed, the witness may never be able to formulate it in so many words, nor is it necessary to do so. In the texts we will encounter, Sebald, Césaire, and Whitman elucidate relatively few direct statements about what is moving them to bear witness. But they *feel* it constantly, and this feeling leads them on. In my experience, the sense of this feeling also leads readers on.

It is not easy to say when a witness begins, nor when it comes to an end. In an important sense, it has no termination, for the summons is existential and not like a problem that can be solved and declared finished. Bearing witness is not a case where first the person gathers knowledge of people's experience and circumstances, and then composes a text. It is not that kind of "research." Rather, the witnessing runs right through the composition: every word, every punctuation mark, is an enactment. To borrow terms from Paul Zweig (1984, p. 10), there is an organic connection between "the shaped entities of language," that is, the written witness, and "the turbulent puzzles of experience" that have given rise to it.

*The Question of Representation*

The descriptive and ethical challenges in writing about other people have troubled writers for generations. The witness encounters multiple aspects of this problematic. Like all writers, they face the fact that human beings and communities are unfathomably complex. The writer will inevitably leave things out of account that might be important to doing justice to people's experience and circumstances. Moreover, unlike the witness in court, or like an historian or journalist, a witness like Sebald, Césaire, and Whitman does not occupy an official or even recognizable role. There is no public office called "witness," save in the technical legal contexts adumbrated previously. The three figures do not organize events or lead causes. Furthermore, nobody asks or invites them to bear witness. People are not waiting around for their presence and insight—though, later, they may be moved by their words. Some people, as we will see, find the witness a rather strange figure at first, for this person doesn't seem to want anything or to be doing anything except hanging around—waiting, lingering, loitering. These predicaments come on top of the compositional conundrums addressed above.

The field of witness studies (cf. the references in note 3, p. 8) features a veritable cottage industry addressing the issue of representation. Scholars and second-order witnesses have been especially concerned not to distort the first-order witness of people who have suffered traumatic events. They acknowledge the limits of what they can accomplish. Jeffrey Librett (2015) captures the gist of this recognition when he remarks, in reference to the Shoah (though he could be, in my view, attesting to many other large-scale traumas of the past and present): "[T]he task of representing the Shoah—the Shoah having been driven to a large degree by an attempt to forbid representation . . . must be undertaken within the larger forward-looking project of assuming the impossible character of representation more generally. For representation as (re)constitution of full presence is always impossible. [It is] forbidden . . . by a dimension of absence that it can never exclude, and that we must affirm as belonging to its proper functioning" (p. 220). The limits of representation mirror the limits of both moral imagination and human expressivity. Like the poet (for example, Paul Celan, among others, who have written of the Shoah), the witness can come nearer and nearer even while falling farther and farther away. There is no overcoming this paradox, for the fullness of touch remains elusive.

However, the witness cannot simply let silence about others' fate obtain. These fellow humans merit a hearing, and their testimony carries invaluable lessons for the prospect of justice. Thus, as mentioned previously, the second-order witness must attempt to speak since so often the affected people lack the circumstances or resources to address the public themselves. By way of anticipation, we will see that Sebald, Césaire, and Whitman are acutely aware of the dangers of what Sebald calls "wrongful trespass" into the lives of others. It seems all too easy, in the attempt to do justice to them, to in effect pin them to a wall for exhibition to others. These writers do not claim to have surmounted such dangers. But I believe they can claim to have composed ethical and trustworthy witnesses, and I hope to demonstrate that in what follows.[7]

*The Vulnerability of the Witness*

Because of their deep personal investment in their witnesses, Sebald, Césaire, and Whitman encounter multiple forms of vulnerability. Simply by ceding control of their respective undertakings to what has summoned them, they put themselves at risk. Their fundamental orientations as persons may be on the line. They may get things wrong, and thereby potentially harm those to whom they are bearing witness. They find this possibility forbidding if not intolerable, and we will encounter their struggles in the chapters ahead.

Because bearing witness is not a clearly defined social role, much less a job or occupation, the witness may experience bouts of self-doubt about both what they are doing and why they are doing it. They may feel drained by the uncertainty and recurring inconclusiveness that characterizes the undertaking. These conditions become weightier when the witness is attending to events of wide, dramatic importance, as is the case with Sebald, Césaire, and Whitman. To accept the responsibility inherent in the process seems to call on the entirety of the persons they are, constituting another reason why ethical self-cultivation accompanies bearing witness.

These remarks do not downplay moments of fulfillment and joy along the road of witnessing. For example, in the midst of Césaire's often painful witness to the people of his native island, he finds himself joyfully overwhelmed—almost to a point of redemption—by the spontaneity of a communal Christmas celebration he encounters (stanzas 23–25). Whitman expresses an extraordinary exuberance across the lines of his *Song of Myself*, and readers will find artful humor in the lengthy works of Césaire and Sebald. These witnesses are not morose, resigned, or forlorn. Of great significance, they persist in their witness right though the last punctuation mark in their writing. There can be an immense sense of meaning that derives from bearing witness, which can feel like it has made life worth living. All the same, bearing witness will not happen without accepting the vulnerabilities it entails.

*The Witness and the Recipient*

The three witnesses addressed here are aware of readers, even if, as we have seen, they sometimes consider other matters far more central. In my experience, they orient themselves toward readers in a manner that echoes how they orient themselves in their witnesses: namely, with frankness and with a fusion of invited proximity and crafted distance. The narrators in their works do not hide their limitations, worries, and failures. Their directness is sometimes stunning and unsettling. But their testimony is not a matter of 'true confessions,' so to speak, because as I have suggested the three authors write from a standpoint of transition rather than of a fixed identity. As witnesses intertwined with the voices of their narrators, they make plain the many-sided challenges in pursuing their labors.

The upshot is that their works draw the willing reader into a participatory rather than spectator's role. The form and style they fashion encourages the reader to accompany them in their witness: to see what they are seeing and to feel its significance, which can lead to integrating the witness into their own lived experience. Whitman is especially direct with the reader in his *Song of Myself*. At times he cajoles, lectures, and provokes the reader in a face to face like manner. In another context he stated that to grasp his poems the reader must allow them to "enter" their being, to "filter their way to the undersoil" (E. H. Miller, 1991, xii). I believe all three witnesses would say, in effect, "Reader, be aware that we have had to be as artful as possible in rendering these written witnesses, both to do the right thing—as best as possible—and to reach you. So be mindful of this art as you arrive at a considered judgment of what you think we have done."

These terms echo the insight that attending to witnesses involves both trust and scrutiny. The latter points to the reader's need to check other sources regarding the events the witness addresses in order to put the witness's testimony in a broader context. This move does not imply prior skepticism or suspicion, but rather an attempt to deepen knowledge and expand perspective on what the witness is undertaking (cf. Josselson, 2004; Van der Heiden, 2022). In this light, it is invaluable from an educational point of view to pair witnesses with historical work about their concerns, a point to which I will return in the concluding chapter. At the same time, a measure of trust is indispensable is order to give the witness a hearing in the first place, and it can be built in the manner sketched previously. Without an inaugurating principle of listening first, and judging second, readers cannot access the witness's experience and insight. They will simply read into the witness their own prior epistemic and moral assumptions; or, they may unawares simply substitute the terms of their own life experience for those the witness is trying to put forward. The next section takes up a particular, and I believe generative, way of reading second-order witnesses.

## Reading Sebald, Césaire, and Whitman as Witnesses

First-order witnesses' testimonies have an inherent autobiographical dimension. They elucidate personal experience directly and often comment on nothing else, since, unlike historians or journalists, they are under no requirement to do so. Their sole and most fundamental commitment is to convey their experience as they underwent it.

Sebald's, Césaire's, and Whitman's personal backgrounds and circumstances do not figure into the equation as straightforwardly. A key reason for this has to do with the summons that calls them to witness in the first place. As I have argued, they do not choose or decide to bear witness. Rather, they respond to a calling to address historical as well as contemporary issues that deeply affect them. As touched on previously, it is not so much the persons they "are" who bear witness, but their persons-in-transformation as they learn to heed the summons. They move both outside the persons they are, or are elsewhere, and deeper into the persons they are becoming *as* witnesses. The transition space between is precisely from where they speak. Their artfulness resides, in part, in keeping that transitional space open as long as possible.

*Bearing Witness Is not an Identity but Rather an Orientation*

The three figures do not refer formally to a summons as that term is characterized here. I have inferred its presence, in part, through the sheer urgency and concern that fires their witnesses. They are aware of the idea of bearing witness, but as far as I have been able to determine only Whitman self-consciously describes his orientation, in his *Song of Myself*, as that of a witness (see chapter 4). However, as this entire chapter shows, to describe the three figures as bearing witness is not to read this orientation into their work. On the contrary, they themselves make plain the pertinence of these terms in responding to them.

The three witnesses also attest to why readers should not approach their works as if they were direct reflections of who they take themselves to be as people, or as others take them to be. At first glance, this claim may appear to undermine if not sunder their moral purposes. If it is *not* Sebald putting forward a witness to the traumas of the 20th century, who is doing so? The answer is that Sebald *is* very much present, but—it bears repeating—precisely as the witness he is in the process of *becoming*. That process—that transition—that transformation, is not reducible to the self conceived as a frozen identity. The witness's development, temporally, is *kairotic*, not solely chronological. That is, it is not a matter of a steady, linear accumulation of more and more sensitive responses. To become a witness is much more unsystematic, unpredictable, and uncontrollable in an engineering sense. (Even people with the most refined attunement to others can regress, depending on the situation, and act blindly.) Thus, the "time" in which the witness moves and, hopefully, grows, has a distinctive pattern and movement that is neither straightforward nor replicable. An enduring aspect of bearing witness is that both witness and recipient must recognize an inherent lack of finality in the endeavor, while not downplaying its potentially powerful truth.

Sebald's texts incorporate various autobiographical allusions and parallels. However, according to many persons who knew him, including numerous interviewers and biographers (see, for example, Angier, 2021, and

Schwartz, 2007), he was an elusive, reserved figure, though evidently with a fine sense of humor. His biographical presence *in* the texts is, in likeness, not easy to pinpoint much less to determine definitively. I will show in chapter 2 just how successfully he moves within the transitional space touched on previously. He speaks from the perspective of an existential journeyer, wanderer, and pilgrim, rather than from a settled personal standpoint.

Consider the following remarks from Césaire and Whitman. Césaire writes: "I am in the habit of saying that I have no biography. And in truth, in reading my poems, the reader will know about me all that is worth knowing, and certainly more than I know myself" (in Davis, 1997, p. ix). "My past is there to show and to hide its face from me," Césaire elsewhere avers. "My future is there to hold out its hand to me. . . . And within the person I am now, the person I will be stands on tiptoe" (1990, p. liii). Césaire echoes what the literary critic Lawrence Lipking says of poets, which in my view can be said of the witness: "Poetry cannot tell us whether the author was a happy person, or a sinner, or justified in his politics, or suffering from bad dreams, but it can tell us all we need to know about the author's ability to convert his experience into vision" (p. x). Alan Trachtenberg (2000) remarks, referring to Whitman's *Leaves of Grass*: "The figure we care most about, the persona of the poems, lives wholly in the lines, the pages, the leaves in and through which he speaks" (p. 124).

Whitman's judgments about his relationship with his poetry are contradictory, in keeping with his frank declaration in *Song of Myself* that he is a person of contradictions who "contain[s] multitudes" (see chapter 4). Late in life he concluded that he himself could not say what his poems mean, or, in an important sense, "who" composed them: "I still think—*I have always thought*—that it [*Leaves of Grass*, which contains *Song of Myself*] escapes me myself, its own author, as to what it means, and what it is after, and what it drifts at. . . . I accept and consider the book as a study. But behind all that . . . remains a subtle and baffling, a mysterious, personality" (in Miller, 2010, p. 248). I interpret "study" to mirror all that has been said here about bearing witness. Matt Miller observes: "Whitman's project is to awaken people to their compound inner makeup, to the . . . all-encompassing diversity that he sees at the heart of identity, and his book, as he saw it, was a separate 'personality' altogether—its own being, related to but not really him" (2010, p. 249).

Consider further these lines from several of Whitman's poems.

- From "Whoever You Are Holding Me Now in Hand" (where "me" refers to his collection, *Leaves of Grass*):

  Whoever you are holding me now in hand,
  Without one thing all will be useless,
  I give you fair warning before you attempt me further,
  I am not what you supposed, but far different.[8]

- From "Myself and Mine":

  I charge you forever reject those who would expound me, for I cannot expound myself,
  I charge that there be no theory or school founded out of me,
  I charge you to leave all free, as I have left all free.

- And from "Poets to Come":

  I am a man who, sauntering along without fully stopping, turns a casual look upon you and then averts his face.

These lines echo Sebald's and Césaire's relationship with the works taken up here. The witness does not "own" what they bequeath to others. It is an offering whose continued life in culture depends on its recipients.

The upshot of this extended excursus is that the works we will encounter walk on their own legs and should not be shackled a priori by predetermined interpretive categories whether they have to do with literary form, biography or autobiography, or anything else. Correspondingly, to refer to these figures as witnesses is not to make claims about their identities, but only about the voices we hear in their written compositions. We learn *from the witness*, not from the vicissitudes of the writer's biography, as such. As argued in this chapter, witnessing is not an identity, or "identitarian" notion, just as it is not a preformed institutional role. Put another way, these witnesses' voices are not reducible to external social or internal psychological effects. To be sure, they do not elide such effects and attain a totally unmediated view of reality. But to perceive their works as mere products of a mechanism of cultural or psychological production means denying them a creative versus a replicative or preset response to their experience. It is true that to attain the transitional space they occupy and from which their narrators speak requires art and artfulness.

It is no simple matter to mediate the power of societal and psychological influence. But it can be done, and to a meaningful, indeed striking degree, as any number of artists, philosophers, and people in the course of their everyday affairs have shown. In likeness, and as alluded to in the Preface, the reader must bring to bear an artfulness that encompasses their own mediation of effects and influences, if they are to interact meaningfully with these figures' witnesses.

Personal and contextual matters are pertinent. Sebald, Césaire, and Whitman are highly singular human beings as well as witnesses. The circumstances in which they dwell differ considerably. I mentioned previously the many-sided nature of their lives as they worked variously as teachers, writers, poets, politicians, journalists, and more. As we will see in the chapters that follow, this background informs their ways of seeing, of knowing, and of composing. But, again, these contextual factors do not *determine* what they do *as* witnesses. The factors position them to act; they do not preset their actions. Precisely because these witnesses give themselves over to a summons, they abandon command over the endeavor. In a manner of speaking, they trust their summons more than they do themselves.

*Vicissitudes of Interpretation*

In the witnesses' active, intense willingness to heed what compels them, they do not attain a view from nowhere, as if they have gained a godlike view of things. But the "somewhere" they are, as touched on above, is always in transition. This fact, alongside the other aspects of bearing witness addressed previously, presents a distinct interpretive challenge to the reader. While there is an inspiring, wide-ranging secondary literature on Sebald, Césaire, and Whitman, the instrumentalities of literary criticism and of philosophy do not map directly onto what it is to come to grips with a witness. The same limitation holds with respect to drawing on the resources of historians, sociologists, anthropologists, art critics, artists, and journalists. Their perspectives can be invaluable, but cannot take the place of the reader's personal response if that reader is to engage the witness on their distinctive ground.

As explained previously, I make no attempt here to provide adequate biographies, though I will occasionally insert telling biographical details. Nor do I offer a considered judgment on the collective oeuvre of the three figures, as contrasted with the specific works I address. Furthermore, I am not suggesting that the lens of bearing witness is the best or only way to approach their efforts. The secondary literature has addressed in depth many aesthetic, moral, cultural, and political questions their work raises.[9] However, no previous study of which I am aware has put forward a systematic conception of witnessing and argued that it pertains to these writers' efforts. Thus, while my conclusions here will not be exhaustive, I hope they will be generative for students, fellow scholars, and, ultimately, anyone who shares the witness's concern for justice. To borrow terms from Ronnie Scharfman (1980, p. 2), I hope to "dilate" elements and challenges in bearing witness.

There are artful exceptions to the general rule I just noted. For example, Matt Miller (2010) regards Whitman as what he calls a "visionary witness" (p. 178). Though Miller does not conceptualize the term, what he has to say illuminates this orientation with respect to Whitman's undertaking. For example, as we will see in chapter 4, the poet's *Song of Myself* is saturated with lengthy trains of pure description of people in their typical activities, as well as descriptions of scenes of tension and sometimes violence. This pattern, Miller argues, "reinforces [the poet's] position as a witness who does not discriminate or judge, but who is [quoting Whitman] 'tenacious, acquisitive, tireless,' returning 'again and again' to both the harsh and pleasant aspects of the human parade" (p. 180). Moreover, Miller adds,

> In the dynamic he establishes the content of these lists is specifically intended to be things he witnesses and includes, not things he creates or projects. They constitute objective, not subjective materials. By disavowing authority over the objects of his catalogs Whitman also disavows the language that evokes them, obviating the conventional prerogative that requires original writing in a literary work. In the context he intends Whitman is the witness, not the creator, of the language of his visionary catalogs. The materials they offer are meant to be as much ours as his. (p. 180)

As we will see, the poet intends these "materials" to serve his fellow Americans in fashioning themselves into democratic-oriented people.

Several commentators on Sebald's oeuvre have noted resemblances between his orientation and the act of bearing witness. For example, Katja Garloff (2004) argues that the narrator in the four stories that comprise *The*

*Emigrants* can be viewed as an "emigrant-witness" who fuses an identity he has as a person born and raised in Germany with his alienation from that very identity. For Garloff, this posture provides the narrator a unique moral perspective on the four figures central to the work. Put another way, it generates a critically sympathetic if tension-laden position from which, Garloff avers, he testifies. Lynn L. Wolff (2014) argues in depth that literature can embody bearing witness in invaluable ways. She perceives Sebald's unusual oeuvre—a hybrid, in her view, of literature fused with historical methods (though not itself history)—as particularly powerful in this regard. Both authors deploy work by Felman and Laub (1992) and others, cited previously, to conceptualize how they understand the idea of bearing witness.

The absence of a considered body of commentary on the three figures as witnesses (I have encountered no studies of Césaire that regard him as a witness) attests to the limits as well as the affordances of what academic framing can accomplish, including in this very book. As touched on previously, there is a valuable scholarly literature on the concept of bearing witness. This theoretical and analytical work differs from the sort of personal response that I have argued Sebald, Césaire, and Whitman call for in their endeavors. These witnesses provoke others to reckon with their own orientations toward the human prospect. Just as every witness can learn from other witnesses but not adopt wholesale their approach—because, as underscored previously, no one else shares their summons point for point—so every reader of a witness can learn from other readers of that same voice, but ultimately must fashion their own existential response since nobody else can do this for them.

*To Read as a Third-Order Witness*

The orientation I will pursue as a reader-interpreter in the chapters ahead is along the lines of a third-order witness. I will attempt to bear witness to the testimony of Césaire, Sebald, and Whitman regarding their own witness. I will endeavor to be a listener, in the full aesthetic, moral, and intellectual sense of that term. Felman and Laub (1992) rightly argue that listening constitutes a necessary ground for testimony to take place in the first place. It cannot exist in a void. Peters (2001) examines this notion as well and argues that no witness is fully realized until "taken in" or received by others. When the latter happens, through the thoughts and reflections of listeners or readers, they "activate"—they bring alive again—the witness's commitment (Etherington, 2018, p. 76).

As touched on the Preface, this approach fuses the philosophical and the poetical. In essaying this mode of reading, I hope to sustain adequate critical distance from Sebald's, Césaire's, and Whitman's work. At the same time, however, I hope equally to maintain a felt responsiveness to what I take to be the profound forms of yearning for justice that underlie their witnesses. To adopt a purely theoretical or clinical stance would preclude me from grasping the play and trajectory of this yearning, however unnamed it remains in formal terms. Put another way, such a stance would block access to the truths of experience these figures disclose. I hope I have heeded their testimony rather than solely analyzed it, though the former relates dynamically with the latter. The witnesses' visions of justice, often implied rather than rendered explicitly, embody wonder and respect for human creativity and the joy it can bring. These visions also incorporate an ongoing, passionate concern about the forces that can destroy the human quest for meaning and justice. Ultimately, to approach a witness such as theirs seems to require a fusion of feeling and criticism: an intertwining of the intimate proximity and the reflective distance they themselves enact as they bear witness.

Is this interpretive orientation an instance of the "in between" referred to above? Does the third-order witness occupy a transitional space or viewpoint in their own right? There is a sense, as mentioned, in which the reader of a witness must themselves cede control and give themselves over to where the witness leads. The reader needs to walk rather than rush to find something predetermined or easily comprehensible. Their task, poetically speaking, is to try to discern the frequency of the summons that has compelled the witness. But this orientation does not mean becoming a blind admirer. It means learning to listen with critical sympathy and critical trust, terms that are hard to define conclusively but which I believe attest to familiar human experience when confronted with testimony that calls for a reckoning. I hope that, finding myself compelled to follow where these three witnesses go, some measure of trust and truth in my account will emerge. This truth will be neither mine nor someone else's to possess. It takes form only at the ever-moving crossroads of communication, for no witness, whether first-, second-, or third-order, is ever complete until received by another. I invite readers to walk alongside as witnesses themselves to the efforts of the three figures. They will doubtless discover meanings I have overlooked or am unable to see.

## The Witness as Educator

The previous sections deployed the terms *educate* and *lessons* on the part of the witness. As I interpret them, Sebald and Césaire did not set out to educate others in their respective witnesses. They pursued a summons, in the course of which they sought to educate themselves, if not to refashion themselves, in the wake of their intense engagement with historical realities. However, whether intentional or not, both figures' work will educate any reader who approaches them in an open- and serious-minded manner. Such a reader simply will not close their texts the exact same person, with the exact same ethical and moral orientation, as when they opened them. The change may not be dramatic, and it may materialize more in shoring up a perspective already in place rather than transforming it, but the educational impact is there.

Whitman did, in my view, have a pedagogical agenda in composing both his *Song of Myself* and his *Memoranda During the War*. He aspired to hold up a mirror to his fellow Americans in which they could see what it means to lead a genuine if inevitably confusing, unpredictable democratic way of life. He sought to show them his best sense of what it means to feel and to act like a democratic person. My experience and that of many other readers suggests that his works provoke thinking about one's personal orientation toward fellow citizens and toward the polity itself. Once again, an educational consequence has ensued.

Writings in all genres, to be sure, can be educative: novels, poems, drama, journalistic accounts, scholarly arguments, personal communications, diaries and journals, instructional manuals, and so forth. The distinctive educational, and edifying, impact of witnesses such as those featured here can be rendered as the following constellation of elements.

*Education as Self-Formation.* As emphasized above, education encompasses more than formal tuition in schools and institutions of higher education. It can happen literally anywhere and at any time in a person's life. As also addressed previously, any reader who takes in hand—and continues to hold in hand—a well-wrought witness such as those touched on here is likely to be changed. Their outlook on the issues at hand, if not on the human condition writ large, will be deepened, broadened, and enriched. They may also be haunted by the witness's testimony. It may accompany them wherever they go, perhaps not at the forefront of consciousness but more like an interior presence that doesn't fade. This outcome can result from studying a first-order witness whose searing account leaves such a mark, or it can emerge from following a second-order witness to the very last syllable of their testimony. These consequences may be even more conspicuous if the reader has brought to the text a strong concern that mirrors that of the witness.

*Historical Consciousness.* To read a witness, and especially to read a wide array of witnesses, can fuel a person's historical consciousness. This term denotes something more than knowledge of historical fact, valuable as that is. To be historically conscious is to see oneself as a being in time, dwelling in the present but vividly connected to the past and future. It is to take on a certain kind of solidarity with people who have borne witness, whether it be to traumatic events or to everyday, ordinary doings that shine a light on human hopes and aspirations. To be historically conscious is to say: "I am not alone. People whose lives I can never know *touch me* if I let them. They teach me to look within, to examine my orientation toward human and other affairs in the world. They speak to me. I can speak back by taking care, by being a person of care, not as a hero or heroine but as a person who can contribute no matter how modest the scale." To be historically conscious is to approach witnesses from the past as *contemporary*, as figures whose voices remain vivid. To be historically conscious is also to imagine voices from the future, posing questions to those whose actions today may affect the world tomorrow. Historical consciousness means steering clear of presentism—the presumption that current views and perspectives are ipso facto superior to those that came before, fused with a tin ear with regard to the prayers of the future.

*Remembrance.* Remembrance differs from memory. Memory often has a life of its own, winging its way into the mind in ways that surprise and sometimes startle. At other times people can call up memory for any number of reasons, or for no reason at all. Remembrance is a deliberate, sometimes even deliberative undertaking. It encompasses both historical knowledge and historical consciousness. It draws on memory, indeed many peoples' memories, though it is not the same as "remembering," despite the close similarity in terms. Remembrance is neither nostalgic nor uncritical. It has an overt moral purpose: to help keep in view suffering and loss, as well as joy and celebration, so that people can act mindful and respectful of such realities. Remembrance can influence present aims and modes of operation. It adds degrees of awareness that such purposes and methods can have unanticipated if not harmful consequences. In this respect, remembrance can fuel active humility: a resistance to hubristic impulse, whether on the part of oneself or others. Ultimately it constitutes a form of love for fellow human beings under pressure: for their efforts, sufferings, and accomplishments. To read affecting witnesses constitutes a powerful road toward remembrance.

*(Re)Inhabiting the World*. Remembrance and historical consciousness, as educational experiences, can help people inhabit their world more fully. The attentiveness and concern the terms embody can lead people not to take for granted their environment, while also taking better care of that environment. All too often, as is common knowledge, most people (the present writer included), most of the time, are too preoccupied with their obligations, interests, and worries to pay much attention to their surroundings, which tend to blur into an undifferentiated background. Though all too understandable given human needs and limitations, this habit constitutes an immeasurable moral, aesthetic, and social loss. It fosters a habit of inattentiveness and indifference that undermines, if not impoverishes, people's capacity to pay attention, with imagination and with tenacity, to things that profoundly matter: from caring for loved ones to broader concerns such as democracy, justice, and the well-being of all entities in the world. The point is not that persons must be attentive 24/7. Such a posture would be exhausting and would interfere with the necessity of practical action. But it does imply cultivating a habit of appreciating more consciously the depths of meaning at play in what can otherwise seem routine.

Self-formation, historical consciousness, remembrance, and (re) inhabiting the world: the witness as educator can fuel or even trigger all of these consequences of engaging them. For educators, witnesses can be that much more impactful when conjoined with historical study. As mentioned, the witness does not replace the historian. There literally is no substitute for the known facts when truth and justice are at stake. As everyone knows, the current world suffers mightily from an epidemic of falsehoods, misinformation, and disinformation broadcast widely via the internet and social media. Witnesses alone cannot make good on the epistemic requirements for humane communication and practice. However, the witness provides something the chronicler of facts cannot: an intensely personalized account of experience that cannot be rendered, without a fatal loss of meaning, in abstract, analytical terms (cf. Felman & Laub, 1992, p. xviii). Witnesses do not describe a thunder shower like a meteorologist does. They describe what it is like to be *in* a thunder shower, without in any sense downplaying the critical value of the meteorologist. In short, the witness's account is not *about* something, in the manner of an analyst. It is *part* of that something, in that every step the witness takes embodies the ongoing influence, or input, of the world. It is in every instance one of a kind even while sharing, as this chapter has highlighted, family resemblances with other witnesses.

## Closing Note

The witnesses featured in this book stand out, in part, because of their acute attention to matters large and small. They respond to large-scale trauma including its manifestations in individual lives. They heed meanings that emerge from attending to seemingly insignificant and everyday moments. With respect to the latter, Etty Hillesum once again shows the way. Like many other witnesses during World War II, she attests to the anguish and suffering due to unjust, wholly unnecessary violence and harm. She shows that while learning to attend more fully to the everyday and ordinary is hardly a direct antidote to injustice, without such concern there will never be justice, because the everyday is where human beings dwell.

In chapter 5, I return to the educational ramifications of bearing witness, equipped at that point with the full-blown accounts of Sebald's, Césaire's, and Whitman's witnesses to which I now turn. I invite readers to keep the question of education in view as they proceed, not in order to instrumentalize these witnesses' efforts—as if they were mere means to an end—but to appreciate that much more their deep value. In a dynamic sense, Sebald, Césaire, and Whitman wrote first and last for themselves. They needed to work out the summons that drew them into their writing in the first place. But thanks to the affordances of publishing and communication, they have bequeathed their testimony to the present generation in whose hands so much of importance will be decided. Education plays directly into the issue of what resources and voices people will draw on, or fail to draw on, in this ongoing task.

Chapter 2

# W. G. Sebald

## Rightful Trespass into the Lives of Others

> I do not have [clarity] today, and I hope that I never will. Clarification would amount to disposal, settlement of the case, which can then be placed in the files of history. My book is meant to prevent precisely this. For nothing is resolved, nothing is settled, no remembering has become mere memory.
>
> —Jean Améry, *At the Mind's Limits*

In this chapter I foreground lessons about bearing witness from the German-born writer W. G. Sebald. Sebald was a professor of European literature at the University of East Anglia in England and turned to nonacademic writing in a major way in his mid-40s. In a series of unclassifiable books that have drawn widespread international acclaim, Sebald examines the many-sided history of Europe and its impact on the world across the last several centuries. He does so through the vehicle of an unnamed narrator who, in his quest for understanding, travels through countless places and, figuratively speaking, wanders through an astonishing array of works of culture, economy, education, and politics from roughly the 17th-century through the present. The narrator is haunted as well as absorbed by the background and events of the Shoah, although in the books I will address he never uses that term (nor the term Holocaust). He ponders the fate of European civilization in the 20th century by investigating everything from urban styles of architecture, to industrialized modes of fishing, to the logic of the rapidly expanding railway system. He meets individuals bruised by historical events and meditates continuously on the unending mysteries in trying to understand another human being.

The narrator's pilgrimage and sensibility resemble those of Sebald himself. However, while Sebald's own life experiences are never far from the texts, the latter are not merely disguised modes of autobiography. What they accomplish, as a mode of bearing witness, is to incorporate Sebald and the reader into the human tableau he sketches. To deploy another metaphor, it is as if he and we become threads in the living history he weaves. Sebald fuses seamlessly practices of the novelist, archivist, literary critic, diarist, philosopher, documentarian, journalist, and historian. The poet and translator Michael Hamburger coined the term *essayistic semifiction* (in Angier, 2021, pp. 347–348) to characterize Sebald's complicated form of composition. It is a form that activates a wide array of responses in the reader. Sebald draws the reader into bearing witness to the past, rather than standing outside events as a placid spectator. The reader is "touched" by the past in the emotional and intellectual senses of that verb developed by Roger Simon and colleagues (2005).

Sebald renders all this in a nondidactic manner that scholars have had difficulty in characterizing. He frustrates the reader's impulse to categorize, classify, or taxonomize his voice and the people and things of the world about which he writes. At the same time, Sebald responds to the reader's concern for justice. They can close his books with a sense of having experienced moral truth, with its fusion of unsettlement, insight, and ungrasping redemption.[1]

Sebald struggles tirelessly against what he calls, in a passage that inspires the title of this chapter, "wrongful trespass" into the lives of others. He writes with sensitive but unsentimental care about people. His concerns are with the dead and the forgotten, but his lessons are for the living. He illuminates ethical symmetries between regard for the past and regard for the present, including one's fellow human beings. His chiseled, tactile accounts of loss veer toward the elegiac, but at heart constitute sharp commentaries on people's present capacities to pay heed to the demands of a humane life. I will suggest that Sebald's unpredictable, unscripted, and deeply compassionate witness embodies a promising way to understand, as well as to practice, rightful trespass in inquiry into the human. It sheds light on the work of teachers, scholars, journalists, artists, and others concerned with people who, if they are to accomplish their work, must enter the experiential terrain of their fellow beings.

## Focus of the Chapter

I draw mainly in what follows on three of Sebald's books: *The Emigrants*, *The Rings of Saturn*, and *Austerlitz*.[2] *The Emigrants* is broken into four parts, each of which could be called a portrait, a case study, a testimonial, an album, and a short story. Each features the troubled life of an émigré, whose names appear in the respective titles of the chapters: Henry Selwyn, Paul Bereyter, Ambros Adelwarth, and Max Ferber. All four chapters are based on actual figures Sebald knew, and they fuse documentary and fictional elements.[3] As portrayed in the book, Selwyn was born in Lithuania, the other three in Germany. All of them save Adelwarth are Jewish or part-Jewish. All of them save Ferber commit suicide because of pressures associated with war, racial persecution, and the vagaries of memory, the latter a recurrent theme in Sebald's work. It becomes increasingly clear to the reader why Sebald titled the book *The Emigrants* rather than *The Immigrants*. None of the four individuals ever feels fully at home in their new settings, which include England, the United States, France, and Switzerland.

Sebald himself emigrated to England from Germany in 1966. He eventually took up a post, as mentioned, as professor of European literature at the University of East Anglia, where before his tragic death in a car accident in 2001 he had helped establish an important scholarly center devoted to the theory and practice of literary translation. The books I draw on here attest to their author's own abiding questions about his identity as emigrant and immigrant. He does seem to have become at home in England, where he became fluent in English and was much appreciated in scholarly and literary circles. At the same time, he wrote all three books touched on here in German and relied on others to translate them into English.[4]

*The Rings of Saturn* features ten parts, which embody portraits of people and places, encyclopedic inquiries, journalistic reports, historical sketches, and more. The book pivots around the unnamed narrator's lengthy walking sojourn along the eastern coast of England, a journey that closely follows one Sebald himself undertook.[5] I use the unfocused word *sojourn* because the narrator often seems to drift from one sight to another, following his intuitions, feelings, confusions, fears, and curiosity. Along the way he muses on the lives and works of writers—some familiar, others now obscure—such as Joseph Conrad, Thomas Browne, Edward FitzGerald, and Charles Swinburne. He ponders the changing forms of English architecture over the past 200 years, while also describing the literal decay of all these forms in the towns and old manor houses he comes upon. He occupies himself with events in English military, political, and imperial history. All of these elements illuminate why Sebald subtitled the book *An English Pilgrimage*. At the same time, the book includes an unpredictable array of commentaries on German history and culture, thus paralleling Sebald's grappling with his own roots. For example, the narrator remarks at length on the history of sericulture in Germany, where the notion of "extermination" comes into ominous play, in this case with regard to the fate of silkworms once they have spun their cocoons.

For ease of exposition in what follows, I will call the parts of *The Emigrants* stories and of *The Rings of Saturn* chapters. They generate moral momentum and exert a cumulating power of impact. The reader who devotedly finishes each book to its very end is left, in various ways, speechless, wondering what sort of work they have been holding in hand, and wondering what sort of world they inhabit. The reader is called, as it were, to speak again, or perhaps to speak for the very first time about their relationship with the past. Sebald is not casual or capricious about the sequence of events, themes, and moments he presents, even if they elude easy systemization.

*Austerlitz* has no table of contents and no chapters. It constitutes a single, continuous, many-sided narrative, often with no paragraph or other breaks for pages on end, a style that reflects some of the literary influences on him, including the work of Thomas Bernhard. Like the other two books, *Austerlitz* includes a gallery of affecting photographs, an aspect I return to later. It also contains direct and indirect references, as do Sebald's other works, to one of his guiding lights—the philosopher Ludwig Wittgenstein. As we will see, Sebald shares with Wittgenstein an intense, moral response to mechanistic and other hardened rationalistic systems which can disfigure the human. In addition, he resonates with Wittgenstein's deep concerns about how language use can confuse, mislead, and distort human endeavors. The book recounts the narrator's many encounters with a figure named Jacques Austerlitz, who was sent to England as a young boy in 1939 on a *Kindertransport*—a train of Jewish children from Central Europe whose parents had managed to arrange for their safe transit. Austerlitz spends his childhood and early youth in Wales, with an austere church minister and his wife, who never refer to his actual origins and show the boy little affection. He eventually attends secondary school away from home and then university. He becomes a professor of architectural history. All this time he is tormented by unaccountable feelings of loss and homelessness, and eventually finds himself compelled to embark on a long odyssey to get back to his roots. He travels repeatedly to Prague, where he was born and lived until boarding a train, never to see his birth parents again. He learns that his mother eventually died in a Nazi concentration camp, while at the book's close he is following, literally, the steps his father took in a bid to escape and perhaps survive.

Sebald, his narrator, and the individuals featured in his work all feel the pull, and the weight, of conventional ways of thinking about, imagining, and remembering people and human events. Time and again, we see the narrator struggling as witness with the question of how to describe what he sees, hears, and reads. He sometimes feels his sensibility compressed, flattened, and emptied out the moment he begins to enunciate himself. Sebald dramatizes the issue in *Austerlitz*, when the protagonist by that name recounts to the narrator something a beloved secondary school history teacher, named André Hilary, said to him about the difficulty of writing history. Hilary was a published writer on the Napoleonic era and tried mightily to help his students see and feel the reality of war (in chapter 4, we will see how Walt Whitman engages this same task). In the end, however, Hilary believed the heavy impress of familiar visual images, combined with the limits of conventional language, were insurmountable. "All of us," Austerlitz reports him saying, "even when we think we have noted every tiny detail, resort to set pieces which have already been staged often enough by others. We try to reproduce the reality, but the harder we try, the more we find the pictures that make up the stock-in-trade of the spectacle of history forcing themselves upon us: the fallen drummer boy, the infantryman shown in the act of stabbing another, the horse's eye starting from its socket, the invulnerable Emperor surrounded by his generals, a moment frozen still amidst the turmoil of battle. Our concern with history," continues Austerlitz in his recollection of Hilary's outlook, "is a concern with preformed images already imprinted on our brains, images at which we keep staring while the truth lies elsewhere, away from it all, somewhere as yet undiscovered" (A71–72).[6]

Sebald enacts a comparable attitude toward much of the conventional discourse about the Shoah. As mentioned, in the works cited here he does not use that term, nor does he deploy the term Holocaust. He seems determined to avoid set pieces, all the painful yet familiar scenes of suffering people, brutal guards, barking German shepherds, and barbed wire fences.

He, like all of us, has been inundated with such images. It is as if their very ubiquity can engender moral indifference, as well as the impatient if whispered question: Must we cover this ground yet again? Sebald even uses the term Jew circumspectly (he was not himself Jewish), as if it were both too well-known and at the same time widely uncomprehended.[7] He seeks what I will characterize below as "rightful trespass," by attending to the precise details of people's experience and what they say about it. Precision becomes not the royal road to truth but the only road he knows that can help him avoid fogging things up. "Unobtrusively," writes Mark Anderson (2003), "his identity shrunk to a bare minimum, the narrator [in Sebald's work] seems to present these lives without mediation, not as they 'really happened,' but as they were 'really reported' to him, without making them a mere foil for his own story. And yet," Anderson continues, "he is the secret center, the thread that holds these narrations together in an implicit gesture of solidarity and identification that is all the more effective for begin unstated" (p. 107).

The discussion below pivots around an in-depth reading of a single story in *The Emigrants*, which I believe can bear the burden of the analysis because of its moral power as expressed, in part, through a brilliant portrait of a remarkable teacher. The latter achievement signals how Sebald's witness can educate the reader. It is an education, among other things, in learning the arts of rightful trespass. These arts are central to the very act of bearing witness, as we will also see in the ensuing chapters on Aimé Césaire and Walt Whitman. In what follows, I will show how this learning appears in the experience of Sebald's narrator, and how it invites the reader into an ethical line of vision.

## The Awareness of Trespass

Sebald's vision as a writer in *The Emigrants*, *The Rings of Saturn*, and *Austerlitz* is turned toward the past. In an interview he once said that only the past interests him, and that he does not believe the future holds much promise (Wachtel, 2007, pp. 41–42). I do not think these words imply he sits in a chair, figuratively speaking, with his back to the present and future. He does not adopt the point of view of Paul Klee's unsettling painting, *Angelus Novus* (New Angel), which the critic Walter Benjamin called "the angel of history. . . . whose face is turned toward the past. Where we perceive a chain of events, the angel sees one single catastrophe which keeps piling wreckage upon wreckage and hurls it in front of his feet. The angel would like to stay, awaken the dead, make whole what has been smashed. But a storm is blowing from Paradise" (quoted in Anderson, 2003, pp. 114-115).

Sebald acknowledges that history can seem like nothing "but a long account of calamities" (R295), and his writing offers no easy consolation. On the contrary, were he not such an artful wordsmith a reader might close his books shattered rather than steeped in thought. Sebald tries to *enter* the past, to walk back into it just as he walks endlessly through fields, villages, cities, battlefields, and ruins across Europe. At times, Sebald's narrator aspires to re-inhabit the past, as if life's secrets, or its redemption, or its only tolerable form, resides there. At other times, Sebald writes of the past, of its people and happenings, as if it stood before him alive and vulnerable, unsure and wondering what he will say of it, how he will treat it, whether he will show respect for it. The past speaks. Will Sebald—*can* Sebald—listen? Can he even hear? And if he can hear and listen, what will he say in reply? What will be the tone, the substance, the trajectory of his witness?

Clinical and humane, scientific and artistic, standing apart and standing in, systematic and spontaneous: the tensions between these terms, all of which pertain to Sebald's endeavor, mirror the tension in his sentences as he tries to handle, to hold in hand, the past in a way that will not damage or disintegrate it. Enough harm has been done already. Enough has been lost. Therefore, it becomes incumbent on him not to injure people and things again. The novelist Alan Paton closes his *Too Late the Phalarope*, an agonizing story of the harshness of Apartheid ideology in pre-1993 South Africa, by having the narrator summon a biblical saying: "That the body of the Lord might not be wounded twice, and virtue come of our offenses" (1953, p. 272).

Sebald carries this image into his writing. In a chapter in *The Rings of Saturn*, the narrator recounts a scene from the memoirs of the Vicomte de Chateaubriand (1768 to 1848), who as a youthful refugee from the French Revolution found himself the guest in a country house in England of a kindly couple named Ives and their young daughter, Charlotte, with whom he fell deeply in love and vice versa. But Chateaubriand, before escaping France, had accepted an arranged marriage, so the love between the English girl and he came to naught. Years later, as Ambassador of the French King in London, Chateaubriand meets Charlotte again, now with grown sons from a contented marriage. She has come to ask him for help in arranging a position for her eldest, and then she leaves, and he never sees her again. "After this painful parting," the narrator reports him writing, "I spent long hours shut away in my study at the embassy and, with repeated interruptions for vain reflection and brooding, committed our unhappy story to paper. As I did so, I was troubled by the question of whether in the writing I should not once again betray and lose Charlotte Ives." (R254–255).

Sebald is obsessively concerned not to "betray" those about whom he writes, so much so that his narrator ends up in a hospital with what amounts to a spiritual and physical collapse (described in the initial pages of *The Rings of Saturn*). He has broken down under the strain of his self-imposed moral strictures about representation, and under the sheer weight of so much destruction across history to which he has born witness. In figurative as well as literal terms, he has risked his footing in the world, and has taken a serious fall. I return to this occurrence on several occasions below.

The first three stories in *The Emigrants* recount the lives of three émigrés who eventually commit suicide. The narratives are not extended obituaries, despite some similarities with that familiar genre of writing. An obituary is a public device for announcing the death of a person and for commenting on their life. It serves a valuable social function, especially in today's world where most people no longer live in small villages and know everybody and everything that happens. While obituaries have their stylistic conventions, the form allows for considerable variation depending on the writer's point of view, background knowledge, relation with the deceased, and the like. The writer's choice of what to recount—and what not to—as well as their interpretive proclivities, are all on display. Some obituaries are terse and almost stenographic; others attain the heights of poetry. Thus, an obituary can be variously understood as a report, a narrative version of a headstone, a commemoration, an appreciation, an assessment of a life, a requiem, an elegy, an encomium, and a duty.

An obituary can also be profoundly misleading and unjust. Put another way, it can enact wrongful trespass. The second story in *The Emigrants*, titled "Paul Bereyter," opens with the narrator reporting on how he learned of the suicide of his 74-year-old former schoolteacher. The news arrived, he says, from the town of S in southwestern Germany, where Bereyter had taught for many years before retiring.[8] The narrator notes that the obituary in the local paper, which had been sent to him, does not mention the fact that Bereyter had committed suicide by what the narrator refers to as either "his own free will" or "through a self-destructive compulsion" (E27). It refers "merely," as the narrator puts it, to Bereyter's tireless work as an educator, his love of music, his inventiveness, and "much else" in a comparable vein. The reference to "merely" may strike the reader as unfair, but it becomes evident that the townspeople of S in fact knew very little about Bereyter and regarded him as an eccentric if not as a stranger. Thus, the praise in the obituary takes on the tone of boilerplate rather than of a sincere testimonial to a distinctive human being—and in the course of the story we learn just how much the narrator esteemed his childhood teacher.

What especially arrests the narrator is that the obituary mentions "almost by way of an aside" and "with no further explanation" the fact that during the Third Reich Bereyter had been "prevented from practicing his chosen profession" (E27). An "aside," "no further explanation," and the passive voice "prevented from": these all-too-familiar expressions, on second hearing, are horrifying given the facts of history. The narrator does not make this judgment explicit. Sebald's usual practice is to let the minute details of individual lives accumulate such that readers are drawn to face the truth and to confront their response to it. Later in the chapter, the narrator reports how he discovered that, according to the infamous statutes of the Nuremberg Laws of 1935, Bereyter had been officially classified as three-quarters Aryan and one-quarter Jewish, on account of a Jewish grandfather in his past. Such a status barred him from employment in state and local public positions, including that of teacher.

The narrator did not know any of this when he was a child in Bereyter's classroom, thus conjuring what numerous commentators have dubbed the massive "silence" about the realities of the Third Reich that descended on Germany in the immediate postwar years. It was a silence that became so deafening and intolerable to Sebald (cf. E225) that—unlike most of the figures in *The Emigrants*—he willingly migrated to another country, a reversal of positions that is never lost on him and that can be detected between the lines of his prose. These facts render all the more mystifying and poignant that the schoolteacher Bereyter, despite being the victim of racist policy, returned to the village of S after the war to his work as an educator.

The people of S who survived the war—which means most of them, since the town is in a remote corner of Germany that escaped becoming a battlefield—knew that Bereyter was unceremoniously fired from his job in their local school and soon after left town, only to reappear out of nowhere a decade later after the shooting was over. They were aware of the Nuremberg Laws and their consequences. When the narrator ends up visiting S to further investigate what happened to his teacher, the townspeople he speaks with say nothing about the prewar or war years, and in general are "not very revealing" (E28). "The only thing that seemed remarkable" to him about their otherwise thin accounts, reports the narrator, "was that no one called him Paul Bereyter or even Bereyter the teacher. Instead, he was invariably referred to simply as Paul, giving me the impression that in the eyes of his contemporaries he had never really grown up" (E27).

To call a person by his or her first name typically connotes a degree of intimacy or at least recognition. The townspeople evidently felt neither close to Bereyter nor did they recognize him, if we highlight the morally pregnant aspect of that verb that has to do with acknowledging a human being's past and their personal experience. The reader cannot help but speculate, with a shudder, that to the townspeople Bereyter's Jewish background implied he had failed to "grow up" into a "real" German. He was like a weed or a strange hybrid in the uniform crop. Oh yes, *Paul* . . . The obituarist in the local paper refers to the circumstances of the Third Reich as if they were "mere" matters of fact. The tone of this kind of writing, which could be taken as a form of antiremembrance, shakes the narrator. Sebald reveals here, and throughout the story of Bereyter, his quest for fair-minded representation of people to whom the Nazis denied all representation and recognition.

Later in the chapter, the narrator has numerous conversations with Lucy Landau, another émigré who left Germany in 1933 as a child and settled with her family in Switzerland. She met Bereyter serendipitously after the war and soon became a close friend (and perhaps lover though the matter is left ambiguous). Landau's memories of Bereyter are highly detailed, moving, and tender, and only occasionally broken by a sudden rush of bitter anger at the Germans for what they had done to him. At one point she tells the narrator she is not the least surprised that he had no idea of Bereyter's past when he was a schoolboy in S. "Do you know," she tells him,

> the systematic thoroughness with which these people kept silent in the years after the war, kept their secrets, and even, I sometimes think, really did forget, is nothing more than the other side of the perfidious way in which Schöferle, who ran

a coffee house in S, informed Paul's mother Thekla, who had been on stage for some time in Nuremberg, that the presence of a lady who was married to a half Jew might be embarrassing to his respectable clientele, and begged to request her, with respect of course, not to take her afternoon coffee at his house any more. I do not find it surprising [continued Landau], not in the slightest, that you were unaware of the meanness and treachery that a family like the Bereyters were exposed to in a miserable hole such as S then was, and such as it still is despite all the so-called progress; it does not surprise me at all, since that is inherent in the logic of the whole wretched sequence of events. (E50)

Landau's remark about the "logic" in events mirrors Sebald's deepest questions about the course European civilization took in the wake of modernity, with its problematic forms of economic and organizational rationality. The remark also calls to mind his concerns about rightful trespass, or what might be called "just description" and its association, in his eyes, with "just remembrance."

A simple obituary about a beloved schoolteacher: not so simple, after all, to a mind caught up in questions of truth and justice. "It was this curiously unconnected, inconsequential statement" about the Third Reich in the obituary, says the narrator, along with his distress at the violent manner of Bereyter's death, that in time compelled him to bear witness. "I had to get beyond my own very fond memories of him," he reports, "and discover the story I did not know" (E28). What the narrator discovers—what Sebald discovers—is the profound difficulty in rendering justly another person's life, especially if it is the life of someone whose experience differs markedly from the inquirer's. As mentioned, Sebald was not Jewish. He was, to use the unhinged language of the Nuremberg Laws, 100 percent Aryan, and this is a language that, as a German born in 1944 when those Laws were still in effect, seems to have marked or branded his consciousness ever after.[9] He seeks to discover what really happened to the Jews of Germany—a story he did not know as a child or youth—and how it could be that his native country would commit itself to tearing out of its very fabric a community that had dwelt there for centuries and had contributed so visibly and profoundly to its arts, letters, and general culture.[10] In his witness, Sebald struggles to comprehend the incomprehensible. He, his narrator, and many other speakers in his books sometimes seem to stutter, to grope for words, and to be reduced to a silence of a different sort than that which obtained in postwar Germany. Sebald's writing enacts his acute sensitivity to differences in experience, and his equally intense awareness of the ethical challenge he took on when he elected to write of people—Jews and non-Jews alike—whose fate he did not share.

However, Sebald implies that he and we share the same world—one world—a world to which we owe our best moral efforts, however paltry our talents, resources, and capacities may be. At least, such is a claim I detect between the lines of his prose. If the quest for truthful and respectful words about people and events remains ever partial and incomplete; if this quest remains vulnerable at any time to slipping into sentimentality and distorting consolation; if it may lead to endless cul-de-sacs, dead ends, and other frustrations; still, Sebald conveys in his writing that the effort is not only worthwhile but, somehow, necessary. Silence will not do. Silence is living death, deathful living. Silence perpetuates injustice, ugliness, and lies. The witness *must* attest.

But to break the silence is a fateful move fraught with dangers of misdescription, of one-sidedness, of adding woe rather than reducing it or at least responding to it. Thus, to know when to keep silent—as Ludwig Wittgenstein evokes at the end of his *Tractatus*—and about what things, and in what ways, becomes as vital as knowing when to speak. Side by side with this knowledge is knowing how and when to provide the right words, the right details, the right observations. In the moral realm, it seems, arts of silence and waiting accompany arts of speaking and doing. This composite knowledge is hard to imagine, much less to attain. I believe Sebald aspires to come as near as he can to such knowledge, while time and again tapping himself on his own shoulder to remind himself and the reader that he is ever underway, and that it is ultimately up to the reader to carry on the endeavor. Sebald has a butterfly stage of understanding: experienced, seasoned, imbued with a sense of responsibility, and transitive rather than caught up in partisan webs. But the butterfly leads a short life. No single Monarch butterfly, for example, can make the epic, annual migration from North America to Mexico and back; it takes several generations. In likeness, no individual person, or generation, can sustain moral grace in human affairs. It is a perpetual undertaking.

To share the same world: right after reporting on the townspeople's habit of calling Bereyter "Paul," the narrator recalls that he and his classmates in school used to do the very same thing. "Not without respect," he adds, "but rather as one might refer to an exemplary older brother, and in a way this implied that he was one of us, or that we belonged together" (E28). But the narrator then says: "I have come to realize" that he and his peers "fabricated" this relation. "Even though Paul knew and understood us," he observes, "we, for our part, had little idea of what he was or what went on inside him" (E28–29). The reader notes the narrator *continuing* to call Bereyter by his first name, right after calling our attention to its inappropriateness. It is in the narrator's remark, "I have come to realize," that we perceive a moral shift. Those words attest to the fact that the narrator is speaking of the past. He is telling a story about what becomes an extended inquiry into the life of his teacher, and, through him, the life of their shared country of birth. He now knows, as it were, what he *now* knows, but did not know as a child. He no longer uses Bereyter's first name as he did then. He uses his first name, here and now, precisely in recognition of the man's humanity. He now knows of this man's painful experience and complicated interiority. He has let himself become Bereyter's pupil once again: to let a compatriot, exiled for the most arbitrary and heinous of reasons, educate him about the meaning of German history, and about the meaning of bearing witness to the human condition.

## Names and Moral Remembrance

Teach, teaching, taught; report, reporting, reported; says, saying, said: the uncanny feeling a reader has in accompanying Sebald has to do, in part, with this writer's skillful sundering of linear time, of traditional storytelling, and of authorial voice. Much of the writing is in the first person, but the person behind the "I" keeps altering, from the narrator to someone speaking to the narrator, to someone speaking about that speaker to the narrator, to someone in the past speaking to someone else in the past or to him- or herself, and so on and so forth. These changes sometimes happen in back-to-back sentences, and sometimes even in the same phrase.

Yet, Sebald takes care not to lose the reader. He is not playing with words or letting them play with him in a manner he associates with a writer he esteemed, Robert Walser, whose prose, Sebald writes, sometimes features "word-eddies" and verbal "turbulence" (like a rough sea) "created in the middle of a sentence by exaggerated participial constructions, or conglomerations of verbs" (Sebald, 2013, p. 139). The voices in Sebald's narratives come across as real, all too real, and they come across as singular, irreproducible, and noninterchangeable. They are voices of experience, of the concrete, and they know about what they say. As the reader turns each page, there comes a point where they almost feel it is their turn to speak—or indeed that they have already become a speaker, or at any rate an active listener, and thus a participant rather than a mere spectator or consumer of words on printed page. As suggested previously, Sebald brings the past alive. He brings the reader into the past and the past into the reader, such that the boundaries between past, present, and future collapse and everything merges into a moment difficult to characterize temporally. It is not a moment "out of time." It is not as if Sebald as writer, his narrator, the affairs at hand, and the reader become suspended in light-saturated amber (cf. Nesaule, 1995). On the contrary, it is to be, somehow, more fully in time, as if temporality has become materiality, has taken on substance in a dynamic and unpredictable movement.

A name for this experience is remembrance. Such remembrance differs from sentimental nostalgia, on the one hand, and fanatical adherence to past precept and example, on the other hand. It is a matter of striking a balance of remembering and forgetting, of respecting the past as making possible the present, but also respecting the present as that which makes possible the future. Put another way, the past can speak *in* the present *for* a better future—but only if people listen to it, heed it, and take it as seriously as they take their own animating interests, concerns, fears, and hopes.

Sebald implies that remembrance fuses a consciousness of the past with a sense of responsibility to and for it. Toward the close of *The Emigrants*, in the chapter titled "Max Ferber" (about an emigrant painter living in Manchester, England, who as a boy was flown out of Nazi Germany in 1939), the narrator finds himself in an old, neglected Jewish cemetery in the German town where Ferber's mother Luisa had lived. The narrator has traveled there after reading the mother's lengthy, handwritten memoir of her childhood and youth, which she wrote in the few short years between sending her young son to freedom in England and her death in a concentration camp. In her writing she says nothing about current events, as if to symbolize how truly unspeakable they were. The memoir had ended up in her now-grown son's hands, and he has passed it on to the narrator.[11] It is a loving, beautiful, almost unbearably heart-breaking portrait of what was without doubt a seamlessly fused Jewish-German, German-Jewish family life, so much so that those qualifiers simply fall away as one reads on. It is a tale of profound rootedness, what in German is called *Heimat*, which contrasts markedly with the existential vertigo that both her son Max, and Sebald himself, often express. Moved by Luisa Ferber's account, the narrator is compelled to seek further traces of her life and soon finds himself, alone, in a Jewish cemetery.[12]

The narrator does not know why he is there, or what he should do. All he knows is that it is a necessity: a summons. He pays his respects, to use the odd English expression. "It was not possible to decipher all of the chiseled inscriptions" on the gravestones, he observes.

> [B]ut the names I could still read—Hamburger, Kissinger, Wertheimer, Friedländer, Arnsberg, Auerbach, Grunwald, Leuthold, Seeligmann, Frank, Hertz, Goldstaub, Baumblatt and Blumenthal—made me think that perhaps there was nothing the Germans begrudged the Jews so much as their beautiful names, so intimately bound up with the country they lived in and with its language. A shock of recognition shot through me at the grave of Maier Stern [a photo of it appears right here in the text], who died on the 18th of May, my own birthday; and I was touched, in a way I knew I could never quite fathom, by the symbol of the writer's quill on the stone of Freiderike Halbleib, who departed this life on the 28th of March 1912 [a photo of her gravestone appears on the opposite page]. I imagined her pen in hand, all by herself, bent with bated breath over her work; and now, as I write these lines, it feels as if *I* had lost her, and as if *I* could not get over the loss despite the many years that have passed since her departure. (E224–225)

The narrator wanders for hours in the abandoned cemetery. Just before leaving, he finds a more recent gravestone, which includes the name of Luisa Ferber. An inscription says that Luisa and her husband were deported in November 1941. "I stood before it for some time," the narrator remarks, "not knowing what I should think; but before I left I placed a stone on the grave, according to custom" (E225).

These passages, along with many others in his oeuvre, lend credence to Susan Sontag's (2003) description of Sebald as a writer "in mourning" (also see Summers-Bremner, 2004). His narrator has absorbed the mourner's ethos so fully in his witness that he participates in a custom—placing a rock on a gravestone—that could be seen as remote from his straightforwardly secular life. He gives himself over to it, though he cannot say why. The narrator mourns Luisa Ferber, whose writing he knows, and Friederike Halbleib, whose writing he does not. This witness is more than a requiem. I believe the narrator intuits, in an inchoate fusion of sadness, innocence, and gratitude, that the sheer fact there is something called writing to do, and the role of writer-witness to take up, is due to his precursors, including those who wrote in German but whose right to be German had been stripped from them. He now sees that *his* forbears include a forgotten writer buried in a forgotten Jewish cemetery in a nation (a world?) pathological and self-destructive in its forgetfulness.

Names, and more names. Paul and Bereyter. Sebald shows there is a way to earn the right to call another person fully by their name. By "fully" I have in mind the accomplishment of the teacher who, when they say a student's name, really sees that student and truly attends to that student. Consider also the lover who says aloud the loved one's name tenderly, again and again, almost caressing the name itself as a symbol of caressing the lover. If the two remain together, and grow in love, the name of the loved one expands and deepens in its meaning, importance, and splendor. Fully to use a name can also be the outcome of an ethical inquiry in which the inquirer learns about others, the world, and self at one and the same time. Here, the inquirer exposes their self-understanding, and perhaps understanding of all things, to influence from others and the world. The inquirer is not a mere spectator or collector but rather is a participant, a respondent.

The theme of naming courses through *The Emigrants* and Sebald's other works; we will encounter this pattern in both Césaire's and Whitman's witnesses as well. For example, in *Austerlitz* the chief protagonist undertakes a piercing, existential investigation into the meaning of his real name (he had been given a Welsh name by his foster parents). On a more low-key but no less significant level, Sebald rarely deploys the word *tree*, not even in poetic formulations such as "tree of life." Instead, he is quite specific about what species of trees are in view (see, for instance, the opening pages of the first story in *The Emigrants*, titled "Henry Selwyn"). Sebald is precise, and he is concrete. In this regard he keeps company with other well-known writers in German, among them Rainer Maria Rilke and Wittgenstein, each of whom cast a moral meaning to the act of naming, of describing, of giving accounts of the things of this world. For Sebald, to use a name consciously, circumspectly, and attentively is a step toward preventing oneself and perhaps others from harming that person or thing that has been named. In short, he does not engage in taxonomy. Rather, the act of naming constitutes a form of moral recognition.

In the same breath, naming can embody witnessing. *The Emigrants* closes with the narrator wondering what the names were of three young women who are weaving a carpet, captured in a photo taken in the Litzmannstadt ghetto in Lodz, Poland, which was a slave labor factory operated by the Nazis. *Austerlitz* concludes with the narrator quoting from another writer, Dan Jacobson, who, years after the war, had gone in search of his Jewish ancestry in Lithuania. Jacobson ends up visiting a former prison where many Jews had been killed. Some French prisoners had etched their names on the walls, which Jacobson, and now Sebald, and now the reader, can see: "Lob, Marcel, de St. Nazaire; Wechsler, Abram, de Limoges; Max Stern, Paris, 18.5.44" (A298). These three names, that close one book, generate a space for the unknown names of the three women that close another.[13]

The narrator has now realized, in his awareness of the moral depths in naming, that he and his classmates did not "belong together" with Bereyter. It was not only that they did not know him. It was that they did not understand that their teacher was in effect ejected from their cultural circle the instant he was born, for their German society at the time discriminated against Jews, and in the Nazi era literally exiled them or killed them. Toward the end of his life, and despite his failing eyesight, Bereyter reads late into the night and takes hundreds of pages of notes on books written by German writers who either committed suicide or had been close to doing so, among them George Trakl, Wittgenstein, Walter Benjamin, Arthur Koestler, and Stefan Zweig. To his close friend Lucy Landau, this intense reading and note-taking seemed "as if Paul had been gathering evidence, the mounting weight of which, as his investigations proceeded, finally convinced him that he belonged to the exiles and not to the people of S" (E59). The reader wonders whether Sebald, a child of S himself, at this very moment during his witness draws the same conclusion about himself.

"And so, belatedly," reports the narrator, "I tried to get closer to [Bereyter], to imagine what his life was like" (E29). But the narrator quickly rejects the route of empathy, at least as he conceives that familiar term. He realizes that to grasp the life of his former teacher is not a matter of trying to get "inside him" or "closer to him." Such a move is but the mirror twin of the townspeople's transparent attempt to psychologize Bereyter's condition—dubbing him "eccentric"—rather than to acknowledge their participation in creating an environment that helped destroy him. The narrator discerns in their remarks about Bereyter their view "that things had happened as they were bound to happen" (E28). But Sebald's entire witness rejects both psychologism and fatalism, even while he expresses a sobered, unoptimistic (not to be confused with unhopeful) view of human capabilities.

The narrator realizes the falsity in his initial steps. First, as he reports, he tried to imagine Bereyter's life in his later years, when the former teacher retained an apartment in S while residing most of the year in Yverdon, Switzerland, near Lucy Landau. The narrator "imagined" Bereyter spending time on his balcony in S, even sleeping there on summer nights under the stars. He imagined him ice skating in winter on nearby ponds. And he "pictured" him stretched out on the railway track where he committed suicide and where the authorities found his body. Bereyter "had taken off his spectacles," the narrator speculates,

> and put them on the ballast stones by his side. The gleaming bands of steel, the crossbars of the sleepers, the spruce trees on the hillside above the village of Altstädten, the arc of the mountains he knew so well, were a blur before his short-sighted eyes, smudged out in the gathering dusk. At the last, as the thunderous sound approached, all he saw was a darkening greyness and, in the midst of it, needle-sharp, the snow-white silhouettes of three mountains: the Kratzer, the Trettach and the Himmelsschrofen. (E29)

The documentary, pointillist style so characteristic of Sebald's writing comes to the fore here, with his use of specific names, places, and details of all sorts, almost as if he were putting in place the pixels of a photograph rather than the words of an account. (He did write by pen and pencil, incidentally, rather than with a computer or typewriter.) We observe time and again this witness's powerful commitment to reality—to both the idea and the reality of reality, as it were—even as he sometimes fumbles with the tools of rightful trespass.

Put another way, for Sebald the commitment to truth and reality seems to spring from a prior or parallel moral mindfulness. He knows that the capacity to describe things minutely and systematically can serve evil as much as good. In *Austerlitz* he crafts a stark portrait of how the Nazis administered the camp known as Theresienstadt, which became a kind of Potemkin village to demonstrate to the world their "humane" treatment of

Jews. Sebald deploys and exposes, in the very same sentences, the Nazis' relentless, bureaucratic precision in their memoranda and reports, with regard to listing things, bodies, and movements. Sebald is aware not only of the dangers of rationalistic description and doublespeak, but also writes with a keen eye for how fine-grained, highly detailed writing can generate illusion and fantasy rather than truth. Thus, Sebald has the narrator pulled up short (cf. Kerdeman, 2003). It is true he cherished his former teacher. But it is equally true that his picturings are taking him away from the truth *of* his former teacher. "Such endeavours to imagine his life and death did not, as I had to admit," concludes the narrator, "bring me any closer to Paul, except at best for brief emotional moments of the kind that seemed presumptuous to me. It is in order to avoid this sort of wrongful trespass that I have written down what I know of Paul Bereyter" (E29).

## The Quest for Truth in Bearing Witness

Sebald could say, echoing his narrator: it is in order to avoid wrongful trespass on the past, present, and future that I have adopted this method of working. His technique includes the use of captionless black-and-white photographs, as well as a variety of drawings, paintings, and other curiosities, which variously complement, trouble, continue, and sidetrack his prose narratives. They complicate the writing, dislodge it, shift it, and keep it from hardening or resting. They are alluring, fascinating, compelling, moving, and confusing. They sometimes appear almost randomly, while at other moments it's as if one were reading an illustrated textbook or travel guide. They help carry the burden of the narratives since, like poems, they compress and hold economically modes of meaning and questioning. To recall a trope used previously, the photos are variously clinical and compassionate, scientific and artistic, distant and intimate.

Several commentators have suggested Sebald deploys photos to question that much more the prospect of truthful and respectful representation of people and events.[14] On the one hand, photographs have what Edward Shils (1965) and others call a charismatic quality. They can persuade us, unawares and in the very instant of looking at them, that they capture truth. On the other hand, Sebald's selection of photographs demonstrates that they are always interpretations of the world, not a stenographic, neutral, or god's-eye representation of it. This claim holds even for a photo that would be as large as the cosmos itself, because it would simultaneously raise the questions of where one is standing to take such a photo and of what is on the other side of the photo. Sebald also seems to be keenly aware that photographs can corrupt human sensibilities as much as words can (see the discussion of this point in Sontag, 2003). Photographs can fall short of the truth. They can distort and undermine ethical concerns.

The chapter on Paul Bereyter begins with a photo of curving railway tracks in a gray countryside. The photo was taken from a camera that must have been placed right on one of the rails, whose near portion is, accordingly, wide and vast. That portion of the rail is also out of focus, thereby recalling the narrator's attempt to "picture" Bereyter stretched out on the rail, having removed his glasses (the narrator surmises) so that things are blurry while in the distance we see a forest and the outline, it seems, of a hill or small mountain. Here and elsewhere in the book there is not a point-by-point correspondence between prose and photograph. For example, we cannot discern in the opening photograph the three snow-capped mountains mentioned in the text, or catch a glimpse of the village named therein. Perhaps the photograph was cropped to make the railway lines stand out.

In the end one is left unsure what to make of the photo, save to remark that it is unnerving, sad, and brilliantly chosen. But the question also emerges whether the photo itself may be part of the "wrongful trespass" that so preoccupies Sebald as witness. As hard as one might try, it is not possible to see the world as another sees it, even if one goes so far as to lay one's head on a rail, as did Sebald, it seems, in order to take the photo—in who knows what kind of emotional frame of mind. One thinks again of the opening of *The Rings of Saturn*, the book that came after *The Emigrants*, with its scenes of the unnamed narrator entering the hospital in a state of spiritual exhaustion from all he has witnessed.

In considering the story of Bereyter as a whole, to me the strange opening photograph is fitting. It is not an accurate representation in and of itself—a mirror of nature—but it constitutes what we might call a true evocation. It has its valuable place as one element in what can be read as an album, like the familiar family album of words, photos, and sometimes drawings, sketches, postcards, and all the rest, which reveal human life in many senses of that verb. In the story on Bereyter we find the following dozen photographs, all in black and white (like all the photos in Sebald's work).

- The aforementioned shot taken from the railway track.

- An oval-shaped photo of 29 German schoolboys from what seems to be around 1950—that is, when the narrator was a child in S—who seem to be in a jovial mood as they squint into the sun that is behind the photographer, who may or may not be Bereyter himself.

- Side-by-side photos (of different sizes) of, on one page, a group of thirteen newly minted teachers (all male) with four of their stern-looking professors (evidently taken around 1935, the time when Bereyter received his teaching license); across the page from this photo is a shot of a crowded classroom, apparently from around 1950, which features in the back a teacher who seems to be Bereyter, along with almost all the fifty children the narrator reports being in his class.

- A photo of a young woman who may or may not be Helen Hollaender, with whom the narrator reports Bereyter fell in love just as he began his teaching career, but from whom he was separated when the Nazi authorities stripped him of his post and he went into exile. (Lucy Landau suggests that Helen Hollaender later died, along with her mother, in the concentration camp called Theresienstadt, to which as mentioned Sebald returns in *Austerlitz*.)

- On the same page we find a set of three photos from a contact sheet, which the reader assumes are Bereyter and Hollaender, who are in a very happy mood.

- On the opposite page is a photo of a very down-spirited, hollowed-out Bereyter (one must always say "or so it seems," since there are no captions) standing alongside the French family for whom he worked as a house tutor after emigrating across the Rhine River in 1935.

- A photo from the 1920s of a classic Durkopp automobile apparently with Bereyter's father at the wheel—he was a successful shopkeeper and bought the car—alongside several friends on a ride through the town of S.

56 | The Witness as Educator

- Two photos, on successive pages, which portray Bereyter during his time as a soldier in the German army. The narrator reports that, like some of the other photographs, they come from a thick album he holds in hand leant to him by Lucy Landau, which Bereyter had assembled and which contains a photographic record of most of his life—and with each photo, unlike in Sebald's text, accompanied by a caption or description.

In one of these two photos, a uniformed, helmeted Bereyter is at the wheel of a truck and has leaned out the window to get a better look at things. In the other, he is shirtless on a bright sunny day, sitting at a table in dark sunglasses. To the narrator's dismay, Bereyter, after tutoring in France from 1935 to 1939, returned to Germany and worked in a garage in Berlin until called up by the army, which the Nazis permitted for "three-quarter Aryans." In a gripping passage, the narrator recounts how Bereyter served—"if that is the right word" (E55)—for the full six years of the war. The narrator might have added "and miraculously so," given the appalling casualties the German army suffered in its complicity with Hitler's dictates; some five and a half million soldiers were killed before the country collapsed in May 1945. Bereyter "was in Poland, Belgium, France, the Balkans, Russia and the Mediterranean," reports the narrator, "and doubtless saw more than any heart or eye can bear. The seasons and the years came and went . . . and always, as Paul wrote under this photograph [of the shirtless Bereyter], one was, as the crow flies, about 2,000 km away—but from where?—and day by day, hour by hour, with every beat of the pulse, one lost more and more of one's qualities, became less comprehensible to oneself, increasingly abstract" (E56). The reader realizes how many train transports Bereyter must have taken across Nazi-occupied Europe, riding the same rails as his Jewish-German brethren on their way to the death camps.

Mark Anderson (2003) recounts the story behind the curious image of being "2,000 km away" no matter where one is: "Two Jews meet after their shtetl has been razed to the ground. One says: 'I've had it. I'm moving to Australia.' The other: 'That's a long way away.' The first: 'A long way from where?'" (p. 111). Anderson notes that Sebald gives the allusion a "citational, interpolated quality" since another character, the narrator's uncle, repeats it almost verbatim elsewhere in the book (E89). As Carol Jacobs (2004) puts it, Sebald endlessly "cross-pollinates" his works with repeated asides, allusions, metaphors, events, and persons (p. 913). We will see this testimonial habit at work in the next chapter on Aimé Césaire's epic poem.

In my view, Sebald aspires in his witness to attain what Wittgenstein (1993) calls a "perspicuous representation." For Wittgenstein, such a representation "makes possible that understanding which consists just in the fact that we 'see the connections.' Hence the importance of finding *intermediate links*" (p. 9e).[15] Sebald provides intermediate links even between his intermediate links in order to assist the reader, and himself, to see his way about in the maze of emotions, memories, uncertainties, and yearnings that mark the human. He does not "explain" what he sees but renders it in such a way that understanding can emerge if one is attentive. At the same time, however, the theme of silk weaving that connects the myriad parts of *The Rings of Saturn* constitutes a reminder that particular sorts of descriptions—like particular framings of memory—can lead to self-cocooning on the part of individuals and societies. Sebald's use of photographs and his tactic of constantly changing speakers disrupt a word-spinning that in its soundlessness might beguile and occlude.

Bereyter's testimony deepens the mystery of his decision, if that is the right word, to return to S after the war and resume his teaching life. Lucy Landau speculates—says the narrator—writes Sebald—that "what moved and perhaps even forced Paul to return, in 1939 and in 1945, was the fact that he was a German to the marrow, profoundly attached to his native land in the foothills of the Alps, and even to that miserable place S" (E57). One notes, parenthetically, that Landau refers to his attachment to the land rather than to the people. The pressing questions for the reader, as for Sebald, remain: What must it have cost Bereyter to keep his dreadful war memories—alongside memories of being rejected by his culture—from his pupils, if not from everyone he knew? What does it cost the narrator, Sebald, Germany, and all of us *not* to recognize such memories as markers of a world for which we share responsibility? The narrator, despite his unknowingness as a child, nonetheless noticed moments when his teacher seemed suddenly moved, distracted, thrown out of his orbit. "At any time," he notes, "—in the middle of a lesson, at break, or on one of our outings—he might stop or sit down somewhere, alone and apart from us all, as if he, who was always in good spirits and seemed so cheerful, was in fact desolation itself" (E42). The child sees with sympathy but without understanding, in a manner that calls to mind Wittgenstein's remark to his sister when she complained about him abandoning philosophy for the sake of a primary school teaching post: "You remind me of somebody who is looking out through a closed window and cannot explain to himself the strange movements of a passer-by. He cannot tell what sort of storm is raging out there or that this person might only be managing with difficulty to stay on his feet" (quoted in Monk, p. 170).[16]

It was not until many years later, in the 1970s, that Bereyter meets Landau and recounts his life to her. He begins to come to grips with his past, as seen in the large album he prepares, in his late-night studies of other German writers fighting for life, and in other investigations such as his intensive study in official archives of the hounding isolation and then oppression of German Jews in the 1930s (all of which, the reader notes when coming up for air, are activities Sebald himself undertook in his witness). With the two photographs mentioned above and accompanying text, Sebald intensifies the almost incomprehensible struggle Bereyter faced—like all the émigrés in the book—in trying to get a purchase on his identity, his roots, his home, his place in the world. Emigrant, immigrant; resident, stranger; homebody, nomad: What is he? Who is he? "Where" in the human tableau is he? "How" is he, whatever he is or is not? The dumbfounding fact that Bereyter joined the army of the very state that repressed him, and fought against those seeking to end that repression, takes the reader to a place of bewilderment and perhaps anguish that is hard to bring into focus.

How "German" was Bereyter? Was that his question? In putting on the uniform of one of the supreme German institutions of the day, was he experimenting with what it felt like to be a "grown" and acceptable German? He had only been able to wear the uniform of teacher—another time-honored institutional role in Germany—for a short time. Did he go to Berlin, at the very heart of the nation, and then enter the army to prove his Germanhood? If so, to whom? Layer upon layer upon layer: Sebald puts before the reader, word by word, photo by photo, just how deep is the damage wrought by injustice, whether it takes the form of brutal oppression or of relentless indifference. And yet, in the very same moment, his acutely attentive, artful witness enacts the (sometimes) requiting beauty and tenderness of which human beings are capable.

In addition to the twelve photographs, which make one think of the twelve Apostles in the Bible who bore witness to Christ, Sebald's album-story includes a student's blueprint-like drawing of Bereyter's classroom, two photocopies of rough, handwritten notebook pages that appear to contain the shorthand style Bereyter deployed in jotting down his hundreds of pages of notes on German writers with whom he felt a life-and-death kinship, and a blueprint-like sketch, on the second to last page of the story, of several buildings including a train station along with several track lines. The reader notes how this sketch of a train station bookends the opening photograph of the railway lines in the countryside. Railways carry Bereyter and other emigrants hither and thither; they cart German soldiers one way and Jews the other; and they convey the narrator-Sebald endlessly around Europe in a quest to discover, to understand, to find meaning if meaning be there to find.

The photographs, drawings, and Sebald's words personalize, humanize, and vivify the man called Paul Bereyter. No single element in the story-album captures the full truth of things. Each element adds something to the whole, which becomes more than the sum of the parts. Consider how a brushstroke of red on a canvas may mean little taken in itself. It may seem utterly wrong compared with the vase of roses the painter has in sight. But when the painting is finished, and if it has done its work, the viewer may realize with a start that they have never truly looked at a rose before. I believe Sebald is asking the reader to consider whether they have ever truly looked into the past and, metaphorically speaking, whether they have ever let it look into them.

Sebald attempts to be "truth-full," to be true to people and things, to be true to life in the multiple senses of that familiar expression. His commitment emerges in his documentary, fact-by-fact, detail-by-detail writing, which steers clear of the sentimental, the consoling, and the comforting, yet without veering into the caustic, the eristic, and the cynical.[17] We get substantive descriptions one can almost touch and feel. Sebald's clinical, scientific tendency does not become tedious or toneless precisely because of his artfulness in organizing, framing, and sequencing events. He much esteemed nature writing—stating that he felt some naturalists write better than most novelists—and he learned a lot from this genre (Silverblatt, 2001). Sebald finds ways to say things just so, like the driver for a professional photographer who, despite the bumpy, jolting terrain of the veldt maneuvers the vehicle such that when he stops, abruptly, the photographer has in their line of vision a view they could never have anticipated. Click, and it's there, and it's right.

## Responsive and Responsible Methods of Attending

Photographs, drawings, sketches, maps, paintings, poems, songs, inscriptions on tombstones, handwritten tracts, newspaper clippings including obituaries; reports from archives, television programs, and the radio;

references to novels, histories, and memoirs; extracts from travel books, scientific treatises and encyclopedias, including some that the reader (but not Sebald) instinctively dismisses as quite out-of-date; what the five senses can discern in the world; and Sebald's prose style with its many voices and tenses, its memories and dreams: such are the materials and methods on display in *The Emigrants* and elsewhere in this oeuvre.[18] They call to mind other peripatetic methodologies, such as those of the sociologist of everyday human life Erving Goffman. Sebald puts forward for the reader tools for excavating and writing the past, not as historiography but as felt remembrance. If used conscientiously, and in the spirit of truthful and respectful heeding, the tools can help make possible rightful trespass. I have sought to indicate thus far how much Sebald accomplishes with them.

However, Sebald suspects their ultimate utility. He questions how much truth they can yield, and how much respect they can in fact evince toward others and the world. He never escapes his underlying sense that no matter how artfully they are employed, they will fall short—that is to say, he will fall short in his witness. I have mentioned several times the moral and spiritual breakdown the narrator undergoes, described on the opening pages of *The Rings of Saturn*. An additional cause of his collapse may have been an unshakeable sense of failure at rightful trespass. A year after his release from hospital—presumably it has taken him all this time to recover—the narrator begins to assemble his notes from his lengthy walking tour of the east coast of England. He cannot help thinking, he remarks, of Michael Parkinson and Janine Dakyns, two faculty colleagues who impress and move him with their complete absence of scholarly vanity, their remarkable, quiet devotion to their studies, and what he calls their innocence—qualities the narrator clearly fears he lacks and whose absence has perhaps vitiated the integrity of the four accounts that comprise *The Emigrants*. Janine astounds him with her "profound understanding" of nineteenth-century French literature, especially the works of Gustave Flaubert. The narrator listens raptly as Janine describes "the scruples which dogged Flaubert's writing, that fear of the false which, she said, sometimes kept him confined to his couch for weeks or months on end in the dread he would never be able to write another word without compromising himself in the most grievous of ways. Moreover, Janine said, he was convinced that everything he had written hitherto consisted solely in a string of the most abysmal errors and lies, the consequences of which were immeasurable" (R7). Flaubert even despairs over his despair, wondering if it is itself hopelessly romantic and narcissistic. The reader senses Sebald gripped by his own uncertain efforts.

In the fourth story in *The Emigrants*, on the émigré painter named Max Ferber whom we met briefly above, the narrator finds himself transfixed by Ferber's moral perfectionism in art, that is, his commitment to depict things justly according to ethical as much as aesthetic criteria. It is so intense that it leads the obviously talented Ferber to erase again and again the charcoal work he has done, or to scrape off layer after layer of paint, until in time the floor of his studio (where he also lives) "was covered with a largely hardened and encrusted deposit of droppings, mixed with coal dust, several centimeters thick at the centre and thinning out toward the outer edges, in places resembling the flow of lava" (E161). This picture resembles the narrator's account of Janine Dakyns's office as "a virtual paper landscape . . . with mountains and valleys" of manuscripts, articles, and books, such that she was reduced to working from an easy chair planted in the middle of "the glacier" of paper (R8). Once when he asked her about it all, Janine replied "that the apparent chaos surrounding her represented in reality a perfect kind of order, or an order which at least tended toward perfection" (R9). The narrator can only shake his head in awe when Janine reports that she never has a problem locating whatever manuscript she needs at a given time. As for Ferber, reports the narrator who often watched him for hours, "he might reject as many as forty variants" he would try of a facial portrait, "or smudge them back into the paper and overdraw new attempts upon them; and if he then decided that the portrait was done, not so much because he was convinced that it was finished as through sheer exhaustion, an onlooker might well feel that it had evolved from a long lineage of grey, ancestral faces, rendered unto ash but still there, as ghostly presences, on the harried paper" (E162; see also E174–175).

Sebald's sentences, it appears, are the outermost layer of an endless series of failed or otherwise inadequate trials, experiments, and attempts. His sentences also embody the "ghostly presence" of the past, not just with regards to the people and doings he describes, but to the countless literary and historical allusions that his words evoke, some of which I have tried to spotlight in the analysis thus far. It is as if every sentence or phrase could be footnoted, and richly so. But that means every expression carries weight—just like every stroke in one of Ferber's artworks—which means Sebald must try to get every word right: not just some of the words, but *every word*.

Near the end of *The Emigrants*, the narrator states that it was "an arduous task" to work on the account of Max Ferber he has framed. Echoing Ferber's travails, he remarks,

> Often I could not get on for hours or days at a time, and not infrequently I unraveled what I had done, continuously tormented [like Flaubert, the reader notes] by scruples that were taking tighter hold and steadily paralyzing me. These scruples concerned not only the subject of my narrative, which I felt I could not do justice to, no matter what approach I tried, but also the entire questionable business of writing. I had covered hundreds of pages with my scribble, in pencil and ballpoint. By far the greater part had been crossed out, discarded, or obliterated by additions. Even what I ultimately salvaged as a "final" version seemed to me a thing of shreds and patches, utterly botched. (E230–231; see also A122–124, R283)

So much for the tools of the trade, it seems. Early in *The Rings of Saturn*, the narrator calls to mind Albrecht Dürer's famous etching titled *Melancholia*, in which an angel sits morosely, her chin in her hand, amid the vaunted tools of science, mathematics, and technology (R9). She is lamenting: What good are all these? What can they fashion that will endure? Do they make us wiser, or do they make us more insane in our ambitions (cf. R181–182)? Why do they seem powerless in preventing cruelty and injustice?

Sebald joins a long list of his precursors, reaching at least as far back as Plato, who seriously question the viability and the justness of the literary enterprise. Does the writer reveal or distort? *Can* the writer engage in rightful trespass, or is she or he or they compromised from the very first step? What makes a writer trustworthy? What is a "good" story? Sebald feels these time-honored concerns even more acutely given the particular tasks of bearing witness and remembrance he has accepted. Such tasks are indeed "arduous," in ways perhaps difficult to imagine for the reader who has never climbed this mountain. Sebald's narrator reports from time to time that he has had "a bad night," that he felt "out of sorts," that he needed "to take a rest." The narrator never states explicitly the causes of his malaise. In time the reader discerns that it is his witness itself that is making him ill—his soul as well as his body—since he stumbles again and again on human perfidy, negligence, indifference, mindlessness, brutality, as well as on individual lives broken by these forces. He has reason to quote the famed writer Wolfgang Goethe, that "our world is a cracked bell that no longer sounds" (E220). One of the epigrams to the book illuminates his condition. It comes from an encyclopedia: "The rings of Saturn consist of ice crystals and probably meteorite particles describing circular orbits around the planet's equator. In all likelihood these are fragments of a former moon that was too close to the planet and was destroyed by its tidal effect (Roche limit)." The Roche limit denotes the distance between a planet's center and a satellite beyond which the satellite cannot approach without being destroyed. The narrator has circled around humanity and its sufferings and has come too close, emotionally and morally speaking. He is shattered and hospitalized.

Through it all the narrator persists in his pilgrimage, which is yet another motif of ethical inquiry that informs his witness. Even in hospital he begins to picture words and sentences formed from the materials memory dredges up from his long sojourn along the east coast of England. His quest pulls him back on his feet. In *The Emigrants* the narrator recalls his teacher, Paul Bereyter, shunting aside the required school textbooks because he found them "ridiculous and hypocritical" (E37). He deploys instead readings from the *Rheinische Hausfreund*, tales of the Rhineland intended for reading at home—all images, the reader notes, of Bereyter's deep sense of rootedness in German soil. What the narrator recalls remembering from the tales, among other things, are "the words said by the passing pilgrim to the woman who kept the Baselstab Inn: When I return, I shall bring you a sacred cockleshell from the Strand at Askalon, or a rose from Jericho" (E38). A cockleshell, discernible in many church carvings, has long been a symbol of the pilgrim, the traveler from distant shores, the seeker of truth. In more ancient traditions the cockleshell was a symbol of birth, as captured in Botticelli's famous painting, *The Birth of Venus*. Askalon refers, among other things, to a landing spot for pilgrims who had arrived in the Levant. The Rose of Jericho is sometimes called the Resurrection Plant. During a prolonged drought it looks quite dead; but with the first watering it springs back to life. Sebald returns from his wanderings bearing many such roses: lives and occurrences lost and forgotten, now reborn and brought literally into our lives through the nourishment of his prose.

At the same time, Sebald surely feels uneasy about the association with resurrection and especially *resurrectionists*, an 18th- to 19th-century English colloquial term for grave robbers who sold corpses to doctors and anatomists. Is that also what he is? Is that how he is treating the past? Are we readers his paying customers? Sebald's unsettlement about the matter perhaps accounts for a brilliant stroke in the first chapter of *The Rings of Saturn*, when the narrator addresses Rembrandt's famous painting, *The Anatomy Lesson* (reproduced in the text on R14–15). Rembrandt immortalized the celebrated anatomy lessons, given to students and a paying public, by Dr. Nicolaas Tulp in 17th-century Amsterdam. Sebald reads the painting as a powerful moral indictment by Rembrandt of an emerging rationalism in science and society. While Dr. Tulp appears to be addressing the audience—forceps in hand—his colleagues and students surrounding him are not even looking at the dead body, that of a petty thief named Aris Kindt ("child" in English) who had been hanged but an hour beforehand—and who is now being wounded for a second time, symbolically speaking, as the doctor makes his incisions. Tulp's confreres are riveted by a diagram off to the side, "a schematic plan of the human being," which the narrator emphasizes would have been of great interest to René Descartes, a budding amateur anatomist who may well have been present at the lesson, and whose "philosophical investigations," the narrator declaims, "form one of the principal chapters of the history of subjection" (R13).

The narrator does not clarify this last, certainly questionable remark. Descartes can be regarded as a profoundly humane thinker whose aim was not rationalistic control of the world but rational ground that could help human beings stop slaughtering themselves in religious and other wars. Be that as it may, for the narrator, newly released from hospital after taking in the "horror" (R3) of so much destruction across modern history, Rembrandt's gaze alone rejects violence and "Cartesian rigidity" (R17). The reader notes yet another play here on the title of Wittgenstein's most famous (and decidedly nonscientistic) book, *Philosophical Investigations* (1953), and recalls how often the narrator and other figures like Austerlitz describe their unusual inquiries as "investigations." Their studies are at once forensic, linguistic, anthropological, moral, scientific, metaphysical, and amalgamations of these and other terms for which we yet lack names. Sebald wonders, in his uneasy incertitude, whether they resemble the work of Dr. Tulp and his fellow anatomists.

The witness-pilgrimage continues. The name and the city of Jerusalem, one of humanity's most iconic sites of pilgrimage, pops up throughout the works. Ambros Adelwarth and his beloved employer Cosmo make a long overland journey there in 1913, faithfully recounted by the narrator in the third story in *The Emigrants*. Adelwarth's journal, from which the narrator quotes, portrays a once beautiful, flowered place that, beginning with the Romans' violent occupation, has declined, Adelwarth sighs, into an arid site marked by religious balkanization. In chapter IX of *The Rings of Saturn*, the narrator visits Thomas Abrams, who for years has been working on an enormous wooden model of the Temple of Jerusalem. It is so well-conceived and executed, although ever unfinished, that it garners international attention and a steady stream of visitors (making their own pilgrimage, as it were). The narrator is so enchanted by both Abrams and the extraordinary model he is fashioning that he wishes, as the man kindly drives him back to town, "that the short drive through the country would never come to an end, and that we could go on and on, all the way to Jerusalem" (R249). Max Ferber refers to Manchester, in its heyday, as "the industrial Jerusalem" to the world (E165). The very first street mentioned in *Austerlitz*, in the city of Antwerp where the narrator finds himself in one of his vertiginous moods, is Jeruzalemstraat (A3). After his journey to Jerusalem in 1807, Chateaubriand plants numerous trees whose names he knows by heart (R265). And in a moment of apparent fusion of author and narrator, we hear about a magnificent brass sarcophagus dedicated to Sebald's "namesake" St. Sebolt, completed in Nuremberg in 1519, that is crowned by a model of Jerusalem (R87–88).

It is *un pèlerinage à pied*—a pilgrimage by foot—an image conjured in the other epigram to *The Rings of Saturn* in which the novelist Joseph Conrad remarks that "we should have compassion for those ill-starred, unhappy souls who have set out on their walking pilgrimage, who skirt the shores of the world and gaze without understanding at the ravages of the struggle between the vanquishing and the vanquished" (original in French, my translation). Conrad's words—he was another emigrant to England, the reader notes—evokes the narrator's meandering walk along the shores of East Anglia—"Eastern England," in the east like Jerusalem. To wander by foot contrasts markedly with the speed of today's transportation options. The narrator slows down in order to see what otherwise would disappear in a blur. Sebald himself remarked that he inserted photographs and other materials into his texts, in part, to decelerate the narrative and the reader's habitual rush to the ending (Wachtel, 2007, pp. 41–42).

Sebald's attempt to receive, to consider things in their moral many-sidedness, reaches an apogee in *Austerlitz*, when the protagonist obtains in the course of his relentless archival work a film made by the Nazis in their grotesque show camp, Theresiendstadt. In a desperate bid to see if he can locate his mother on the screen, Austerlitz not only views the film repeatedly but slows it down so radically that it almost becomes, in effect, a slide show, wherein he can discern individual features and gestures. Sebald slows his writing down in just this manner, in his own pilgrimage toward the truth of things. He also realizes the pitfalls of trying to get "too close," just as the narrator learned to respect them in his quest to understand his teacher Bereyter. In a mirror image to the video scene in *Austerlitz*, in the chapter on Henry Selwyn in *The Emigrants*, the narrator and others are transfixed by a slide Selwyn shows of a beautiful valley in Crete—taken during a trip there years before—so much so that while they stare silently at the scene, the heat of the projector light suddenly shatters the slide (E17). The past disappears.

What is this pilgrim's progress? What is the witness-narrator's Jerusalem, and does he arrive? Like Wittgenstein and the figure Austerlitz, both inveterate wanderers, the narrator carries with him everywhere a beloved rucksack, a miniature symbol of home in an unpredictable, seemingly vagabond life. Sebald includes a photo of Austerlitz's rucksack (A40) and describes a deeply painful moment in the man's life when, as a boy just off the *Kindertransport*, his foster parents took away and hid his rucksack, just as they did his natal identity (A137–138). Ultimately, for the narrator, Wittgenstein and Austerlitz appear to walk hand in hand, almost as if they represented a single uncanny figure. He notes many resemblances between their manner of being (A40–41). At the start of the book, he remarks on "the fixed, inquiring gaze found in certain painters and philosophers who seek to penetrate the darkness that surrounds us purely by means of looking and thinking" (A5)—and in between these words is a well-known photograph of Wittgenstein's eyes (along with a photo of the eyes of the painter Jan Peter Tripp, Sebald's long-standing friend and collaborator [Sebald & Tripp, 2004]).

Like the two figures, the narrator also is going somewhere, even if the destination remains over the horizon and not yet nameable. The narrator is summoned to journey and to witness by his need to come to grips with history's trajectory that has shaped the terms of his and so many other people's lives. Earlier in the chapter I referred in passing to the last paragraph of *The Emigrants*, in which the narrator recalls a photo he had recently seen of three young women weaving a carpet in the Litzmannstadt ghetto in Lodz. He reports that before the war the industrial city of Lodz had been called "the Polish Manchester," and he is recollecting the photo and the exhibit of wartime photographs in which it appeared while he is in Manchester itself, the city where the emigrants Wittgenstein, Ferber, and Sebald—as well as a great many Jews—first found a footing in English soil. The exhibit featured the contents of a suitcase of photos, discovered in 1987, taken by a Nazi accountant named Genewein, of Jews at work in the ghetto. Here is the narrator's concluding description, worth hearing in full as I bring this chapter to its own close.

> Behind the perpendicular frame of a loom sit three young women, perhaps aged twenty. The irregular geometrical patterns of the carpet they are knotting, and even its colours, remind me of the settee in our living room at home. Who the young women are I do not know. The light falls on them from the window in the background, so I cannot make out their eyes clearly, but I sense that all three of them are looking across at me, since I am standing on the very spot where Genewein the accountant stood with his camera. The young woman in the middle is blonde and has the air of a bride about her. The weaver to her left has inclined her head a little to one side, whilst the woman on the right is looking at me with so steady and relentless a gaze that I cannot meet it for long. I wonder what the three women's names were—Roza, Luisa, and Lea, or Nona, Decuma and Morta, the daughters of night, with spindle, scissors and thread. (E237)

The narrator symbolically replaces the cold, instrumental, and deadly efficient regard of the Nazis with that of one who would bear witness. In the same instant, the writer reveals the moral vicissitudes in trying to comprehend the lives of others. He may be guilty of wrongful trespass, not only presuming to guess at the women's names but bestowing on them the power of the Fates—Nona spinning the thread of life, Decuma measuring it out, and Morta cutting it at death. The narrator signals a strain of ambivalence, or unsettlement, in revealing that he could not hold the third weaver's gaze for long. He cannot fully become one with her. They do not belong together, or so it seems.

To me, the reference to the three Fates reveals that the narrator was fated to end his pilgrimage right here, face-to-face with those he has helped call out of the darkness. From the time he turned his soul, whenever that was—while a boy with Bereyter the unusual teacher? while a young man recently planted in England? when he bought a rucksack not knowing how many miles it would travel with him?—he was, as it were, destined to be held by the past he sought. It is a particular, ethically charged form of fate, or destiny, that differs radically from the view of the townspeople of S. They were wrong that "things turn out as they are bound to happen." Paul Bereyter was not marked to "end up on the railways" by a cruel turn of history. The three young weavers were not prefigured to end their short lives trapped in history's web. Sebald shows that fate can become a name for a self-accepted path of inquiry, a quest for rightful trespass that leads, if not directly to repair, to remembrance and the sense of hope and redemption it can enshrine. The witness-inquirer can look, listen, and wait. Perhaps they will come upon a weaver who, like they mythic Ariadne, will cast a thread of life that leads them out of the labyrinth where past and present meet, to a moment of clarity, of insight, and even of love.

## Conclusion: Bearing Witness and an Education in the Arts of Rightful Trespass

Sebald as witness walks a fine line between two forms of wrongful trespass, both of which haunt inquiry into human lives past and present. The first encompasses sentimentality, self-consolation, and the sheer power of the ego to slant reality to its own bent. The narrator realizes that this possessive approach distances him from the truth of his teacher's life. It becomes noteworthy that Sebald time and again refers to heights in his writing: mountain vistas, the view from various towers and high buildings, scenes looking out an airplane window. In some of the very same passages he emphasizes closeness to the ground. His first encounter with Henry Selwyn, for example, is when the man is laying on a lawn counting blades of grass as, ultimately, Sebald himself does in his absorption with the apparent minutia of human lives.[19] Using this periscopic method, Sebald centers the idea that rightful trespass implies a circumspect step, a sense of discretion, an acute attention to detail, awareness and respect for distance, and a commitment to steer clear of emotional assimilation (which is not the same thing as the absence of emotion). These hardy demands call for a method of investigation, as the narrator discovers, that embodies modesty and that is ever responsive to all that he encounters. As we have seen, the latter includes the cultivation of an ethically informed sense of what matters, or is at stake, in the lives of the people one witnesses (cf.

Crary, 2012). Last but not least, rightful trespass requires disciplined, sometimes difficult writing exquisitely evoked in a photograph in *The Emigrants* (E171) of a schoolboy bent over his prose, his face so close to the words that they almost touch.

The second form of wrongful trespass into the human is an unselfconscious, rationalistic method of classifying, categorizing, labeling, sorting, organizing, placing, and summing up whose a priori logic provides the inquirer safety from the travails of self-examination. Sebald resonates strongly with Wittgenstein's view that understanding others constitutes an ethical rather than purely epistemic affair. In his *Remarks on Frazer's Golden Bough*, Wittgenstein (1993) takes the famed anthropologist James George Frazer to task for producing volumes of alleged "explanation" for so-called primitive customs, both ancient and contemporary, that, for Wittgenstein, leave the reader baffled rather than enlightened. In his drive to explain unidirectionally, rather than also opening his self-understanding to criticism, Frazer trespasses wrongfully. He resembles the anatomist Nicolaas Tulp, at least as Sebald interprets Rembrandt's intent. Frazer will not put aside his schematic framework, at least for a time, and try to see the body of the past as a living body, as a body posing questions to us, as a body calling for an ethical response rather than for a scalpel. Thus, he fails to assist the reader, and himself, in coming to grips with how the people he investigates saw and experienced the world. Wittgenstein lauds Frazer's tremendous diligence in unearthing ethnographic details, from ancient Europe and elsewhere, but he is distressed by what Frazer then does with them. "I think one reason why the attempt to find an explanation is wrong," he concludes, "is that we have only to put together in the right way what *we know*, without adding anything, and the satisfaction we are trying to get from the explanation comes of itself" (1993, p. 2e).

Sebald's narrator discovers that, though his tools are limited and limiting, they can help him "put together" what he has witnessed. They help him describe human realities ungraspingly and systematically, with patience and with sympathy. To borrow terms from the historian Simon Schama (1996), the narrator brings to bear "a dispassionate eye, [which] is the condition of a compassionate intelligence" (p. 98).

The narrator has had to learn these arts, just as Sebald reveals his instructors. It is striking how earnestly Sebald writes of the narrator's teachers, as if the influence of a teacher can retain a presence in an ever-shifting world. First and foremost is Paul Bereyter. The very instant after the narrator speaks of "wrongful trespass" (E29) he launches a lengthy remembrance: page after page of colorful, beautifully rendered detail, yielding one of the most affecting portraits of a teacher I have read in a long history of reading about teachers. Bereyter did lose his temper at times, and at other moments positively despised his charges (yet another parallel with Wittgenstein!). But he had, it seems, an inspired pedagogical touch, knowing just how to address a student, how to spot and act on a strength or a weakness, how to identify something for the curriculum, and how to create an enriching environment. He brought probity, discretion, and integrity to his daily work. Time and again he evinced scientific, artistic, and psychological insight. Like a good gardener, which he also was, Bereyter-as-teacher *grows things*, in marked contrast with the destruction Sebald's work unsparingly registers. As Lucy Landau observes, the man was "a veritable Melammed," a Hebrew term for a good teacher of children, "who could start from nothing and hold the most inspiring of lessons" (E56). Late in life, when he has lost most of his eyesight, Landau reads aloud to him from the well-known educator Johan Pestalozzi, a splendid symbolic touch on the part of Sebald. To the narrator, as he looks back, "Paul's teaching was altogether the most lucid, in general, that one could imagine" (E38).

Tellingly, the narrator reports that Bereyter's first act as a teacher, upon returning to the school after the war, was to scrape the whitewash off the windows of the classroom that the previous teacher had slapped on (so that the children, one wants to say, would not be distracted by the real world). Bereyter sought to let in light, and he brings much light himself through his knowledge and talents. Slowly but surely the reader sees that the narrator himself absorbed a love of light, in its moral as well as aesthetic senses, in Bereyter's classroom. He learned from Bereyter the very qualities that later, in a way he could never have anticipated, would outfit him to bear witness and to understand something about his teacher and the history they shared. These qualities include a responsive sensibility, a serious intellectual curiosity, and a commitment to truth-seeking. What the narrator learned would equip him to remove whitewash.[20]

I referred in passing at the start of the chapter to André Hillary, a gifted history teacher who not only showed Austerlitz—and, through him, the sponge-like narrator—what it means to be a scholar but who also, when Austerlitz divulged his real name and origins to him, fully embraced the news and henceforth did everything he could to pave Austerlitz's path to university (A69–74). The narrator refers to Austerlitz himself as "the first teacher I could listen to since my time in primary school" (A33; see also A12–13). He finds himself utterly absorbed in listening to Austerlitz's disquisitions about capitalism and architecture, about the joys and difficulties of writing, about the engineering logic that has given rise to the railway system, about the intricate biological marvels of moths, and many other subjects. Austerlitz, on his part, reports cherishing school. He found it a place of intellectual adventure after his pinched childhood in Wales (A61). And the reader discerns in Austerlitz an astute, mindful enactor of rightful trespass.

Finally, the narrator-Sebald learns from his intensive reading, especially the work of fellow writers in German such as Wittgenstein, Benjamin, and Kafka. He develops esteem for literature in its manifold forms and in its relation to the human quest for mutual understanding. What the art critic Peter Schjeldahl says of the contemporary German artist Gerhard Richter's approach to painting could be said of Sebald's view of literature. "Richter's life and times," writes Schjeldahl (2005), "forced thought upon him, complicating a reverence for painting that stands guard against uses of the medium, even by himself—as propaganda, for example—that would violate its mysterious integrity" (p. 98).[21] In a lecture at the opening of the House of Literature in Stuttgart, in 2001, Sebald concluded a reminiscence about the city, which featured his usual unpredictable array of figures and events, by posing and answering a question that had preoccupied him his entire career: "What is literature good for? . . . There are many forms of writing; only in literature, however, can there be an attempt at restitution over and above the mere recital of facts, and over and above scholarship" (2005, p. 205).[22] Sebald suggests that while literature cannot bring an end to suffering and catastrophe, it does allow for an enduring response rather than mute acquiescence. Literature is educative and edifying. Among other things, Sebald signals, it helps us to remember how to remember in an ethical spirit. His viewpoint can be applied, virtually point for point, to the witness, including his own.

Chapter 3

# Aimé Césaire

## Witnessing Transformation in Self and World

> . . . I probe I probe
> I the burden-bearer, I the root-bearer
> I weigh I press I hide
> I navel.
>
> —Aimé Césaire, "The Body Lost"

In this chapter I attend to Aimé Césaire's witness in his now-legendary, book-length poem, *Cahier d'un retour au pay natal* (*Journal of a Homecoming*). Césaire was an acclaimed poet, critic of colonialism, and politician in his native Martinique. He received a classical French education at the Lycée Victor Schoelcher, the only secondary school on his island at the time, then was awarded fellowship support to further his education in Paris. He studied the humanities, first at the Lycée Louis Le Grand where he prepared for university entrance exams, and then after graduation at the renowned École Normale Supérieure. He immersed himself in French letters, especially poetry with which he had a profound, lifelong relationship, as well as in Latin, Greek, and classical studies. At the same time, during this Parisian period (1931 to 1939) Césaire encountered numerous other black students from both the Antilles (the island archipelago in the Caribbean that includes Martinique) and Africa. He also met African American writers, such as Langston Hughes and Claude McKay, who were seeking fresh creative horizons as well as a break from the relentless weight of American racism.

These experiences constituted a second education for Césaire. They opened his eyes to the fundamental injustices immanent in European colonialism. They gave rise to what he came to call *negritude*: a mode of black consciousness as an orientation toward being in the world. His *Cahier d'un retour au pay natal* constitutes, among other things, an extended meditation on his own education, including its painful moments as he realizes how his acquired Frenchness (*francité*) has alienated him from his black community and historical inheritances. As he works his way through his *crise de conscience*, he bears witness to the process of creative self-transformation in the face of severe inner conflict, even as he also learns, in the very same movement, how to perceive justly the material and spiritual condition of the people of Martinique. As we will see, Césaire's undertaking parallels Sebald's quest for rightful trespass, and it complements Walt Whitman's witness, addressed in chapter 4, to democratic and cosmopolitan possibilities in dwelling in community with others.

## Context and Structure of the *Cahier d'un retour au pays natal*

I will draw here on the initial or primordial version of *Cahier* published in August, 1939, in the Parisian magazine *Volonté*, when the author was 26 years old. I call it primordial because Césaire made additions in the subsequent editions of 1947—two different versions were published that year, one in New York and one in Paris—and of 1956. As I will suggest, in the original version the poet is at his most vulnerable and heartfelt. He is deeply marked by the concern and the wonder of the witness adumbrated in chapter 1. He finds himself on a pilgrimage, with echoes of that of Sebald, to come to grips with his people's past and with his own identity as a black man straddling the cultures of Martinique and France.

Some of the additions made in 1956 are more overtly political than what a reader would find hitherto, though, crucially for the poet, the political and the aesthetic are intertwined across his oeuvre. The more explicit expressions of 1956, such as the new in-your-face opening stanza, reflect the poet's increasing international stature as a voice of black consciousness and liberation from the European colonial system. His influential, searing, and still timely anticolonial polemic, *Discours sur le Colonialisme* (Discourse on Colonialism) had come out in 1955 in a newly edited, more accessible volume than the initial version of 1950.

He would go on to compose several widely noted plays critical of the imperial project, including *La Tragédie du Roi Christophe* (The Tragedy of King Christophe), about the rise and fall of an early 19th-century Haitian leader; *Une Tempête* (A Tempest), in which Césaire rewrites Shakespeare's play from the point of view of the slave Caliban; and *Une Saison au Congo* (A Season in the Congo), about the murder of Patrice Lumumba, the first prime minister of the independent Republic of Congo and much admired by democratic-thinking people the world over.

The 1956 version of the *Cahier*, like those of 1947 in which Césaire introduced new surrealist elements (see below), retains almost everything in the poet's first version. In this respect, Césaire mirrors the practice of Michel de Montaigne (1533 to 1592), whom he read closely as part of his journey through the French educational system (I return to this point in the concluding paragraph of the chapter). Montaigne invented the essay form of writing as we know it and was truly a great wordsmith. He deleted very little as he revised several times over his collection of essays that grew substantially in length with each successive edition from 1580 to 1595. Césaire's epic[1] grows in length, too, from 109 stanzas (using the translation structure by A. James Arnold and Clayton Eshleman [2014]) in the 1939 version to 174 stanzas in 1956 (using N. Gregson Davis's [2017] translation structure—Césaire himself did not number them). But many of the latter stanzas are quite short, merely a line or two, and some of them were inserted in the 1947 editions. Like the famed essayist Montaigne, Césaire plumbs his interiority in an unsparing, frank manner. Moreover, as he proceeds from edition to edition, he does not eject his past selves, so to speak, but rather retains and learns from them.

Césaire's various deletions and additions do not compromise the poet's fundamental orientation as witness, since the great bulk of his poetic testimony remains intact across the editions.[2] Thus, while I focus on the original 1939 version, translated by Arnold and Eshleman (2014), in order to approach the work as the poet primordially conceived it, I will rely on the translation of the 1956 edition by Davis (2017). In my experience, Davis does a compelling job of rendering the substance, tone, and spirit of Césaire's oeuvre (see his affecting appraisal of the poem in Davis, 1997). From time to time, I will deploy a word or phrase from other well-known translations, including those by John Berger and Anna Bostock (2014), Clayton Eshleman and Annette Smith (1983), and Mireille Rosello with Annie Pritchard (1995). Berger and Bostock translate the title of *Cahier d'un retour au pays natal* as *Return to My Native Land*;

Eshleman and Smith translate it as *Notebook of a Return to The Native Land*; and Rosello and Pritchard work with *Notebook of a Return to My Native Land*. Davis deploys the title *Journal of a Homecoming*.

Each translation of the title has its virtues and limitations. Berger and Bostock, Eshleman and Smith, and Rosello and Pritchard nicely capture the *action* in the poem by foregrounding the verb *return*. This term denotes coming back, circling back, as well as bringing something back. The poet brings back to what he perceives as his downtrodden, dispirited island people, still under the colonial heel of France at the time, the gift and power of poetry, which he studied and refined during his lengthy sojourn in Paris. He will aspire to inspire them and, like the classical demiurge, to participate in creating a new world with them (cf. Diawara, 1998, p. 6). This "new world," I sense the poet imagining, will turn on its head the colonialists' use of those very terms when they first crossed the Atlantic.[3]

The image of "turning" runs through Césaire's endeavor. There are many references to a turn, a re-turn, and a turning of the soul, to recall Plato's famous image. Some of these refrains are spiritual in tone and trajectory. I think especially of the biblical story of the return of the prodigal son, which in my view the poet has in mind throughout. To echo the terms of the parable, the poet was lost, and then is found—though he himself must do the work of "founding," or fashioning, a reconstructed self.

This hypothesis calls to mind Davis's title with its emphasis on "homecoming." We will see that the poet's homecoming is anything but easy. He will have *to make his way* home, not just literally in shipping out from Le Havre in France to Fort de France in Martinique, but emotionally, spiritually, intellectually, and culturally. His *Cahier* recounts the phases of this journey, which has overtones of Homer's *Odyssey*—another thorny homecoming—and of Dante's *The Divine Comedy*, with its powerful images of a descent into darkness and an ascent into lightness that Césaire will mirror to poignant effect. Césaire knew both texts intimately, as well as other classic works such as Virgil's *Aeneid* that feature dimensions of *katabasis* (a withdrawal or retreat), *nostos* (the return of a hero), and departure-and-return.[4]

Many people the world over have kept journals of their journeys, whether the latter be literal and/or spiritual. Césaire's choice of *cahier* for his epic poem conjures notions of a record: a series of descriptive reports of events and experiences. This possibility coheres with another meaning of the French term, namely, *notebook*, which points to the practice of regularly jotting things down. Césaire regularly used a notebook to gather images and ideas that he later deployed in his work (Irele, 2017, p. 16). (Sebald and Whitman were determined note-takers, too, and write of how reliant they were on this habit.) Yet another connotation of the word *cahier* is "exercise book." This term implies a working out of an idea or problem which, as Ronnie Scharfman (1987, p. 30) points out, could be a deeply personal conundrum or crisis—a conception that mirrors Césaire's intense self-examination, and indeed search for self, in his poem. Davis (1997, pp. 21–22) further suggests that the idea of a "notebook" or "journal" implies something incomplete and sketchy, which in his view nicely captures the experimental nature of the poem as well as the fact the poet revised it several times. Finally, if we consider how a journal can morph into a diary and back again—as seems to be the case with Etty Hillesum, whom we met in chapter 1—the use of *cahier* can signal intimacy with the reader, and thus also the poet's vulnerability.

We will see how the poet traverses a rocky path toward justifying his witness to the situation of the people of Martinique. In this light, his use of *cahier* in the poem's title anticipates his struggle to attain the right voice as witness.[5] It is true that journals and notebooks are typically informal, unpolished, and not shared with the public. But Césaire *will* be sharing his poem with the public. Will it be unpolished and inadequate? Will it fail the test? Is the poet's title, perhaps announcing the work will be informal, a way of restraining readers' expectations? He does not project himself as *the* authority. He calls his poem "journal of *a* return" not of "*the* (most important, most interesting, most enlightening) return." It will become plain that the poet does not begin his journal-poem with his sense of authority, or authorization to speak, in place. He discovers that he must earn it through the very act of bearing witness. To recall a trope from the previous chapter, he will have to learn how to wed dispassion with compassion.

What might readers' expectations and assumptions have been had Césaire titled the work "The Story (fr. *histoire* or *recit*) of a Homecoming"? I sense the poet would worry that such a title might conflate fact and fiction in an unhelpful way, or perhaps suggest that that the project is nothing but autobiographical. In other words, the use of story might render his oeuvre parochial, thereby draining it of the universal reach that clearly animates him (see below). Moreover, journal and notebook have a more empirical aura than story. They appear down to earth, straightforward, unadorned, unembellished, and factual. To be sure, stories—whether fact or fiction or a fusion of the two—can be deeply true to life, as we saw with Sebald's texts (as mentioned, in the original German edition of *The Emigrants* he refers to the four chapters as stories). But the poet here is after something other, or something more, than a story, as such. As with Sebald, there are autobiographical elements at work in poem, but it is not reducible to that genre. The poem has features of a confession or "confessional documentary," of a *Bildungsroman* or coming of age, of a socio-anthropological inquiry, of a political critique—and of a witness.[6]

A final contextual note has to do with the form and style of the *Cahier*. The text features both prose and verse often intertwined, with a marked orality that echoes ancestral roots in Africa. Irele (2017) suggests that the poem incarnates a view of poetry as "*charged utterance, in turn narrative, contemplative, incantatory, prophetic, and much else besides*—in short, with an expression whose mode of existence restores the immediacies of the imaginative impulse as it moves the poet" (p. 68). Irele further remarks, in another telling insight: "[The *Cahier*] remains a work whose energy of poetic statement ultimately reflects the pressure on human speech of strong emotions and of an intensely held apprehension of the world" (p. 2).

As mentioned, the text is divided into stanzas, though they obey no consistent rule regarding length or poetic scheme. They feature the poet moving in and out of linear time. They show him looking to the future, looking back, and attending to what faces him in the moment. Striking and sometimes disturbing images proliferate from start to finish. They are variously violent, halcyon, sexualized, hateful, loving, explanatory, obfuscating. They resound with "percussive" (Echleman & Smith, 1983, p. 13) and other melo-poetic effects emblematic of the poet's preference for parataxis over standard syntax and his attunement to the physical aspects of language.[7] Emotions and images detonate before the reader's eyes. Words avalanche down the page, "still warm with the heat of their birth" (Simmons, 1973, p. 74). Stream of consciousness morphs into philosophical reflection and back again.

In keeping with his attraction to surrealism,[8] Césaire gives play to spontaneity and to unconstrained metaphorical association, seemingly letting his unconscious mind lead the way. The result is that there are hermetic passages almost impossible to interpret even for the most seasoned exegete, whether literary critic, philosopher, or psychoanalyst. They are like shouts and cries, whispers and murmurs, dreams and wishes. They are *there*, as markers of the poet's unguarded response to reality. This point is not to suggest the poem is at times capricious or random in expression.

Quite the contrary, it is purposive from start to finish, including in its moments of apparent gratuitousness. As Lilyan Kesteloot writes, Césaire's "language is sculpted, worked, kneaded like dough" (1991, p. 341).

This intense labor does not, paradoxically, imply that the poet is in control of the narrative he recounts. Not unlike Sebald's narrator, he is at times like a billiard ball being struck repeatedly by unanticipated emotions and reactions, including to his own words on printed page. As Schafman (2000, p. 30) alerts us, the title of the poem—*Cahier d'un retour au pays natal*—has no grammatical subject, and no evident reference to the poet himself. It is a tale of what happens to him despite his own conscious efforts to remain in charge. And yet, while the poet cannot orchestrate matters—he does not know at the start what "home" will be or look like—he is the one on the path and he knows it.

The poem is not an easy read, and nor is it intended to be. The poet makes it clear that the subject matter is hard to handle. It can burn. At times the poet insists that it *should* burn. Césaire suggested in one of his other poems ("Patience des signes" [Patience of signs]) that his work is "always accessible to the sincerity of great thirst" (in Kesteloot, 1991, p. 193). By "thirst," he means an urgent existential desire for meaning, purpose, understanding, and justice. However, at times in *Cahier* the poet places extensive if not excessive demands on himself and on his readers, particularly when the surrealist impulse takes hold of his writing. All the same, as mentioned, the poet's gestures are neither arbitrary nor haphazard. They are *fateful*: something real, decisive, determining, is always at stake as the poet confronts what he regards as his people's dire poverty and spiritual malaise while also facing his reaction to these conditions. As we will see, his response evolves from disappointment and dejection to a love he had no idea was possible. Put another way, he transforms from spectator to witness. As we follow this movement, the poet encourages readers to share with him "the courage of the imagination" (Eshleman & Smith, 1983, p. 19).

## The Face of Alienation

Paris, France is often called the City of Light. At dawn, at sunset, and in between, the daylight plays in captivating ways on the city's refined architecture. So do the human-made lights at night as they illuminate the city's churches, monuments, boulevards, and the flowing Seine River.

Paris is also associated with light because of its intense intellectual and artistic life that "shines a light" on human thought and creativity. For these and other reasons, Paris has for centuries been a magnet to people who seek to expand their horizons in ways they anticipate will be surprising, exciting, and rewarding.

Césaire was thrilled to be awarded financial support to study and live in the city. "I left Martinique with rapture," he later wrote (in Snyder, 1970, p. 198). He was enthusiastic about the prospect of "blossoming" there in his studies (in Larrier, 2010, p. 39). At the age of eighteen he set sail from Fort de France. For the next eight years he enjoyed a rich intellectual and artistic life in Paris. As mentioned previously, he systematically studied French letters, especially poetry.[9] He developed his own poetic oeuvre. He participated in countless, wide-ranging conversations with fellow French-speaking black students, teachers, writers, and others from the Antilles and Africa. He met and interacted with writers associated with the Harlem Renaissance such as the aforementioned Langston Hughes and Claude McKay (Césaire's entrance essay to the École Normale Supérieure focused on the American South as depicted by these and other African American auteurs). Césaire organized a student-run if short-lived newspaper, *L'Étudiant noir* (The Black Student) with his new comrades Léopold Sédar Senghor, a fellow poet and future president of Senegal, and Léon Damas, also a poet and later a politician in his native Guyana. They and others explored in depth fresh ideas about black consciousness and identity, drawing on newly published work on African history and culture that for them was a revelation. They began to articulate conceptions of justice and liberty for their colonized homelands. Their thinking was influenced by several dynamic Antillean women who also studied in Paris during those years, especially Paulette Nardal and her sisters who, of great cultural significance for these fledgling leaders, hosted a flourishing salon that brought the figures mentioned here together for free-flowing dialogue.[10] For Césaire, the overall experience was profoundly formative.

Unawares, however, it also set him up for an existential trial upon his return home that shakes him to the roots so thoroughly that he finds himself forced to confront the question of what his roots in fact are—and, indeed, whether he has *any* roots at all. His journey becomes more than the familiar tale of the deracinated intellectual trapped between worlds. Rather, the poet is summoned to bear witness to the travails of self-alienation, self-confrontation, and self-transformation, side by side with witnessing the hard circumstances yet underlying humanity of the people of Martinique.

On first stepping off the boat, figuratively speaking, in Fort de France, the poet is in the grip of an emotional response over which he has no control. *He feels no connection whatsoever with the people.* He finds himself surveying them through a lens that is at once detached, clinical, and chagrined, yet also marked by a deep if inchoate yearning. In a desolating, unguarded manner, he tells us graphically and bluntly what he first sees after his long sojourn in the inspiring, beautiful capital of the French world.

The poet perceives nothing but dirt and degradation. Though he had been born and raised on the island, he is mortified by the poverty and the rubbish-strewn streets and seaside of Fort de France. The first 20 or so stanzas feature a devastating commentary that leaves him seemingly drained of any prospect, as if to try to make something positive of the scene would be like a "senseless reawakening" (stanza 4; hereafter all solo numbers in parentheses refer to stanzas). He observes: "At the close of foreday morning (*au bout du petit matin*), burgeoning with frail bays, the starving Antilles, the Antilles pockmarked with smallpox, the Antilles dynamited with alcohol, run aground in the mud of this bay, in the dust of this town ominously grounded ["sinisterly grounded" in Arnold & Eshleman's translation, from *sinistrement*]" (2). The words *ominous* and *sinister* connote a threat, a danger, as if the port and island where he's returned are on the verge of collapse. Worse, it is as if the island were itself an eyesore, an "outlandish, masking scar on the wound of the waters" (3).

The material poverty, in the poet's unsettled state of mind, mirrors the spiritual poverty he discerns.

> At the close of foreday morning, the aberrant running aground, the high stench of corruption, the monstrous sodomies of host and sacrificer, the insurmountable beak-head of prows of prejudice and stupidity, the prostitutions, the hypocrisies, the lecheries, the treasons, the lies, the deceptions, the peculations—the loss of breath induced by cowardly ineffectual acts, the lackluster enthusiasm in redundant pushing, the greeds, the hysterias, the perversions, the comic routines of poverty, the cripplings, the itchings, the hives, the lukewarm hammocks of decadence. Here passes by the ridiculous parade of bubonic

scrofulas, the cultures of unfamiliar microbes, the poisons without known antidotes, the oozing pus from very old sores, the unpredictable fermentations of species prone to rot. (17)

This bleak, surrealistic vista—which Ruth Jean Simmons likens to a doctor describing a spreading disease (1973, p. 100)—reveals starkly the gap between the poet's anticipations upon his arrival and the physical and social ugliness he perceives and unsparingly registers. He allows no check on his reactions. He opens the door to his consciousness fused with his subconsciousness. He speaks swiftly and candidly, as if to cannon-shoot his way beyond scruple and hesitation. He portrays exactly what he sees.[11]

Césaire had taken ship from Martinique eight years previously as a literary-minded youth with ambitions to become deeply learned. After his seasoning in Paris, including his awakening to the realities of his African origins and of the depredations of colonialism, he was returning to accept a formal offer to become a teacher at the very secondary school he had himself attended in Fort de France, the prestigious Lycée Schoelcher. He would enjoy renown during his five-year sojourn there as a teacher of Latin and French as well as of philosophy and literature. Among the students at his school during this time were Frantz Fanon, Édouard Glissant, and Georges Desportes, all of whom would go on to become influential writers, and all of whom composed critical, appreciative commentaries on Césaire's work (Larrier, 2010, pp. 39–40). It seems clear that Césaire got off the boat with high hopes and excitement.

Just as clearly, his angst and impatience at the realities on the ground drum like hail on the page. He does not yet realize that he had in fact never truly seen his island people before, though this truth will impress itself upon him with suddenness and force in due time, that is, as part of his homecoming. The poet writes: "In this inert town, this boisterous crowd whose cry is so shockingly displaced, like this town from its movement, from its meaning, oblivious, displaced from its true cry, the sole cry that you would have wanted to hear because you feel it is unique to this town; because you feel it dwells within some deep inner refuge of darkness and pride; in this inert town" (7). The poet regards the crowd on the dirt roads and dusty squares as "strange" (8). He feels estranged from them. "This crowd," he judges, "that does not know how to behave like a crowd" (8). In the poet's disappointed eyes, the people do not act, or apparently know how to act, like a community with a sense of purpose and with a vision of possibility—precisely the sensibility he feels himself to embody.

"[T]his crowd so eerily talkative and silent" (7), he adds with a paradoxical twist. The crowd is full of gossip about the affairs of the day, but utterly mute with regard to speaking consciously of its constrained condition and what they might do about it. To the poet's ears, they chatter but do not speak. They pour out words but say nothing. They are, to him, "martyrs who fail to bear witness" (3).

As touched on in chapter 1, the term *witness* has long-standing associations with the term *martyr*. The poet knows that most of the townspeople are descendants of slaves. They are martyrs all, in a manner of speaking, to the principle of equality and shared dignity, and they are still locked in impoverishment. He is frustrated (cf. 35) that they seem unaware of their claim to speak truth to the world, to stand tall in their humanity. The poet regards them as *the* persons truly appointed to speak and to bear witness to terrible injustices, more so than him since the people are wholly tied to the town, the land, and their history (they have not studied and resided in Paris for eight years). For the poet, the crowd is "displaced from its cry of hunger, of poverty, of revolt, of hate" (7). The crowd in its ramshackle town "crawls along on its hands without any desire to stand tall and pierce the sky with its protestations" (25).

Tragically, in the poet's eyes, the people appear supine, passive, and alienated from the very ground on which they dwell. The poet implies that they have slipped away from both civilization and from nature: "[T]his inert town with its hinterland of lepers, of consumption, of famines, of fears cowering in gullies, of fears perched in trees, of fears buried in the ground, of fears drifting in the sky, of accumulated fears and their fumaroles [volcanic openings releasing sulfuric gases] of anguish [10] . . . this town flat . . . where the trickling gutter-water grimaces among feces all along its length" (26). Whatever dignity and pride remain for the people is sealed and hidden in an unspoken "inner refuge," to recall the terms above. Their life is so "prostrate" that they do not know "where to dispatch [their] aborted dreams" (27).

Martinique is an island whose physical beauty the poet will go on to extol, in part as a symbol of the beauty he had longed to see in his people and which, in due course, he will try to invigorate.

> . . . this town flat—spread out: slipped, fallen, from its common sense, inert, out of breath under its geometric load of a cross eternally to be picked up, refractory to its lot, without a voice, cross and crossed in every way, unable to grow with the juice

> of this earth; cut short, reduced, ruptured from its flora and fauna [5] . . . this town flat—spread out . . . (6)
>
> . . . this inert town, this crowd doleful under the sun, sharing in nothing that is remotely self-expressive, self-affirming or self-liberating in the full daylight of this land it calls its very own . . . (9)

The poet conjures a forbidding image of a body lying prone on a crucifix, flattened into the burning soil. The questions this specter evokes force themselves on him: Are the people truly rooted? Are they weeds, merely parasites on the earth? Or can they fructify?

Put differently, are the people educable? The poet presses home this harsh question. He appears to mock the very idea of the teacher he is himself on the way to becoming at his former school.

> And neither the teacher at school nor the priest at catechism
> will succeed in dragging a word out of this sleepy little nigger,[12]
> despite their common method of drumming strenuously on
> his shaven skull; for his voice has been bogged down in the
> swamps of hunger . . .
> his voice dies away in the swamps of hunger
> and there is nothing, nothing of worth to drag out of this
>     worthless infant
> only a hunger that can no longer climb up the rigging of his voice
> a hunger weighty and infirm,
> a hunger buried in the deepest layer of the Hunger of this
>     famished mount. (16)

Despite their caustic tone, the poet's words disclose a yearning he discerns beneath the surface, denoted by the capitalized word *Hunger* of the mount, the latter a term of reference to an elevated portion of Fort de France marked by the impoverishment of its inhabitants. This hunger recalls once more the "inner refuge of darkness and pride" (7) which the poet had earlier highlighted. The poet also reverses the apparent mockery, identifying not the teacher *he* aspires to become but the kind of insufferable pedant students encounter from time to time in school, who, rather than questioning and encouraging, "drags out," and who, rather than listening and conversing, "drums on." All the same, the destitute image drawn here of the muted child remains harrowing.

The quasi-apocalyptic beginning to the poem, with its movement down to the Cave (Plato) or Purgatory (Dante), soon finds the poet standing in front of the patchwork shack in which he grew up. He senses a "joy of old" from childhood, but it immediately makes him "cognizant of [his] present poverty" (21)—that is, of his alienation from his natal world (*pays natal*). His memories turn sour.

> . . . the carcass of wood, ludicrously perched on tiny paws of cement, which I call 'our house' . . . the rough floorboards gleaming with nail heads . . . the streaking of glazed cockroaches with their nauseating whir [21] . . . a minuscule house that shelters dozens of rats within its rotten wooden entrails, and the turmoil caused by my six brothers and sisters . . . and my mercurial father . . . whom an unpredictable magic spell might charm into a melancholy tenderness or kindle into giant flames of anger . . . and the harsh bite into the soft flesh of the night taken by a Singer sewing machine that my mother pedals and pedals for our hunger, by day and by night." (28)[13]

How utterly remote all this is from life in the well-built apartments of Paris that line its boulevards and spill out into its cafés, shops, and parks. How far removed are the muted people from the stimulating and life-changing dialogues the poet enjoyed with his fellow black students as they rapturously spoke of poetry and art, and as they fielded dreams of becoming leaders in the struggle against colonialism. From the cliff tops of high ideals and hopes, he has descended to the ruined beach below his old home, "with its heaps of rotting trash, its behinds of people stealthily relieving themselves" (31).

## Turning the Soul

The poet's homecoming has been crushing. As he remarks, his shock in getting off the boat is like "the startled face of an English lady who peers into her soup tureen to find a Hottentot skull" (36). Appalled by the scenes before him, the poet has described them in excruciating detail. He has incised them into the body of his narrative.

Have they been etched into his own body, too? In saying them, does he share in them? *Is* he them, in some fundamental way, for *where else* does he come from? He is not a Frenchman and does not presume to be, though he learned much from his lengthy residence in the capital. He has come home—but *who* has come home and *what* is home?

As he rounds out his withering judgment of the island culture, the poet takes a second look at what he's composed in his emerging journal. He seems to find something awry or missing in this notebook of a return. He reimagines what his homecoming could and perhaps should have been like, had he left for France in the first place with a more whole-souled, informed comprehension that, for better and for worse, he will always be a child of the island.

> To leave. My heart murmured with pronounced altruism (*générosités emphatiques*). To leave . . . I would arrive [back] suave and young in this land of mine and I would say to this land whose mud is an ingredient of my flesh: "I have wandered for a long time and I am coming home to the abandoned ghastliness of your sores."

> I would come to this land of mine and I would say to it: "Embrace me without fear . . . And if I only know how to speak, it is for you that I shall speak." (37)

> And I would say to it also:

> "My mouth shall be the mouth of adversities that have no mouth, my voice, the freedom of those who languish in the dungeon of despair." (38)

The poet would not deign to *replace* the voice of the people that has been "displaced," to recall the term he deployed previously. But he would offer language that can guide them toward truth, that can awaken them from the torpor he sees all around. He would show them they are not resigned to what he calls "the burdensome neutrality of boredom, dispensing darkness on all things indiscriminately" (27). He would teach them to discriminate, to see that their impoverished material condition does not imply an impoverished soul or spirit. He will use his own education in Paris, his own awakenings, to help point the way.

The turn is not instantaneous. He cannot will it into form. He struggles to describe things in a different register. He reaches out, figuratively speaking, to what he calls "my own" (42, 44, 45). He means all that, spiritually speaking, in fact "owns" him and to which he would give himself over, thus exchanging the cocooned comfort of a spectator for the vulnerability yet also dignity of a participant-witness.[14] He refers to a sense of solidarity with the other Antilles where things are "no less wretched than ourselves" (42). He spotlights Toussaint L'Ouverture (1743 to 1803) who helped lead a rebellion of slaves and freedmen that liberated Haiti from France in 1803. Toussaint had taken the name "L'Ouverture" because it means "the opener" or "the liberator." For the poet, Toussaint represents far more than political freedom, meaningful as that is. He also signals the cultural, spiritual, and intellectual release of the people from all the fetters—material, social, and psychological—of the long horror of slavery. It was in Haiti, the poet avers with a palpable touch of pride, that "for the first time negritude stood up tall and straight and declared that it believed in its humanity" (42). The poet tenderly bears witness to Toussaint's sad ending, as the great leader was eventually tricked and captured by the French and then imprisoned in a lonely cell in the Jura mountains of France. The poet joins Toussaint in his cell, figuratively speaking, to pay homage. The poet virtually cries out: "When shall the splendor of this [man's] blood burst forth?" (46).[15]

As indicated previously, Césaire played a leading role in the conceptualization of negritude in the 1930s. His *Cahier* is where the neologism makes its most dramatic initial appearance, though Césaire had coined it in a short essay in the aforementioned student paper, *L'Étudiant noir*. He deliberately integrated in the term's construction the pejorative French term *nègre*, which had for centuries been associated with slavery, rather than the word for black, *noir*, and he had wanted to name the student journal *L'Étudiant nègre*. His intent in so doing was to provoke people to confront colonialism and racism while reimagining black identity and prospects.[16] Brian J. Reilly (2020) helpfully illuminates how Césaire's extensive engagement with poems and prose in English composed by African-American writers strongly influenced his conception of negritude. Reilly suggests that Césaire encountered the term Negrohood during his research, and fused the Latin root of the noun-forming suffix *hood*—namely, *tudo*—with nègre (p. 387).

In due course, the concept would take on varied and sometimes contested meanings and valence in the writing of leading figures in Antillean and African letters. These meanings range from essentialist understandings of what it is "to be black" or "to be African," to metaphorical or symbolic uses that shine a light on aspects of black identity, resistance, and cultural, spiritual, and personal reconstruction.[17]

Césaire enacts the latter orientation in the *Cahier*. For him, negritude means movement, motion, activity, rather than denoting a frozen state or condition. It lives as a verb of consciousness, thought, and vision, not as a noun of permanent or fossilized substance. "My negritude is not a stone," the poet declaims; it is "neither a tower nor a cathedral" (115). The poet rejects fixity, just as he disassociates the term from a preset political stance ("a tower" as in a castle) and a prefigured religion ("a cathedral"). At the same time, however, the poet does entertain images of a generalizable black identity or mode of being. He enacts what might be dubbed a "strategic" (Spivak, 1990, pp. 11–12) or contingent essentialism in which the writer provisionally pushes a strong, seemingly settled claim about identity in order to dramatize a particular point.

Stanza 42 marks the first use of the concept negritude in the *Cahier*, though not the last. The first is dramatic enough, with (a) the image of "standing tall and straight" contrasting with the prostrate posture he perceives in the people of Martinique, and (b) the anthropomorphic "declaration" denoting the exact opposite of his people's muteness about their fundamental humanity. The next appearance of the term is in stanza 99, where the poet speaks of an old, impoverished man he notices on a streetcar whose blackness, that is, whose negritude as the poet puts it, is in the poet's eyes slowly disintegrating (see my analysis of this stanza below). The final three references to the concept are after the poet's turning of the soul, and I address them in the next section. Ultimately, as we will see, the term becomes a repeated road sign on the poet's odyssey back home.

The poet's recollection of Toussaint L'Ouverture coincides with his introduction of direct references to slavery and its legacy, which haunt him with an intense immediacy throughout the oeuvre. This history has brought his own family to the very condition he bitterly describes: "the shack breaking out in blisters, like a peach tree racked with blight, and the rooftop shrunken, patched up with bits of gasoline can, that make swamps of rust in the pasty grey straw, nauseating and squalid . . . and the bed of planks where my race was brought up, my entire race from this bed of planks . . ." (28). The reference to planks attests to the wooden ships that brought slaves across the Atlantic to the poet's island, while the grim details of his description of his home evoke the foul conditions in the holds of those ships. An image pierces him to the bone: "I hear rising from the hold the curses in chains, the hiccupping of the dying, the sound of a slave being thrown overboard . . . the baying of a woman in labor . . . the scrapings of fingernails groping for throats . . . the tauntings of the whip . . . the rummaging of vermin amid the spells of exhaustion . . ." (96). As with Sebald, the poet-as-witness at times almost drowns in his acute consciousness of historical tragedy, which accompanies him everywhere on his odyssey and saturates his sensibility. A previous image had held him wholly in its grip.

—I on a road as a child, chewing on a sugarcane stalk

—as a grown man being hauled along a bloodstained road a rope around my neck

—standing up in the middle of a gigantic circus, on my black brow a crown of daturas (62)

He rejects picturesque, colonialist-pleasing images such as ponds covered with pretty water lilies, with colorfully dressed women walking along with "smiles on their lips, infants at their breasts" (69) (cf. Kesteloot, 1991, p. 166). Not so for the poet: "So much blood in my memory! In my memory there are lagoons. They are strewn with skulls. They are not strewn with water lilies. In my memory there are lagoons. On their banks there are no displays of women in loincloths. My memory is ringed with blood. My memory is bound with corpses!" (82) The poet's sense of reality teeters as such images flood his consciousness. They threaten to poison (daturas) his soul's internal system. He recoils at the Christ-like image of humiliation in the vicious "circus" of colonialism.

At the same time, the poet cannot shake his chagrin and borderline resignation at what he perceives as the sheer lack of material and spiritual resources among the people of Martinique. He speaks again of the corruption that in his view rots their lives. He rejects "puffed-up appearances," broadcasting that his people have "never been Amazon squadrons of the king of Dahomey, nor princes of Ghana with eight hundred camels, nor scholars of Timbuktu under the reign of Askia the Great" (93). The poet adds that because he has "made a vow to conceal nothing in our history," he "freely admit[s]" that the people have been "from time immemorial [a temporality initiated by slavery], a race of grubby dishwashers, shoeshine boys lacking in ambition—at best we were scrupulous witch doctors, and the only undisputed record that we broke is that of endurance under the whip" (93). In these grinding lines there is not, to say the least, "nostalgia for a plenitude that never was" (Scharfman, 2000, p. 14). The upshot is that the poet, having now juxtaposed the bitter memories of slavery with an acerbic view of the people's plight, contemplates closing his notebook right then and there. "How mad of me," he cries out, "to dream up a marvelous caper (*merveilleux entrechat*) above the degradation!" (89). Despite his best efforts, the poet's imagination seems arrested, grounded, and frozen in place by the ugliness, the squalor, the lassitude, and the pervasive boredom he perceives.

And yet: all along this dolorous route of return, the poet continues to be troubled by the sense of missing something crucial. He feels keenly a yearning not to betray the dead whose suffering remains vivid in everything around him, and in him. As we saw with Sebald, the poet does not want to wound twice, and it seems clear he is marked by grief and mourning as much as by anger and frustration.[18] Earlier, he had appeared to perceive the distance his initial orientation as poet was creating: "This above all, my body and my soul: beware of crossing your arms in the sterile pose of a spectator, for life is not a show on stage, for a sea of troubles is not a proscenium, for a screaming human being is not a dancing bear" (38). As heartfelt as these lines feel, however, they evince a staginess that constitutes yet another form of distance. Who can forget the immortal lines from Shakespeare's *Hamlet*: "*This above all*: to thine own self be true. . . . take arms against *a sea of troubles*/and by opposing them end them" (act I, scene 3 and act III, scene 1, emphasis added). Césaire may well be criticizing or even mocking his earlier self for its judgmentalism. In any case, the poet resorts here to romanticized cliché rather than truly confronting how he is going to reconcile himself to his island people. The poet cannot simply declare himself a spokesperson for them, as if by fiat or divine dispensation. He will have to earn his way back home, truly *into* home, if he is to speak *of* them justly as the necessary ground for speaking *for* them in one manner or another. The odyssey the poet has put himself on won't obey his wishes or fantasies. It will insist on a full reckoning.

The poet recalls an encounter from his time in Paris that becomes, in his present circumstances, "an unforeseen and salutary involutional turn (*bienfaisante révolution interiéure*)" (90). It will prove to be transforming. "One evening," he recollects, "in a streetcar opposite me, a nigger" (98). I quote in full.

A black man as huge as a great ape was trying to make himself small on the bench of a tramcar. He was trying to shed, on this filthy tramcar bench, his gigantic legs and his shaking, starved boxer's hands. And every bodily part had deserted, was deserting him: his nose, which resembled a peninsula adrift, even his blackness (*négritude*), which was becoming discolored under the action of a relentless tawing. And the tawer was none other than Poverty (*Misère*)—an enormous bat from hell whose claw marks on his face had scarred it with islets of scab. Or rather, Poverty was an untiring artisan working on some grotesque cartouche. One could clearly make out how a sedulous and malevolent thumb had molded his brow into a hump, pierced his nose with two parallel, discombobulating tunnels, prolonged the lower lip out of all measure, and, by a masterstroke of caricature, planed, polished and varnished the most delicate and dainty little ear in the whole world.

He was an ungainly black man without measure or proportion.

A black whose eyes rolled in gory fatigue

An indecent black and his toes sniggered in a very foul manner at the bottom of the cracked housing of his shoes.

Poverty—it was unspeakable—had gone to perverse lengths to construct him.

It had dug out the eye socket, then rouged it with a makeover of dust and mucous.

It had stretched empty space between the solid hook of the jaw and the bones of an old sordid cheek.

On top it had planted the tiny gleaming stumps of a beard a few days old. It had driven his heart to distraction, arched his back.

The net effect was the perfect image of a hideous black, a sullen black, a melancholy black, a collapsed black, his hands joined in prayer on a gnarled stick. A black buried in an old tattered coat. A black comical and ugly, and some women seated behind me snickered at the sight of him.

He was COMICAL AND UGLY.

COMICAL AND UGLY that's for sure.

I spread a branching smile of complicity . . .

My cowardly self rediscovered! . . .

My heroism, what a farce! (99)

The capitalized terms toward the end of these shocking lines mirror a disturbing image in a poem Césaire knew well, Charles Baudelaire's "The Albatross." A majestic seagoing bird by that name has been trapped on a ship's deck. A true artist of the skies, the albatross is pure clumsiness on solid ground. It flaps around ungainly and out of control, to the cruel laughter of the crew, a mockery now copied by the women seated behind the poet and indeed by the poet himself, whose initial appellation "great ape" had already cheapened the old man's dignity.

In the 1939 but not 1956 version, there is a line that comes before the capitalized words: "Me I turned, my eyes proclaiming that I had nothing in common with this monkey" (*Moi je me tournai, mes yeux proclamant que je n'avais rien de commun avec ce singe*) (in Césaire, 2013, 52). My sense is that Césaire ultimately judged the stanza in question shattering enough without this particular line, since he had already crudely referred to the ape family. All the same, the repetition itself remains telling. The poet realizes, suddenly and sickeningly—marked by the ellipsis in the next to last line—his "complicity" in racism, doubtless because of the lingering colonial imprint on his sensibility, that is, his "cowardly self" that won't give up the tie to French identity. Note how the very term *negritude* has shifted from denoting pride and achievement, associated with Toussaint L'Ouverture, to utter abjection (Arnold, 1981, p. 161). The poet immediately lacerates himself: "This town is my measure / And my spirit is prostrate . . . This town, my face of mud. / For my face I lay claim to the erupted tribute of spit!" (99). He perceives how appalling his account of the old man has been, a direct result of his powerful poetic gifts applied so meanly.[19] The poet's humiliation is doubled by his intuition, intimated previously in the poem, that there is something rich at work in his people's "inner refuge," if only he can learn how to see it and attend to it.

Recall the poet's terms for this painful yet revelatory experience: "an unforeseen and salutary involutional turn (*bienfaisante révolution interiéure*)" (90). Arnold and Eshleman, and Rosello and Pritchard, translate the terms as "beneficent inner revolution," connoting an image of a turning (revolving) of the soul. Berger and Bostock prefer "unforeseen happy conversion." *Bienfaisante* can also be rendered as "regenerative," "nurturing," "making good," or "making better." The poet apprehends that, however heartfelt, his reflections on his heritage and his outrage at colonialism and slavery have until now had an inauthentic quality to them. He has not yet fully heeded the *address* his homecoming is making to him, which he must "hear" if he is to truly bear witness (more on this point below). He had felt great chagrin and injury in seeing his people prostrate, wanting them to stand upright and take their place in the world. But it is he who needs to come down to earth: to see the world *with* them rather than standing outside looking *at* them. He has enacted a false solidarity. Unawares, his ego appointed him presumptively to the post of spokesman from on high. But his ego, his prideful sense of self, was like a canker in his eye, or as the novelist George Eliot (*née* Maryann Evans) writes: "Will not a tiny speck very close to our vision blot out the glory of the world, and leave only a margin by which we see the blot? I know no speck so troublesome as self" (1985, p. 456).

The poet drops the pose of the returning hero who will give his people the word so they can rise up.[20] He transforms into a prodigal son who had lost something bequeathed to him by his *pays natal*, namely, a solidarity that began long before he was born. The great painter Rembrandt van Rijn, in a work he completed in the 1660s, poignantly and movingly portrays the prodigal son going down on his knees before his forgiving father. The poet goes further: "My spirit is prostrate," to recall the words quoted previously (99). His mind and body have become as flattened and prone as he once perceived his people. Barbara Cease (1980) pens a grim if apt summary of the poet's trial: "[H]e had witnessed a denuding striptease of his assimilationism, and it was not a pretty sight" (p. 54). However, the supine poet does not become a supplicant. As he looks up, for the first time, from the ground to the sky rather than the other way around, he now discerns the true work of homecoming.

Consider again the very first words of the poem: *Au bout du petit matin*.[21] Davis's translation of these terms—"at the close of foreday morning"—is comprehensively sound. But one virtue of Arnold and Eshleman's translation of the terms, "at the end of first light," is the very image it creates of "first light." I read this as the first light that makes possible the poet's first seeing when he gets off the boat and walks back into his natal world. That first light was dim and limiting. It set too narrow a spectrum. It did not allow the full play of color, including of black as aesthetic, as cultural, as beautiful despite its stereotyped associations with darkness, night, and the forbidding. Now, with second light, comes second sight. As the poet makes the soul-turn to which he attests, in which he lets dissolve his initial self-expectations as well as sense of self-as-poet, a fresh light now floods the scene. He can see more truly, if not clairvoyantly (there is still work to do). Morning gives way to the fullness of the day. The poet is now able to say in a single breath, unreservedly and unguardedly, "'It's beautiful-and-good-and-legitimate-to-be-black'" (172)—a point Césaire conveyed to students at the Lycée where he taught (Larrier, 2010, p. 40), and which he had first enunciated, word for word, in his early 1935 essay in *L'Étudiant noir* (Rexer, 2013, p. 8).

## Cri de Coeur, Cri de l'Esprit

The black American poet Countee Cullen, in his well-known poem "Heritage" first published in 1925, asks himself: "What is Africa to me?" In the course of his rhymed inquiry, he questions radically his Christian upbringing, but does not see himself at home in African religious traditions. He questions his Westernized, what he calls "civilized" condition, but does not yearn for a return to village life. He projects no images of an Edenic present, past, or future, either in America or Africa. He does not despair, but he has not arrived at a settled outlook. Wrenched from Africa, set down and put down in America, he is a searcher: "Lord, forgive me if my need / Sometimes shapes a human creed." The poet accepts the trials, losses, and joys of making his own way, of fashioning a "creed" that can lead the way rather than passively following the dictates of others, whether they are malevolent or well-intentioned.

Cry of the heart (*coeur*), cry of the mind and spirit (*esprit*): Cullen illuminates the existential experience of coming to grips with one's orientation in the world rather than assuming it unreflectively and uncritically. Part of that experience is conceiving one's roots, or one's sources of "being," so to speak. As we have seen, the poet of the *Cahier*, upon first stepping off the boat, could not touch the land and its people. His polished shoes kept him from feeling the black sandy coast and the red soil interior. His Frenchified, spectator posture, of which he was scarcely aware, compromised his vision of the people. He had no answer to the question What is Martinique to me? However, after his stark awakening, touched on previously—his "salutary involutional turn" (90)—he has heard the address his homecoming is making to him. It is asking him: Who *are* you? Where *do* you come from? How *will* you conduct yourself now that you are back? The remainder of the epic poem constitutes a sustained response that reflects the turning of the soul the poet has undergone. He realizes that involutional—denoting that which is complex, involved, intricate—parallels *in-volitional*, meaning not a matter of will, of decision, or of choice. It is a matter of being summoned and bearing witness.

The poet now begins to respond directly to his addressor, with the latter constituting the people, the history, and the prospect of Martinique as a place in which he might learn to (re)dwell. He admits or, better, confesses to his addressor his initial stance upon his return.

> I was hiding behind an obtuse vanity; destiny was calling me;
>     I was in hiding in the back, and look at me now: man flat
>     on the ground, his frail defense dispersed,
> his most revered maxims trampled underfoot, his pedantic
>     declamations blowing hot air through every gash
> look at me: man flat on the ground
> and his soul is virtually bare
> and destiny triumphantly contemplates
> this soul that defied it molting in the ancestral slough. (104)

He makes no apology, asks for no forgiveness—again, he does not become a supplicant—but he does see he must start over. He embraces the task: "I declare that this is just fine (*Je dis que cela est bien ainsi*)" (105, repeated in 106). "I toss overboard my alien wealth / I toss overboard my authentic self-deceptions" (109).

In so doing, the revelations initiated on the streetcar continue: "But what strange pride illumines me all of a sudden?" (110). The poet's "authentic self-deceptions" give way to an authentic setting aside of his will as he takes on, instead, a posture of receptivity. Compassion, feeling-with, being with, replaces spectatorial, clinical distance. Echoing the image above of second light and second sight, the poet writes the following:

> O friendly light
> O pristine source of light
> those who invented neither gunpowder nor compass
> those who have never tamed steam or electricity
> those who have not explored either seas or sky
> but without whom the earth would not be the earth (114)

The turn to earthy imagery rushes on as he characterizes his new sight, naming its main organon (and deploying anaphora as he increasingly does in the poem's movement):

> My negritude is not a stone . . .
> my negritude is not a film of dead water on the dead eye of earth
> my negritude . . . delves into the red flesh of the soil . . . (115)

He fairly shouts out how he now sees his people, affirming that their human condition he had hitherto cast as utterly fallen in fact discloses possibility. He begins with a direct link to Africa, highlighting a well-known mahogany tree associated in local customs with notions of purification, of life force, of nourishment, and of the intimate link between humans and the natural world. The poet then repeats a refrain, which he will later do a third time.

> Hurray (*Eia*) for the majestic Cedrate (*Kailcedrat*)!
> Hurray for those who have never invented anything
> for those who have never explored anything
> for those who have never vanquished anything
> but they surrender, possessed, to the essence of every thing
> ignorant of surfaces but possessed by the movement
> of every thing
> unconcerned to vanquish, but playing the game of the world (116)
> truly the elder sons of the world (117)

The poet celebrates the nonimperial qualities of the people. They are not interested in vanquishing others. They are not interested in creating instruments for doing so. They remain "ignorant of surfaces" rather than seeking the particular knowledge that would give them power to dominate others and nature. They play "the game of the world" constituted by the rhythms of life and death, of family and friendship, of kin and stranger, of hunger and satiety, of thirst and quenching. They are not at all ignorant of such things, which reside not on the surface—the realm of theory and explanation—but in the very marrow of quotidian life. In the poet's view, their material and spiritual poverty perdures, as does their current lack of ambition and rebellion (148). He does not replace his prior disdain with a sentimental, romanticized view, much less an exoticized one, which elsewhere in the poem (69, and see 80) he makes plain is repugnant, and which he grasps would announce, in effect, a failure to bear witness. But he discerns nothing romantic in the people's ability to move in tandem with the world around them rather than manipulate it in the violent manner of colonialism.

In likeness, there is nothing sentimental in the poet's discovery that his people's naturalistic way of being in the world positions them to show others the importance of mutual openness. "Permeable to all the breaths of the world," he writes of his people, "fraternal compass points for all the breaths of the world / deep lake bed for all the waters of the world" (117). The poet perceives how this humanist-cosmopolitan spirit has survived slavery, and perhaps even been fueled by it though not by intent. The revelation has an unanticipated effect. The realization of the people's infinite suffering juxtaposed with their infinite resilience moves the poet beyond his previous hatred toward the colonialists and, in a way, toward his own people and island—and toward his own self, or self-that-was. He now sees "the white world / grotesquely worn out from its enormous effort" to control and own things, and from its "false victories" and "grandiose alibis" as part of that effort. "Pity for our vanquishers," the poet declares, "omniscient and naïve" (119). The colonizers' (mis)use of their power in seizing faraway lands reveals, as touched on above, their moral bankruptcy: how they thoroughly tarnish and diminish their own humanity and thereby alienate themselves from the earth. They know so much ("omniscient"), but live as if they know nothing ("naïve").

The poet turns from resentment, bitterness, and bile—to prayer.

> . . . and here at the end of this foreday morning is my robust prayer
> that I may hear neither mockery nor howling, my eyes focused
> on this town that I presage, beautiful,
> grant me the crude faith of the conjurer
> grant to my hands the faculty to model
> grant to my soul the power in the sword's tempering
> I shall not shirk. Make of my head a prow's head
> and, o my heart, make of me neither a father nor a brother
> nor a son, but the father, the brother, the son
> not a husband, but the lover of this unique people. (122)
> Make me eschew all vanity, yet be open to its power,
> like a fist at the end of an outstretched arm!
> Make me commissioner of its blood
> make me trustee of its resentment
> make of me a man of closure
> make of me a man of beginning
> make of me a man of reaping

> but also make of me a man of sowing (123)
> Make me the one to implement these lofty plans
> now is the time to gird one's loins like a stalwart—(124)

The poet continues to drop all pretense of being a privileged spokesperson, much less a savior. As a witness, he aspires to be one who takes care, handles with care, advocates with care. He would be the "lover" of the people (more on this theme below). He hopes not to suffer the brunt of "mockery" or "howling" in light of this aim, referring here to Baudelaire's concluding lines in "The Albatross" about the poet's fate of being jeered whenever they put forward meaning and possibilities that reach beyond typical human satisfactions and preoccupations. Above all, the poet of the *Cahier* will persist. *Someone* must bear witness to the noncolonialized world that remains seeded everywhere on the island. The poet intensifies his charge by fusing space and time into a single point of action. The quoted lines above are bookended by "here" (122) and "now" (124).

The task is much larger than what he had initially set himself before his turn. The poet grasps the necessity of the witness to prepare themselves, to make ready continuously to heed the humanity before them. The image of prayer dramatizes his commitment to receptivity, his suspension of a will to power, his willingness to wait for insight and truth to arrive and to become their vehicle. "At the end of this foreday morning," he repeats, "my robust prayer":

> grant me the muscles of this canoe on the turbulent sea
> and the triumphing cheer of the conch of good news

The poet draws explicitly on local cultural symbols to render his hopes—the canoe of a fishing people that sets out to bring them life from the sea, the conch sounded on the beach at a happy return. He continues,

> Hear me: I am just a human being, unperturbed by any
>    humiliation, by any disgusting spit,
> I am just a human being who accepts, who has relinquished
>    anger (in my heart there is only love, immense, ablaze) (132)

The poet-as-witness identifies himself here with humanity writ large. "I am just a human being," he writes, rather than "I am just a black man or a man from Martinique." He gestures toward expanding his moral remit qua witness beyond his island people, a point I also return to below.

At the same time, the poet's new consciousness, his negritude as he names it, emerges side by side with his new perceptivity. It transforms from a theoretical to a lived idea. While in Paris, Césaire had learned of the alleged "scientific" basis of white supremacy associated most controversially with the blinkered theories of Arthur de Gobineau (1816 to 1882) that were built, in part, around the "science" of head measurements. Césaire had also read critics of racism such as the Haitian philosopher Anténor Firmin (1850 to 1911), whose pioneering book *De l'égalité des races humaines* (On the Equality of Human Races) was both a direct attack on and creative response to Gobineau's notorious *Essai sur l'inégalité des races humaines* (Essay on the Inequality of Human Races). Earlier in the *Cahier* the poet had thoroughly repudiated the latter's ugly outlook.

> I belong to no nationality foreseen by the chancelleries [of Europe].
> I defy the craniometer. Homo sum etc. (97)

"Homo sum" is doubtless a reference to a much-quoted line from the Roman poet and playwright Terence (second century CE): "*Homo sum; humani nil a me alienum puto*—I am a human being, therefore nothing that is human is foreign to me." The poet reveals both the depth of his familiarity with ancient texts and his emerging anticolonial humanism and cosmopolitanism. Perhaps the poet's deliberate deployment of the Latin he knows so well also points to his claim to a place in the pantheon of world poets (cf. Scharfman, 2000, p. 54).

In any event, if not by name the poet criticizes geographers, historians, anthropologists, psychologists, biologists, and all others whenever they arbitrarily create borders, boundaries, categories, and types, all of which run counter to his new sense of the spontaneous movement of people and of all things in the world. He speaks of "the geometry of my shed blood" (146), which instantly encompasses Africa, the Atlantic crossing, the setting down on the island, and all that has since transpired. His blood is that of many people, places, and times, and a pox on anyone who insists on typecasting him. "I accept," he writes,

> both the determination of my biology, no longer confined to
> a facial angle, or a texture of hair, or a nose sufficiently flat,

or a color sufficiently melanian, and my negritude, no longer tied to a cephalic index, or a plasma, or a soma, but measured with the compass of suffering. (147)

The poet's "acceptance," not to be confused with resignation (cf. Arnold, 1981, p. 163), encompasses every facet of his negritude, his consciousness and his awareness and embrace of his people's history. He launches once again into a registry of specific acts of violence done to the slaves and, in effect, imprints this train of harm onto his very being. "I accept . . . I accept . . . entirely, without reserve," he declaims, ". . . I accept. I accept [133] . . . I accept, all that I accept . . ." (149). The staccato physicality of the poet's repetitive "I accept" recalls Echleman and Smith's remark mentioned previously about the "percussive effects" of the poet's idiom. In this moment of epiphany, the repetition underscores the fact that the poet accepts the martyr's cause: he will bear witness. At the same time, his gesture is one of remembrance: the Greek origin for martyr, *martis*, also means "to remember."

The weight is not light to bear, for as mentioned, the circumstances on the ground remain dire and abjection is always just around the corner. A forlorn image of a pietà (Arnold, 2013, p. xv) crosses the poet's eye as he sees "the body of my country magically nestled in my despairing arms, its bones rattled and, in its veins, the blood holding back, like the droplet of vegetal milk at the tip of the damaged bulb" (150). But the poet's acceptance of truth in all its many sides, from crushing to joyous, triggers another revelation on his journey home. "And now all of a sudden life and force rush upon me like a bull" (151). Césaire tips his hat here to his comrade Senghor, who would revel in the idea of "life and force," or natal life force, making an appearance and breaking through. Metaphorically speaking, the bull tosses the poet into the air, and he has a vista and vision which expresses a new grasp of possibilities.

> And we are upright now, my country and I, hair in the wind, my tiny hand in its gigantic fist, and the force is not within us but above us, in a voice that pierces the night and the hearing like the invasive wasp of the apocalypse. And the voice announces that Europe has for centuries gorged us with lies and bloated us with afflictions,
> for it is by no means true that the work of man is finished,
> that we have nothing left to do in the world,

    that we parasite the world
    that we need only keep in step with the world (152)
    instead the work of man has only just begun
    the task remains for man to overcome all taboos rendered
        powerless in the corners of his fervor
    and no race has a monopoly on beauty, or intelligence, or vitality
    and there is room for all at the appointed place of conquest,
        and we
    now know that the sun revolves around our earth illuminating
        each
    parcel by the dictates of our will alone, and every star that
        falls from
    sky to earth does so at our unconditional command. (153)

Several themes expressed in these lines are worth highlighting as part of the poet's witness.

    1. The poem has shifted from an emphasis on being prostrate to being "upright," as seen in the first line above. In stanzas 165–166, the poet will enunciate the latter term 16 times, with the very shape of those stanzas, vertical in their height on the page, mirroring the standing tall the poet had longed to see. Carrie Noland (2019, p. 420) reminds us that this accent on standing upright—*debout* in French—contrasts with the refrain repeated earlier, *au bout* (*du petit matin*) denoting "at the end," a term whose relative passivity differs from how the poet now evokes the beginning of something new, *a standing up*.[22] The biblical references and allusions are also noteworthy, with mention of the "apocalypse" which, in this case, suggests a complete obliteration of colonial mentalities. The poet will speak of "the old negritude," denoting by these terms the obsequiousness and racial shame that whites called being "a very good negro" (156, 157, 159), but which now, as the people begin to stir, "is gradually becoming a cadaver" alongside colonialism itself (156, 162). This point syncs with Césaire's reconstruction of the French language itself, including its expression in traditional poetic forms that the previous generation of Antillean poets ("very good negroes" in the poet's view) adopted. Those forms, too, are old and cadaverous.

    2. The poet sees himself and his people engaged in "the work of man." They are not parasitic on the world. Again, unlike "the very good negro"—which the poet admits might once have described him, at least in part—they do not "need only keep in step with the world" but can

help give it direction. For "no race has a monopoly on beauty, or intelligence, or vitality"; all are needed for the work that "has only just begun." "[T]here is room for all" in the "conquest," which refers not to imperial or exploitative moves but to the emergence of collective agency, a true participation, a flowering of solidarity.[23]

Césaire anticipated the images of humanism and cosmopolitanism that come to the fore in the latter stages of *Cahier* in his aforementioned 1935 article in *L'Étudiant noir*. He had argued against self-cocooning versions of race consciousness, contending that negritude's true promise lies not only in material and spiritual uplift for blacks but also in how it can guide them into "the beautiful headwaters of universal humanity" (quoted in Rexer, 2013, p. 11). The poet's humanist orientation that is so bound up with his people's well-being is not anthropocentric, as seen in his countless appreciative references to the flora and fauna of the island and, especially, in how he comes to see his people—and himself—as organically tied to the natural environment, moving with it and alongside it.[24] At the same time, the poet conjures the cosmopolitan idea of a human crossroads marked by the general and the particular, the universal and the local, in which the aim is neither homogeneity—or a false, assimilationist universality such as that characteristic of colonialism—nor a self-sealed wholeness given the fluidity, or permeability, of persons and communities. Rather, the idea points to the acknowledgment of difference as that which puts in relief what humans share, even as the acknowledgment of similarity puts in relief what is different and singular about individuals and communities.

It is true that the particular can constitute a negation of the universal, and vice versa. But like the grain of sand that starts a beach to form, the particular can be understood as the very condition for the possibility of the universal (cf. Garraway, 2010, p. 77). The latter simply loses meaning and coherence in the absence of diffuse, diverse reality. It disappears in a spiral of abstraction. The poet's cosmopolitan sensibility, saturated by his formative time on both sides of the Atlantic, stands in marked contrast, on the one hand, to the colonizers' hyperparochial, acquisitive mind-set that has somehow persuaded them they own the world and, on the other hand, to purist, hermetically sealed conceptions of culture and identity that regard any outside influence as acidic rather than as potentially both nonthreatening and generative. In this sense, the universal constitutes the condition for the possibility of the particular.[25]

The poet's universal gesture originates in his intense commitment to his local world, now (re)discovered and (re)vitalized through the rough and tumble of his return home. He had already expanded his sense of the local by incorporating in his concern-full vision black communities across the Americas, which for him share a common experience of violent oppression and attempted revolt, as well as hope for freedom: "red lands, blood-red lands, blood-brother lands" (43 [cf. Dease, 1980, p. 42]).[26] The poet had also gestured toward a universal solidarity with the downtrodden in a stanza which began with terms from an African myth: "As there are hyena-men and panther-men, I would be a jew-man, / a kaffir-man, / a hindu-man-from-Calcutta, / a Harlem-man-who-does-not-vote" (33). Moreover, and crucially for the poet, he had anticipated his humanist-cosmopolitan turn in his refusal to let his life be guided by hate. That refusal did not constitute a change in his critical position. On the contrary, in his own view it *matured* his outlook. He had said: "Make me the one to implement these lofty plans / now is the time to gird one's loins like a stalwart" (124). "But in so doing," he continued,

> heart of mine, preserve me from all hate
> do not make of me that man of hate for whom
> I have only hate
> for though I am quartered in this unique race
> you know nonetheless my domineering love
> you know that it is not from hatred of other races
> that I make myself the husbandman of this unique race
> that what I most desire is
> to meet the universal hunger
> the universal thirst
> is to commit my race, free at last,
> to producing from its cloistered intimacy
> the succulence of fruits. (125)

The reference to fruits recalls the moment when Césaire coined the term *negritude* in his 1935 essay mentioned earlier. He had forecast that the idea would blossom "like a beautiful tree until it bears the most authentic fruit" (quoted in Rexer, 2013, p. 2). Much later, in an interview, he would say that negritude embodies "universalizing, living values" that will "bear fruit" if he and his confreres make the effort to "irrigate" their cultural field (2000a, p. 92). Here, the fruits to which the poet refers will be not only for local consumption but for any person or community, near or far, who seeks to stand upright, who aspires to a voice, who knows they can contribute to "the work of man."

The poet hates the hating he had done. In its place, his love has become "domineering" over everything else in his being (in the 1939 version, the phrase is "catholic" love, denoting not the religion by that name but a general, universal outlook). The poet has given himself over to this love in a moment of transcendent and we might say participatory negritude (cf. Dease, 1980, p. 44). This love would lead him now to be a "husbandman"—a tenderer, caretaker, nurturer—as he readies himself for the work of cultural reconstruction that faces him and his fellow islanders, if not black communities everywhere under colonial rule. In due course Césaire took literally the self-ascribed role he conceives. He "took care" by serving for several decades as Mayor of Fort de France and as a deputy in the French parliament, even while continuing his poetic and literary endeavors.

"I now grasp the meaning of my ordeal (*ordalie*)" (154). Yes: the poet's odyssey, his *retour*, has been far more complicated and painful than he anticipated. It has been an ordeal in two senses of the term. On the one hand, his fundamental life commitments, his very sense of being, have been on trial: like Odysseus and so many others who would seek a homecoming, he has been put to the test (cf. Rosello, 1995, p. 148). On the other hand, he has suffered what the philosopher Michael Oakeshott (1989) dubs, following Henry James, "the ordeal of consciousness" (p. 9). Oakeshott means the ways a person's own mind, through the process of becoming educated, will challenge their complacency, their self-understandings, and their view of the world. The poet's often searing testimony constitutes a now matured response to finding his feet back on the ground of his island. The bleak poverty is there, both physical and spiritual. *But so is the abiding humanity and inheritance.* The poet names explicitly, for the first time, who he comprehends to be his forbears: "my Bambara ancestors" (154), referring both to a West African people and to a kingdom by that name that flourished from the 17th to the 19th centuries. His *pays natal*—his inaugurating home—has expanded imaginatively from Martinique to encompass Africa, however irretrievable in actuality is such a connection (cf. Scharfman, 1987, p. 37). The poet also acknowledges his "new growth" (172), which is at once ethical, aesthetic, spiritual, and political. He has shriven the self. He has let the scene "in." He has let the people in. He has let love in. "Hurray for joy / Hurray for love" (121).

## Conclusion: An Education in Self-Transformation as Witness

A central experience of those who bear witness is that while summoned to testify, they are accompanied by questions and doubts about how to heed this call. In the previous chapter, I highlighted Sebald's concerns about his bona fides as a witness. He fears the siren power of a falsely consoling resolution to his quest to come to terms with Germany's past. He worries that this drive distorts his capacity to balance passion with dispassion in the name of truth. He suspects the core instrument at his disposal: writing itself. Words can express what an author does not intend; what an author intends can elude expression in words. Caught in the middle of this tension, which seems to operate independently of the author's control, Sebald struggles to keep the door open rather than have it shut prematurely on an ill-formed thought that could vitiate his entire endeavor.

Césaire's homecoming is riddled with comparable questions. For example, as countless Antillean and African writers have attested, he feels the challenge of using the colonial metropole's language to convey his authentic thought. He wonders whether his resort to French and to the literary and poetic traditions behind it compromises his undertaking from the start.[27] His studies of the emerging ethnographic and historical literature on Africa in the 1930s, with their revelations about long-standing oral traditions as well as about ancient kingdoms, had had a marked effect on his consciousness as it did on his fellow black students in Paris. In due course, the poet became aware of the limits as well as the potential in language. He saw that ways of thinking, examining, imagining, and questioning can have dramatic ideational and practical consequences.

In the additions Césaire inserted in the poem in 1956, which I characterized previously as a metacommentary on his endeavor linked with some overtly political stanzas, he engages the very idea of "reason" itself.

> Words?
> Ah yes, words!
> Reason, I anoint you "wind of evening."

> The name you claim is "mouthpiece of order"?
> For me you are "corolla of the lash." (48)

The poet attacks the same rationalistic impulse that Sebald's narrator discerns in Dr. Nicholas Tulp's anatomy lesson (chapter 2, p. 64). To the narrator, as we saw, Rembrandt dramatizes the objectifying if not deadening gaze of rationalism when it is unmoored from ethics. This gaze converts reason into a surgical weapon, as it takes things apart and rearranges them in a will to power and control, even as it presumes an uncoercive posture. For the poet, this conception of reason becomes a "mouthpiece of order" as it drowns out the voice of justice and humanity—and of poetry and witnessing. The poet fashions an incredible and devastating image of what he regards as the colonists' rationalistic and rationalizing imperative. The poet conjures a corolla, that is, the colorful petals that protect a flower's interior reproductive organs, grown in this case *from a whip* and protecting its self-reproducing use against slaves.[28]

Then, the poet clinches his critique:

> Because we detest you, yes you and your reason, we repossess ourselves in the name of dementia praecox (*démence précoce*), of flamboyant madness of inveterate cannibalism. (48)

The poet pulls out an extreme stereotype that the colonialists manufactured—that the Indigenous people are cannibalistic, out-of-control savages—and throws it in their faces (cf. Jahn, 1990, p. 144). He makes plain to them that their entire imperial project with its underlying modes of rationalization is what is truly demented. The colonialists, in effect, cannibalize their own moral humanity in suppressing that of others. The poet will fight against their mental as well as material force as he unleashes a barrage of metaphors that constitutes a complete rejection of the imperial assumption that as a black man and black poet he can only "mumble words" (71).

> [W]ords, ah yes, words! but fresh-blooded words, words that are tsunamis and erysipelas malarial fevers and lava flows and brush fires, and burnings of flesh, and burnings of cities . . . (72)

He declares to the French language itself: "Adjust yourself to me: I refuse to adjust myself to you!" (74).[29]

Reason, logic, and reasonableness are not reducible to rationalism, nor to any "ism" that comes to mind (Splitter, 2022). The poet realizes the differences across his oeuvre. He is careful not to conflate reason and reasoning *tout court* with the colonial mind-set. In addition, he is far too well-read to confuse colonial reason with "Western reason," since there is no such thing as the latter taken as a totality (cf. the long critical tradition in European philosophy). The poet flirts with but does not enact an essentialist variant of negritude in which reason and reasoning are sharply demarcated from an emotional-intuitive mode of mind characteristic, or so some allege, of Africans and people of African descent.[30]

To be sure, the poet will not privilege reason and logic considered in isolation: "recalcitrant Reason: you shall not hinder me" (141).[31] Put another way, he knows poetry is not theory or vice versa, even though the one can provoke the other as he demonstrates. But while not presuming the post of theoretician or logician, the poet will not simply hand his trajectory over to caprice, which as discussed previously is not a synonym with surrealism because the latter constitutes an *intentional* break from conventional orderings of thought. He is as deliberate as any writer can be, including when he silences his reflecting mind to let the precognitive speak. The precognitive denotes an instantaneous, immediate aesthetic-ethical response to experience, which can then be brought into reflective consciousness. It should not be confused with the irrational, though Césaire allows—through prior rational consideration—the latter to break in from time to time, often when mocking colonial caricatures of his people (cf. 51). His use of scare quotes in the first lines above from stanza 48 constitutes a beautifully thoughtful way of intensifying his theme precisely by not reifying what he is saying of reason. The poet appreciates that, alongside other cultural resources, it will require careful reasoning, sustained arguments, and numerous modes of communication for the people to "repossess" themselves in the wake of colonialism. His tight, Cartesian-like logic at certain phases, which sometimes has the feel of a hammer blow, does not contradict but complements his trust, at other times, in the soul's pre-analytical spontaneity.

In the poet's distinctive manner, formed in the crucible of bearing witness, he fuses active passivity with passive activity. He gives himself over to the "ordeal" he experiences. But he also guides his way. He *responds* with mind, heart, and spirit to what is addressing him. In an astonishing, transfixing moment toward the close of the *Cahier*, the poet transforms his "acceptance" of the witness's charge into a willingness, as he puts it, to be *bound* by this task:

> bind, bind me without chagrin
> bind me with your vast arms to the luminous clay
> bind my black vibration to the very navel of the world
> bind, o bind me, bitter fraternity,
> then lassoing me with your noose of stars
> ascend, Dove
> ascend
> ascend
> ascend
> I follow you, who are inscribed in my inherited white cornea. (173)

The poet's previous smoking hot words call up the image of melting the chains (bonds) of slavery and its legacy. But this act is not in the name of a purely personal liberation. Rather, the poet-witness will let his accepted task bind him, hold him, lead him, in the name of his people and of the oppressed everywhere—*all* who "hunger" and "thirst" (125).[32] The poet realizes that it is a "bitter" fraternity that links them, given so much suffering, but the key here is fraternity. He rescues this image of solidarity from its hitherto unrealized state as one of the core terms, alongside equality and liberty, in the famed trilogy enunciated during the French Revolution.[33] The poet's active passivity reveals how he has learned to heed truth. He takes advantage of what I characterized previously as second light—compare his reference here to the cornea, which lets light into the eye—informed now by a consciousness of his Antillean and African inheritances. The biblical image of the dove of peace attests to his ascension to a new understanding.

The poet has let dissolve his self's partially colonized gaze, but, importantly, not the education he received through the French language with its literary traditions. He has benefited from Gustave Flaubert's example (also mentioned in chapter 2, p. 60) of what it means to seek le mot juste—just the right word for what is at issue. He has learned from the surrealists' example of identifying that word (*mot*) through trusting in the unconscious mind and in the precognitive in general, rather than solely in the abstract cogitations of logical mind. As countless other writers have discovered, the poet realizes nobody owns a language. The lissomness of language, when joined with the poet's imaginal bent, can be liberating. The key is *artfulness*, an unending labor that faces the witness and every other writer who aspires to truth. Césaire's pas de deux with French, expressed in every line of the *Cahier*, has opened him to truth.

The poet wholeheartedly embraces his lessons, and he brings his rich education to bear as fully as possible. The *Cahier* is a literary and philosophical cornucopia that is at once both poetic and encyclopedic. It embodies the thought of a cosmopolitan-minded witness who has been in dialogue with ideas from countless sources. It reads as if the poet would squeeze out of himself every pertinent insight about art, beauty, goodness, suffering, injustice, and truth that he has absorbed through years of study, contemplation, and constant conversation. The reader observes, and perhaps can come to witness, the poet's conviction that humans can and should learn from cultural resources from anywhere (including Césaire's own offering), *and that they can make them their own*—not as commodities to consume pulled off a market shelf, but as gifts that can deepen and transfigure their self-awareness and their awareness of community, with all the accomplishments, shortcomings, and promise that self and community feature.

The poet had asked of himself and his people: "Who and what are we?" (52). He had asked himself as poet: "What can I do? / I have to begin / Begin what?" (67). He had wondered about his qualifications as a witness: "Tell me: am I humble enough [he does not say strong enough] . . . To grovel in the mud? To bear up in the thick of the mud? To bear the load?" (134). As we have seen, out of an apparent wasteland of muted voices and crushed hopes, he arrives at a lived response (not to be confused with a final "answer") to the questions. In so doing, he experiences one final revelation. As he closes his witness-notebook, his long journal-journey home, he concludes.

> Master of laughter?
> Master of dread silence?
> Master of hope and of despair?
> Master of laziness? Master of dances?
> That's me! (170)

The poet riffs off the French word for master, *maître*, which like its English counterpart can denote a teacher or instructor whose identity comes from working in a formal educational institution. The poet's formal institution is poetry. Through his long struggle to find his voice and the right poetic idiom, he has become—to his surprise—a *maître* of laughter and joy, suffering and pain, hope and action, despair and resignation, motion ("dances," as in the dance of negritude) and energy.

In this respect the poet echoes the aforementioned Michel de Montaigne, who over 300 years previously had been a severe critic of the colonial rapacity just getting underway in his era. Montaigne had argued that every human being "bears the whole form of the human condition" (1991, p. 908)—that is, all the aspects listed above, from laughter to despondency, none of which are in principle foreign to any person (cf. Terence's adage touched on previously). Playfully speaking—with play understood as deeply serious—we might say that human beings are creatures who feel hope and joy on even-numbered days, and despair and despondency on odd-numbered ones. To reconfigure the poet's words: That's us! Montaigne suggests that this humanizing truth opens a path to mutual moral recognition and support. He anticipates Césaire's powerful summons to himself and his people to stop looking outside themselves—for example, to the colonial metropoles—for meaning and self-identity. "It is an accomplishment," Montaigne writes, "absolute and as it were God-like, to know how to enjoy our being as we ought [in his 16th-century French: *C'est une absolue perfection, et comme divine, de scavoyr jouyr loiallement de son estre*]." He adds: "We seek other attributes because we do not understand the use of our own; and, having no knowledge of what is within we sally forth outside ourselves" (pp. 1268–1269).

It is indeed an accomplishment, never a foregone conclusion, to realize the sources of one's being. The poet-witness of the *Cahier* grasps this truth. He had cited Montaigne, without naming him, in his earliest published writing in 1935, when he proclaimed that with the coming revolution of black consciousness he seeks, "we will 'loyally take joy in our being'" and thereby "triumph over all slaveries born of 'civilization'" (quoted in Rexer, 2013, p. 10). Now, in his poetic *tour de force*, the poet draws on all that he has metabolized: his life-altering studies of the emerging literature on his African and Antillean inheritances, and his deep work in Latin, classical literature, traditions in French poetry, and surrealism. The poet shows us that the ethical labor of self-criticism and self-cultivation that is immanent in bearing witness can lead to a living issue. In the same moment, his witness helps build conditions that can support what was suppressed under colonial rule but which, as Césaire stated in a speech in 1956, "is characteristic of every living civilization: the faculty of renewal" (in Irele, 2017, p. 31).

Chapter 4

# Walt Whitman

Democracy, Remembrance, and the Witness

> An old man bending I come among new faces,
> Years looking backward resuming in answer to children,
> Come tell us old man . . . Now be witness again . . .
>
> —Walt Whitman, "The Wound-Dresser"

Walt Whitman is the United States' most widely cited poet. His collection *Leaves of Grass*, which he self-published in 1855 and revised several times thereafter, has been translated in part or in whole into every broadly spoken language in the world. It has constituted a source of inspiration, and provocation, to countless wordsmiths from every corner of the globe, among them Jorge Luis Borges, Syl Cheney-Coker, Rubén Darío, Kahlil Gibran, Joy Harjo, Langston Hughes, June Jordan, D. H. Lawrence, Federico García Lorca, Vladimir Mayakovsky, Czesław Miłosz, José Marti, Pablo Neruda, Ngugi wa T'hiongo, and Oscar Wilde. They have regarded his poetry as politically prophetic, as breaking precedent in generating fresh modes of poesis, as bold and enlightened on sexuality and the erotic, as an encomium to American vernacular and by extension to all vernaculars, and more. Gay Wilson Allen and Ed Folsom (1995) rightly state that "[n]o other poet in English since Shakespeare has appealed to so many people in so many places in so many ways" (p. 6; and see Folsom, 1994; Miller, 2010; Robertson, 2010; and Santi, 2005).

Along with eleven shorter poems (in the 1855 edition), *Leaves of Grass* includes Whitman's lengthy, justly famous poem, *Song of Myself*. This pioneering oeuvre enacts an extraordinary witness that is at once particular and universal in its reach. The poet aspires to grasp the nature of the United States, his then 80-year-old country, and the character and spirit of its diverse people. In the same breath, he seeks self-understanding and bears witness to this process in a manner that mirrors though does not replicate Sebald's and Césaire's self-examinations. In between these intersecting endeavors, which in due course fuse, the poet opens himself to the human condition writ large. He fields or, better, absorbs into his vision fundamental questions of what it is to lead a human life—to eat, drink, sleep, dream, love, hate, work, play, hope, despair, build, destroy, pray, neglect, appreciate, scorn, embrace, and so much more. He witnesses fellow Americans embodying all these human aspects. He "receives" their humanity: he would let it speak through the lines of his poem, against the backdrop of a societal ethos marked by injustice, suffering, and indifference, as well as by joy, celebration, and mutual support. *Song of Myself*, like *Cahier d'un retour au pays natal*, *The Emigrants*, *The Rings of Saturn*, and *Austerlitz*, constitutes a witness of the very first order.

In this chapter, I will attend to features of Whitman's witness in *Song of Myself*. I will then draw on this analysis to approach a lesser-known work by him: *Memoranda During the War*, which he published in 1876. This short text is a compilation of impromptu notes Whitman composed during his hundreds of visits to military hospitals in Washington, DC, and to nearby battlefields during the American Civil War (1861 to 1865). Whitman became an unpaid attendant who made himself available to assist hospital staffs in any ways that might be useful, whether it be emptying bedpans or helping to dress wounds. But he was an "attendant" of an unusual sort. His main purpose, as it turns out, was *in deed* to attend: to pay attention, to heed, to bear witness. He sought "simply" to be with the wounded, fearful, bewildered, and suffering soldiers—"Poor ruined lengths of paltry men" (Barry, 2017, p. 149)—who, for the most part, were too far from home to be visited by family and friends. He brought them small gifts, he wrote letters home for them, he listened to their stories, he told them stories of his own, he held their hands, he kissed them, and he cooed them to sleep. He gave them comfort and companionship—a human presence—in the midst of a brutal national conflict. And he left a written record of this singular, compassionate involvement.

As mentioned, Whitman published *Song of Myself* in 1855, a few short years before the outbreak of the Civil War. We will see that the poem's ethos deeply informs, albeit indirectly, Whitman's commitment to visiting Union hospitals during the conflict. It becomes a source of moral and existential support for his fateful encounters with dying soldiers carried back from the battlefields. The poem's ethos helps steady him in this endeavor as he comes to grips, in broad terms, with the profound challenge the Civil War represented to his beliefs about the nation's identity and trajectory. Like many other Americans, although in a much more flesh and blood manner than most, Whitman was shocked and stunned by the scale of the fighting. Over 600,000 soldiers perished in the war, a staggering proportion of the still nascent country's population.

Whitman found himself questioning the viability of American democracy, which for him was a beautiful, confusing, frustrating, and hopeful experiment in governance.[1] As he remarked in his introduction to *Leaves of Grass*, he regarded the nation as itself a poem about human possibility, and he charged himself with doing it justice in his oeuvre (1986, pp. 5, 6). Like his famed contemporary, Ralph Waldo Emerson, Whitman believed that this experiment required self-transformation on the part of everyone, himself included. The political revolution that created the United States demanded an interior, ethical revolution on the part of each person: a turning of the soul toward what it is to be a citizen in an experiment. Like his philosophical successor, John Dewey, Whitman judged that this transformed American self should aspire to *live* in a democratic spirit.[2] This task, and invitation, embodies an existential commitment far more comprehensive—and, to Whitman, majestic—than just being sure to vote every few years. Rather, as Mark Edmundson (2019) writes, *Song of Myself* constitutes "an evocation of what being a democratic man or woman *feels* like at its best, day to day, moment to moment" (p. 102, word in italics changed into present tense). Whitman bears witness in the poem to what he sees as the inspiring possibilities built into the very fabric of democracy. As we saw with Césaire, he conjures the image of a demiurge who would create with the people a fuller version of a unified community. The hospital visits which he begins several years later will confront these convictions. He will discover in the course of them what he regards as a redemptive truth: *the experiment will continue*. But a crucial necessity in this process, he will foreground, is remembrance of those who have suffered to keep it going.

## Lineaments of Whitman's Poetic Witness

It is not possible to weigh up or fathom Walt Whitman the poet, as he himself declares.

> I know I have the best of time and space—and that I was never measured, and never will be measured.
> I tramp a perpetual journey. (46)

Whitman's free verse idiom, which was radical for his time and strongly criticized for that, outruns fixed modes of classification and genre-fixing. Like Sebald and Césaire, and as a mirror to his conception of democracy, Whitman plays continuously with form even as he himself is played by the press of reality. He accepts a summons to bear witness and to do so justly. His self-as-witness and his self-as-writer—so intertwined in his endeavor—remain elusive and impossible to pin down definitively. Nonetheless, it is possible to trace the contours of his witness, and to do so there is no better place to begin than with his own beginning.

But before turning to it, let me offer a few textual notes that will be helpful for what follows. I will draw on Whitman's original edition of 1855, rather than the six revised editions of the poem he later produced, the last being in 1891 to 1892, shortly before his death. The principle here is the same as that which informed the decision discussed in chapter 3 to work with Césaire's original version of *Cahier*. Both first editions have a freshness, vibrancy, viscerality, and spontaneity about them that embodies the primordial, unselfconscious, initial move of the witness.[3]

With respect to technical matters, I will deploy brackets to mark particular stanzas cited; Whitman marked out 52 of these for the 1867 edition, which critics regard as symbolizing the full cycle of the year. In the quotations to come, the reader will note the poet's extensive use of dashes. These dashes, observes Lawrence Lipking (1981), "democratically affirming that all punctuation was created equal," demonstrate "that no clause should be subordinate to any other" (p. 122; and see Miller, 2010). There are also repeated ellipses of four dots inserted by the poet. They appear to have multiple functions. Like Sebald's use of captionless photographs, the ellipses slow readers down, giving them time and space to consider what has been said, and perhaps to imagine what the poet has in his mind's eye. The ellipses also slow the poet himself down in order to catch his breath, given the surging, sometimes staccato-like movement of the poem. Finally, the device may highlight what the poet realizes he cannot (yet) say. It symbolizes the fact that he lacks the words for certain insights, intuitions, intimations, and feelings. After all, the poet is not divine. The world does not obey his will, and nor does his pen at all times. But the poet can at least mark those moments where what cannot be said resides invisibly within the interstices of the said, thereby helping to hold things together.

## The Poet as Singer

> I celebrate myself,
> And what I assume you shall assume,
> For every atom belonging to me as good belongs to you. (1)

The many pronouns in these oft-quoted opening lines reverberate: I . . . myself . . . I . . . you . . . me . . . you. They pivot around the intentionally repetitive "belonging" and "belong." The poet implies that "I" and "you" belong together. In the same breadth, he addresses both himself and the reader or listener. To address is to speak directly to another, with no hesitation or false decorum. It is to provoke in a generative manner.

In due course, the poet will confound the pronouns such that it becomes difficult to sort out addressor and addressee. It sometimes appears that the poet, in his capacity as a witness, has become a vehicle or conduit for something speaking through him (more on this point below). At other times, the poet asserts his singular identity directly and boldly, for example, in stanza 24 where he appears to leap out of the poem, for a moment, by stating "Walt Whitman, an American." (These specific words constituted the original title Whitman gave to the collection he later named, in a subsequent revision, *Leaves of Grass*.) At the close of the poem, the reader circles back and realizes that the very first word of the poem, "I," mirrors the very last word of the poem, "You" (52). In naming I, myself, and you at the very start, the poet transforms them into *a relationship*. He says: the poet's self, and the self of every other person, are fundamentally permeable and porous. He says: the self is not self-contained—"every atom belonging to me as good belongs to you." The poet echoes the laws of physics that demonstrate how permanently connected everything is down to the atomic level. But in his vision, atoms transform from particles to be measured and analyzed into entities that are shared. They become, in a manner of speaking, democratic entities. The poet will transfigure the biological reality that humans breathe the same air into a political possibility called *democracy*.

The poet also points, in a manner that echoes Césaire's concluding vision in *Cahier*, to what he regards as the moral unity of humanity. He does so by referring to a celebration: "I celebrate myself." We soon learn he is celebrating *everyone*. To celebrate means to acknowledge, to recognize, to name, to esteem. It has an air of seriousness but also of joy. It conjures the long-standing phenomenon of a festival. It also evokes a ritualized undertaking (Christians "celebrate" the Mass). The poet celebrates the particularity of each human being and the universality of what it is to be human. *All can sing this song*. As the long poem unfolds, we encounter one image after another of humans at work, at play, in love, in friendship, in loneliness, in joy, in sorrow, in suffering, in closeness, in separation, with each image highly singular and unique yet also speaking of all and to all.

As the poet well knows, the world in general, and his nation in particular, remain discordant terrains. He names "Song" as the first word in the title as if he would institute a new ritual, a new singing, a new anthem (perhaps a reconfigured "Star-Spangled Banner"). Here he inherits a call from Thomas Jefferson. Whatever else one may think of this contradictory thinker and politician, who beautifully immortalized the idea of freedom even as he owned slaves, he bequeathed the nation a profound challenge. He urged every generation of citizens to launch its own revolution, not in the military fashion of 1776 to 1783—the long series of battles before Britain let go—but in the sense of a serious taking stock of where things stand with the people and reconstructing the polity in light of such inquiry (cf. Burch 2020).

In drawing on the motif of song, the poet also echoes the cultural centrality of singing since the very dawn of human culture. Songs carry histories, memories, projections, warnings, paeans, hopes, fears, dreams, and more. As modes of music, they affect emotion and mind: they set them in motion. Songs comfort and console, they delight and please, and they inspire and strengthen. All of this gives the very notion of "song" powerful symbolic and metaphorical potential. For example, in W. E. B. Du Bois's *The Souls of Black Folk* (published in 1901), every chapter begins with several bars from the "sorrow songs" composed by slaves across the generations of their forced servitude. The songs are richly soulful, and they bear witness to terrible suffering as well as to ecstatic redemption.

The recurring pattern of musical bars across Du Bois's text dramatizes his suggestive claim that this mode of music is the most genuinely American of all, or at least as American as any other tradition emergent in the land. The songs constitute a source, or well-spring, for Du Bois's own deepest thought and feeling, just as they summon readers to rethink their relationship with one another and with society itself. In figurative terms, Du Bois asks whether the sorrow songs can become everyone's song in the nation, in an as yet unattained solidarity.

Consider, as another example, Plato's dialogue *Phaedo*. This work recounts in moving, artful form Socrates's last day before his execution by the Athenian authorities for allegedly turning young people against the city and its conventions. Song appears on the scene at a fateful moment. Socrates and his young interlocutors have been inquiring into the nature of the soul: what it is and whether it survives the death of the body. All of their attempts to prove the soul's immortality fail, a devastating development for Socrates's comrades who are about to lose a man whom they deeply venerate and whose soul, they imagined, would live on. At this juncture, Socrates reminds them that there are many other philosophers in Greece whose community they can join, and he urges them to remember to "sing" in the face of their deepest disquietude. He refers to how the swan, according to their cultural lore, sings more sweetly than ever at the approach of its death, for it harbors no fear but rather feels joyful gratitude for its life as well as hope, if not certainty, for another form of continuity after it is gone from the earth. For Socrates, philosophizing with others can itself be this kind of singing.

For the writer of *Song of Myself*, poetry can constitute a mode of singing that has transformative effects, including on the poet himself. He "sings" himself *into* the role of witness, and he sings *in* this register. However, he does not choose this role, as such, but rather accepts it, not unlike what we beheld with Césaire and Sebald. He does not control things in the familiar sense of that term. He is not a solo composer or conductor. As anticipated in chapter 1, he lets himself be controlled through his precognitive response to all that he witnesses even as he renders the latter process into written form. He heeds human significances in the quietest, most ordinary of events and actions as if they were prophetic, even while acknowledging the import of loud public doings and events. In figurative terms, the sheets of paper on which the poet writes start with the horizontal lines typical of musical scores; and it is the world to which he bears witness that teaches him what notations to make.[4]

Put another way, the poet is a player. He is a participant, albeit of a unique sort. Even while plucking the strings of the proverbial lyre as he weaves his words and stanzas together, he challenges his reader to respond—not to sing *his* song, but to sing *with* him.

> Stop this day and night with me and you shall possess the origin of all poems,
> You shall possess the good of the earth and sun. . . . there are millions of suns left,
> You shall no longer take things at second or third hand. . . . nor look through the eyes of the dead. . . . nor feed on the spectres in books,
> You shall not look through my eyes either, nor take things from me,
> You shall listen to all sides and filter them from yourself. (2)

"This day and night" has a biblical tone that transcends chronological time. Like Césaire, Whitman knew the Bible well and was a keen reader of Homer, Virgil, Dante, Milton, and other composers who responded in their epic works to the human condition as they perceived it (see his late poem, "Old Chants"). Whitman aspires to something comparable, even if the concept "epic," as contrasted with "lyric," may be less apposite than it is with Césaire's *Cahier* (cf. Miller, 1991, pp. xv–xvi). "This day and night" refers temporally and spatially to the poem in its entirety—a mirror, of sorts, to how Plato's poetic dialogue known as *The Republic* unfolds over a single night. *Song of Myself* embodies the poet's self-questioning and his questioning of the reader, alongside an extraordinary series of vivid descriptions of Americans at work, in play, and in everything else that people do. As if he were a new, democratically minded Adam of biblical fame, the poet *names* them all: blacksmiths, tanners, carpenters, teachers, children, farmers, escaped slaves and freedmen, deckhands, factory workers, married people, single people, solitary people, Indigenous people, tall and short people, happy people, angry people, coachmen, peddlers, drovers, suicides, soldiers, prostitutes, thieves, opium eaters, priests, politicians, fishermen, pedestrians, swimmers, ruffians, caregivers, hunters, cowboys, and much more from all over the country (see, for example, stanzas 7–13, 15–16).[5]

The sheer diversity of these people nearly bursts the bounds of the poem, which like many creatures in nature must repeatedly shed its skin as it grows. The microscopic richness of the portrait informs the poet's claim that the reader of *Song of Myself* "will possess the origin of all poems." For the poet, the latter just do originate in wonder at the fabulous, unfathomable, mystifying, challenging, inspiring, and confusing phenomenon-experience called "being alive as a human being." In the same breadth, the poet strives to spark readers to consider their own origins: that is, to discover and truly heed their own minds, hearts, and spirits, to be alive in their distinctive fullness as human beings rather than to follow cultural inheritances or societal conventions unthinkingly. He fairly cries out,

> What is a man anyhow? What am I? and what are you?
> All I mark as my own you shall offset it with your own,
> Else it were time lost listening to me. (20)

Rather than experiencing life "second-" or "third-hand"; rather than letting past traditions and conventions ("the eyes of the dead") substitute for one's own bent; and rather than letting books like the Bible or poems like *Song of Myself* ("spectres") do one's thinking, the poet beckons the reader to *participate* in the world as a thinking, feeling being. Yes, avers the poet, by all means *read deeply*, read everything you can—books, the events of the day, the sky, your friends' faces, your own soul. Yes, read these "leaves of grass," these leaves of the book. But then move on: "[W]hoever hears me let him or her set out in search of this day" (25).

The poet bears witness to the nation and its people, and he casts himself as a would-be witness of his readers' response to his call. He repeatedly refers to his readers and to himself as being on a "journey." That journey begins with self-awareness and awareness of the pulsating, vital life all around. Its destination is not later or down the road, but in the very movement of the moment. "This minute that comes to me over the past decillions / There is no better than it and now" (47). "Sit awhile wayfarer," the poet beckons to the reader.

> Here are biscuits to eat and here is milk to drink,
> But as soon as you sleep and renew yourself in sweet clothes I
>     will certainly kiss you with my goodbye kiss and open the
>     gate for your egress hence.
> Long enough have you dreamed contemptible dreams,
> Now I wash the gum from your eyes,

> You must habit yourself to the dazzle of the light and of every
> moment of your life. (46)

For the poet, dreams are "contemptible" when they are in fact others' dreams rather than one's own. More to the point, the poet urges readers to abandon dreams and to awaken. When they do—when the gum locking their eyes shut dissolves—they will be "dazzled" by the brightness of reality.[6] The poet urges the reader to stay the course, to keep their eyes open, to not be thrown by the sometimes demanding tasks of thinking and feeling meaningfully. He declaims: develop the "habit" of attending with care to all that is around you, to facing the broadness of life in all its multicolored and sometimes challenging reality. In a word: your life can be merely fleeting, like the wink of an eye, or it can be full.

The poet's theme is not easy to formulate, for experience ever outruns what words can catch. It also outruns attempts at self-fashioning, which can only be partially successful. The journey to which the poet refers is unavoidably messy and uncertain. Social, psychological, political, and biological factors weigh in nonstop. Humans as living beings are both vulnerable and fallible, though not in the same ways or to the same degree. Human beings are inconstant; they will never remain entirely fixed in nature, however microscopic each alteration may be as they encounter the world 24/7. This fact implies, in turn, that if we look carefully enough at ourselves and at others, we will time and again discover that we humans are inconsistent and contradictory, a condition the poet embraces as he has no interest in mechanistic perfection (a truly repellent image, for him). Humans simply do gyrate unpredictability between happiness and sadness, irritability and calm, gentleness and roughness, trust and suspicion, and all the rest. They may say or believe something now, only to change their minds tomorrow, and perhaps change them back the day after. As the poet observes,

> Do I contradict myself?
> Very well then. . . . I contradict myself;
> I am large. . . . I contain multitudes. (51)

For the poet, contradiction and inconsistency are natural; they come with the territory of being human (cf. Lipking, 1981, p. 121). He does not say persons are fated to them. On the contrary, human agency is equally real in ironing out contradictions or inconsistencies that may be harmful to others or, for that matter, to the self. His lines point again to how "myself" encompasses a shared or common self, an "ourself" that reflects the mark on all persons of the human condition, even as every person influences that condition however infinitesimally. Every person contains, participates in, and contributes to the "multitudes" of the world. That world depends on their presence, just as they depend on it.

All of these lessons and insights are for the poet as much as for the reader. He is singing himself into them in the face of his own limitations, which have become that much clearer to him through his literal and poetic journey through America.[7] He will not hide his blemishes. He will trust the reader.

> This hour I tell things in confidence,
> I might not tell everybody but I will tell you. (19)

The poet can safely conclude that he is no expert on human life, on American life, or on the meaning and practice of democracy. He takes the measure of what he sees not as a sociologist, economist, psychologist, or statistician, but as a poet-witness.

Put another way, the poet *imagines*, and he does so in at least three ways that inform his *ars poetica*.

1. He forms images of lived reality to which people are often blind. To recall the discussion of re-inhabiting the world in chapter 1, most persons, most of the time, are too preoccupied with their concerns, obligations, and interests to pay much attention to their surroundings, which in time tend to blur into an undifferentiated background. Though quite understandable given human needs and limitations, this habit constitutes an immeasurable moral, aesthetic, social, political, and personal loss. It fosters a habit of inattentiveness and indifference that undermines, if not impoverishes, people's capacity to pay attention with imagination and tenacity to things that profoundly matter: from caring for loved ones and strangers, to broader realities such as democracy, justice, and the well-being of all entities in the world. The point is not that persons must be attentive 24/7. Such a posture would be exhausting and might interfere with the necessity of practical action. But it does imply cultivating attunement to the particulars in everyday experience. I referred at the start of chapter 1 to Etty Hillesum's remarkable responsiveness to the expressivity of so-called ordinary life, a capacity that, coincidentally, attests to the positive influence that sustained reading of poetry can have on a

person (in Hillesum's case, her absorption in the poetry of Rainer Maria Rilke).

2. The poet imagines what *could* be, in a manner captured by the 19th-century orator, writer, and abolitionist Frederick Douglass. "Poets, prophets, and reformers are all picture makers," he writes, "and this ability is the secret of their power and of their achievements. They see what ought to be by the reflection of what is, and endeavor to remove that contradiction" (in Slate, 2012, p. 253). Again, the poet does not generate images out of nothing. He must wait for reality to come to him. But his waiting is intensely active.[8] He thinks, recalls, and connects things seen and heard, and he experiments with poetic form and substance (in a late notebook entry, Whitman called his entire life's work a "language experiment" [Zweig, 1984, p. 209]).[9] He "recollects in tranquility," an image of the poet composing at a desk in solitude evoked by William Wordsworth in his "Preface to Lyrical Ballads" (first published in 1800). But Whitman also composes in a state of perpetual turbulence. We might call the energy behind the poem's lines "tranquil agitation," an oxymoron he might appreciate. The poet does not aspire to build institutions or lead causes. Through his capacity to wait, he hopes to catch signs and symbols in everyday life that help point the way to how to realize (make real) generative human possibilities.

3. The poet imagines what people have long known but are apt to forget and to neglect, sometimes at great cost. Foremost here is what we have already seen: the poet's strong urging to readers to remember the potentially powerful, creative expressions of mind, heart, and spirit of which they are capable, and how all this can help enact democracy on the ground. For the poet, people have the capacity to sing if they let themselves do so, no matter what their circumstances. To recur to a previous reference, the "sorrow songs" contribute to democracy understood as an ongoing amplification of all voices and a building up of just conditions and relations.

To imagine what is right before our eyes but to which we are blind; to imagine how the human condition could be transformed for the good; and to imagine, or reimagine, forgotten values and purposes: such is the poet's inspiration at work as he bears witness. His moral attentiveness and moral imagination merge into one. The poet's notions of song and journey fuse as metaphors for transformation, for awakening.

Time and again, readers come upon lines that speak directly and intimately to them, with no mediation.

> My signs are a rain-proof coat and good shoes and a staff cut from the woods;
> No friend of mine takes his ease in my chair,
> I have no chair, nor church nor philosophy;
> I lead no man to a dinner-table or library or exchange,
> But each man and each woman of you I lead upon a knoll,
> My left hand hooks you round the waist,
> My right hand points to landscapes of continents, and a plain public road.
> . . .
> Not I, not any one else can travel that road for you,
> You must travel it for yourself.
> It is not far. . . . it is within reach,
> Perhaps you have been on it since you were born, and did not know,
> Perhaps it is everywhere on water and on land.
> . . .
> You are asking me questions, and I hear you;
> I answer that I cannot answer. . . . you must find out for yourself. (46)

The poet has no ideologies or creeds to proffer. He has no "church" or "philosophy." He is not seeking followers, nor is he trying to convert the reader into something they are not.[10] On the contrary, he would lead them to vistas where they can see themselves, perhaps for the first time, in full illumination. Like a philosopher, he can pose the right questions to them. As a poet-witness, he can foreground images he has beheld of life's movement and contours, its hardships and its beauties, which become mirrors in which readers might see their world from a more vivid slant.

## The Democratic Pulse and Impulse

> I speak the password primeval. . . . I give the sign of democracy;
> By God! I will accept nothing which all cannot have their counterpart of on the same terms. (24)

Primeval calls to mind the primordial, the primal, the primitive, the most ancient and most basic of things. A password is a secret, sometimes confidentially shared between persons. What is "the" (not "a") password to which the poet refers? Why is it needed? Why does the poet have it but, apparently, not us? I return to these questions below, but a preliminary response here is that in *Song of Myself* the poet becomes a primeval, primitive being himself. He embarks on a journey or search for understanding, but he pares down his will to the barest minimum so that he can receive what the world—rather than what his will—can bring him. The sparks triggered by the connection, and sometimes collision, of the world and his poetic self light up the blank page so that he can see what to write. Put differently, the sparks become the password needed to enter the space of poesis. The poet can now work *with* the world, as a participant moving both within it and alongside it, rather than work *on* the world, as a clinical spectator.[11]

This perspective may conjure an apotheosis of romanticism, but it points directly to another aspect of the poet's effort to find his voice as a witness. In a number of stanzas, he contrasts nature and everyday experience with theory, theology, science, and philosophy. He distinguishes attempts to explain things formally from a quest to be at home in the world. Put another way, he does not need to explain home to be in it. His identification with the most commonplace of nature's inventory—the grasses beneath our feet—illuminates his resonance with the fundamentals of being alive in the first place.

The contrast with the forlorn figures Sebald's narrator encounters could not be more stark. For example, Dr. Henry Selwyn—the central character in the first story in Sebald's *The Emigrants*—is lying outside on his lawn, counting blades of grass, when the narrator and his wife first come upon him (they were seeking to rent an apartment in Selwyn's house that had been advertised locally). Selwyn explains that he counts the blades of grass as a "pastime" (E, p. 5). It soon becomes apparent that he has so lost any sense of meaning in life that he literally just wants to "pass [the] time." Where Whitman is inspired by what he regards as the beautiful "ordinariness" of the leaves of grass on which he loafs, for Selwyn the grass symbolizes not plenitude but a void.

For Whitman the poet, it appears that, like Socrates, he had sought out in his youth final answers: "Backward I see in my own days where I sweated through fog with / linguists and contenders" (4). Unlike Socrates, he does not aim to burrow deeper into what we can know and justify philosophically or scientifically, valuable as those endeavors are in their place. Nor does he seek to supplant or dismiss the effort of a Socrates: "I have no mockings or arguments. . . . I witness and wait" (4). The poet aspires to come nearer to the truths of felt and lived experience, just as it is, which he perceives link rather than separate people and the events of the world. For the poet, this linkage is a core image of democracy itself.

In brief, the poet is not anti-intellectual, only anti-alienation, anti-isolation, anti-objectification. He would like nothing better than to help dissolve the harmful forces in society: misanthropy, greed, nihilism, discrimination of all sorts, jingoism, and fundamentalism in its various religious and secular guises. But as he evoked previously, he offers a poem rather than an argument, diatribe, or exhortation.

> Logic and sermons never convince,
> The damp of the night drives deeper into my soul. (30)
> . . .
> Oxen that rattle the yoke or halt in the shade, what is that you express in your eyes?
> It seems to me more than all the print I have read in my life. (13)
> . . .
> To walk up my stoop is unaccountable. . . . I pause to consider if it really be,
> That I eat and drink is spectacle enough for the great authors and schools,
> A morning-glory at my window satisfies me more than the metaphysics of books. (24)

Every entity literally "speaks volumes," and the poet is astounded by every existence. "To *be* in any form," he wonders, "what *is* that?" (27).[12]

For the poet, nobody has the last word on the nature and meaning of being human.

> Writing and talk do not prove me,
> I carry the plenum of proof and every thing else in my face,
> With the hush of my lips I confound the topmost skeptic. (25)

All the theories and categorizations in the world can never "prove"—that is, explain—a human being. The poet will not have his language reduced to convention, where words have hardened like lava that once burned hot.

And he insists that no amount of skeptical doubt, suspicion, or cynicism can deny the truth of our human presence to one another and to ourselves. That truth helps constitute the password toward a genuinely democratic life. All can make public this secret, in both their words and deeds.

The poet responds continuously as a witness whose sense of wonder deepens the longer he looks, contemplates, and composes.

> Apart from the pulling and hauling stands what I am . . .
> Both in and out of the game, and watching and wondering
>    at it. (4)
> . . .
> And I know I am solid and sound,
> To me the converging objects of the universe perpetually flow,
> All are written to me, and I must get what the writing means.
>    (20)

We might conclude that the whole poem embodies "the password primeval." That is, the poet does more than deliver it. He *speaks* the password, not just about it. He enacts the truths incorporated in his ongoing address.

> The facts are useful and real. . . . they are not my dwelling. . . .
> I enter by them to an area of the dwelling.
> I am less the reminder of property or qualities, and more the
>    reminder of life. (23)

The poem becomes something other than a mere means toward cultivating a democratic imagination. Rather, the reader participates *in* the password, shares in it, experiences it, while responding to the poet's words and images.

These remarks shed light on the "sign" of democracy that the poet "gives." A sign can be a pointer toward something, a symbol or indicator, a source of direction. It can also be a manifestation or enactment of that same something—in this case, democracy as the poet perceives it. Recall the original Greek meaning of the latter term: rule by the people (*demos*). In anticipation of the likes of John Dewey, the poet moves far beyond the question of governance because he regards democracy as more than a form of government. Rather, it constitutes a way of moving in the world marked by ethical awareness and responsiveness to others (Dewey, 1985, p. 93; Dewey, 1988). For the poet, democracy as a way of being is *everywhere* if people look with care, including in nature itself. He devotes whole stanzas (for example, 31–33) to painstakingly naming natural creatures and forces: leaves of grass, toads, blackberries, mice, trees, moss, roots, birds, wind, water, earth, seagulls, snakes, elk, wolverines, flowers, weeds, corn, wheat, and much more. They all belong in the house of the poem, and in the house of democracy. They all have an absolute right to being—thus, the mode of primordial-sounding naming and describing in which the poet engages, as if we humans have simply forgotten the equal right to existence of all beings and entities and, educationally, have forgotten all that they can teach us and inspire in us (the cow's deep eyes, the morning glory's glory). Nothing in nature is unnatural. Nature rejects nothing, though everything may be continuously evolving. Nature has been egalitarian from the start, giving and taking with no favor. It features no dictators, autocrats, or tyrants, nor is it animated by ideologies and dogmas.

As touched on previously, there are many more stanzas, again like rolling trains across the land, where the poet lists in fine-grained detail Americans of all stripes and persuasions doing what they do in their quotidian lives. The poet wheels all of them, too, into the house of the poem, and the house of democracy. The forms of mutual- and self-isolation that are so damaging to democracy—which the poet has also noted—cannot gain a foothold in the poem's tightly knit pattern of connections and connections on top of connections. "Every condition promulges not only itself. . . . it promulges what / grows after and out of itself" (45). The poet shows that none of the connections he repeatedly draws out are forced or arbitrary. As a witness, he records them, or, better, transcribes them into the composed poem. To recall an earlier motif, in an important sense he does not create the poem. He is the parchment on which the world writes, the world he has let in, for which he gives himself over as a receptacle, conduit, vehicle. In an echo of what we heard in Césaire's *Cahier*, Whitman writes: "Through me the many long dumb voices" (24), referring to those fellow Americans dwelling in silence ("dumb") because they have no platform to speak. "Through me the forbidden voices" (24), he adds, spotlighting all who reject social conventions that have dehumanized them, yet in ways unharmful to others or to the polity itself, with the latter understood as more than governmental institutions alone but as encompassing the constitution of actual human relations. If "found art," in one of its meanings, denotes the artist taking up materials scattered on streets and byways, "found poetry" is what the poet seeks in the vernaculars of *all* the people in the nation.

As the poet emphasizes, he harbors "no mockings or arguments." He witnesses and waits. He does not set himself up as a judge of anything or anyone. He does not approve or disapprove of anything or anyone. The poet's radical, democratic inclusivity comes to the fore when he describes his endeavor as

> the meat and drink for
> natural hunger,
> It is for the wicked just the same as the righteous. . . . I make appointments with all,
> I will not have a single person slighted or left away,
> The keptwoman and sponger and thief are hereby invited. . . . the heavy-lipped slave is invited. . . . the venerealee is invited,
> There shall be no difference between them and the rest. (19)
> . . .
> What blurt is it about virtue and about vice?
> Evil propels me, and reform of evil propels me. . . . I stand indifferent,
> My gait is no fault-finder's or rejecter's gait,
> I moisten the roots of all that has grown. (22)

For the poet, all persons have a "natural hunger" for meaning and purpose, however smothered or distorted this impulse may be. The poet's office, in part, is to honor and respond to that hunger, which Césaire also saw as part of his witness. Whitman's inclusive solidarity, combined with the unabashed sensuality of many of his free form images, rendered *Song of Myself* controversial in its time and made it difficult for him in the years after its initial appearance to find a publisher for his subsequent work. Whitman was condemned publicly by various critics for his praise of bodily experience and was fired from a government position when his superior got hold of the poem (Morris, 2000, p. 233; Zweig, 1984, p. 344; the work was officially declared obscene by a court in Boston in 1882, even as Whitman's fame was expanding). The poet may well have anticipated this outcome, and thus speaks directly to the shocked, confused, or uncertain reader:

> Do you guess I have some intricate purpose?
> Well I have. . . . for the April rain has, and the mica on the side of a rock has.

> Do you take it I would astonish?
> Does the daylight astonish? or the early redstart twittering through the woods?
> Do I astonish more than they? (19)

The poet asks: Can humans (re)learn to feel wonder about one another, rather than cede the stage to fear, suspicion, and resentment? Can they feel the sheer, astonishing fact of their mutual existence, that they are here rather than not here? Can they reimagine the meaning of "here" itself, and render that here, now, into an inhabitable, democratic space?

While the poet is careful not to condemn anything outright—which, again, does not imply approval or disapproval, as such—he does not say to the reader: do not judge. Citizens in a democracy must judge between the better and the worse, and they must determine what is better and worse. Nobody else can or should do this for them. The poet reminds them: judge not lest ye be judged, which is to say avoid judgmentalism. Rather, judge always mindful of the full reality of other persons and communities, that they resemble you at least as much as they differ from you (they eat, sleep, laugh, cry, talk, are silent, and so on). Judge through refined perception, and through awareness of how all touches all, organically, and that from your judgments waves of ramification will flow to all sides, and then back to you.

While the poet's role is not to judge, there is one thing he will not tolerate. "By God!" as we heard him say, "I will accept nothing which all cannot have their counter-part of on the same terms" (24). In one sense, this declaration implies that he rejects everything, for the radical egalitarianism he evokes does not exist. The nation is marked by egregious inequalities and inequities. But as discussed above, for the poet organic equality is the very form of the world, including humanity. Everything and everyone always already have an absolute existence and a right to that existence. The world needs everything and everyone in order to be whole. Humanity alone, the poet makes clear, is the only species to rupture continuities and connections through a will to power not shared by anything else known. It is a will that isolates one entity from another, that separates causes from effects despite the fact that any given cause is only the effect of another cause, and vice versa, such that the very terms cause and effect are exclusively of heuristic value (a real value for some practical purposes) but do not name anything isolatable or discrete in nature. The same holds for all entities. For the poet, all things touch all things in one way or another.

A change in perception or orientation will not in itself reduce injustice in the nation. But there can be no diminishment of injustice without a sensitive perceptivity and a democratic commitment, at least on the part of those in a position to alter things. In this respect, purposeful perception is not willful but will-less in the sense of being marked by receptivity rather than by a desire to control. At one of many dramatic junctures in the poet's "perpetual journey," he imagines,

> I am the hounded slave. . . . I wince at the bite of the dogs,
> Hell and despair are upon me. . . . crack and again crack the marksmen,
> I clutch the rails of the fence. . . . my gore dribs thinned with the ooze of my skin,
> I fall on the weeds and stones,
> The riders spur their unwilling horses and haul close,
> They taunt my dizzy ears. . . . they beat me violently over the head with their whip-stocks.

He continues:

> Agonies are one of my changes of garments;
> I do not ask the wounded person how he feels. . . . I myself become the wounded person,
> My hurt turns livid upon me as I lean on a cane and observe.
> (33)

Like other democratic-minded people, the poet is profoundly agonized by others' suffering. As he indicates, he needs a cane, metaphorically speaking, to keep him upright as a witness.[13] He does not pretend to stand in the desperate slave's place nor in the place of the wounded person. Such a move is impossible literally and spiritually. Rather, he stands *alongside* them, in a figurative sense that he further illustrates in a remarkable sequence where he imagines himself as a participant, rather than spectator, accompanying firemen, soldiers, mariners, convicts, and cholera patients (stanzas 33–37).[14] The poet is endeavoring *to see* the reality of those who surround him, as well as those who came before him, in the fullness of their pain, their joy, their very existence. This seeing is prior to all empathy and sympathy, as those terms are conventionally understood, and can discipline them from becoming patronizing or sentimental. It is a direct seeing not fully achievable or sustainable, and yet buoyed by the witness's steady self-questioning and self-cultivation.

The poet-witness balances his sense of wonder with an equally deep sense of concern:

> Whoever degrades another degrades me. . . . and whatever is
>     done or said returns at last to me,
> And whatever I do or say I also return. (24)

As we have seen, the theme of reciprocity saturates *Song of Myself* (of Ourself). The poet bears witness to the play of the particular and the universal, of the individual human being and the world. These connections illuminate how the poet's vision is not only democratic through and through—again, in his vivid sense of democracy—but also cosmopolitan. The poet's cosmopolitanism, built on his monist view of the cosmos, is not homogenizing. On the contrary, it renders distinctions and particularities in a much more powerful and dynamic manner than can be done from a presumption of the "many" versus the "one." For the poet, the presumption that the world is composed of discrete, untouching entities, including human beings and cultures, betrays a failure of perception brought about either by fear or by a will to power. "*This* is us, *that* is you, full stop": for the poet-witness, this all-too-familiar refrain is the inevitable consequence of seeing things atomistically rather than reciprocally or relationally. The atomistic view pre-essentializes self and other, and thus hamstrings perception from the very start.

As we saw, the poet offers a contrasting "atomistic" view in the very first lines of the poem. Every person, every thing, is indeed singular like an atom. "Every existence has its idiom," he writes in a poem he called "Song of the Answerer," ". . . every thing has an idiom and tongue." But atoms, or existences, are not *divided*. They belong—be-long, as in their very being—together. Far from leading to the appropriation of others and their existence, this cosmopolitan orientation embodies an abiding respect for their dignity. It harbors a commitment to trying to bring others and their reality into moral focus.[15]

Wonder and concern fuse into love, a word the poet deploys frequently. It is a word that he knows causes some to flee the room because it can smack of maudlin cliché and has led to many obscure claims and strange doings. But Whitman embraces what gives rise to his love: namely, his "acceptation" (3) of both the indescribable fullness of human beings in all their rational, emotional, sexual, soulful multiplicity, and the unfathomable diversity constitutive of the nation.[16] For the poet, love's negative connotation boils down to a refusal to reject any expression of the human as nonhuman, which, as we have seen, has nothing to do with approval or disapproval. He simply will not hate. Love's positive connotation has to do with acknowledging human propensities for caring, laughing, crying, cheering, touching, holding, dreaming, and deciding. It has to do with all people, young and old, and with weeds and woods, mountains and streams, winds and snow, farms and towns, vegetables and fruits, insects and birds, worn-out shirts and shiny shoes. Behold the scene as I have, invites the poet, and ask: Where do you find yourself? Where do you wish to be? What do you hope to be? And: Can you love all this? Are you capable of love? Because of the splendor in the grass, which has touched and inspired me, all the world should learn to love the way I do. Can you?

The poet's conceit is not egoistic, stark appearances to the contrary.[17] He invokes the *way* he loves, not *what* he loves. His commitment is based on what his odyssey across the nation's past and present, and across the contours of his own many-sided being, have shown him. At the beginning of the poem, he finds himself "observing a spear of summer grass" (1). At the poem's end he concludes, with a final direct address to the reader.

> I bequeath myself to the dirt to grow from the grass I love,
> If you want me again look for me under your bootsoles.
> You will hardly know who I am or what I mean,
> But I shall be good health to you nevertheless,
> And filter and fibre your blood.
> Failing to fetch me at first keep encouraged,
> Missing me one place search another,
> I stop some where waiting for you. (52)

The poet appreciates the difficulty of taking one's own measure, and of hearing the pitch of the democratic love song he has recorded. He passes on to the reader, like a baton, these themes and his poem as a whole. (The French word for witness, *témoin*, also means baton.) Indeed, the poet would bequeath poetry itself, if not all art, to readers. He and his readers have met *in* his poem. But that is but one experience, the poet underscores; "search another" and another as you journey. "I"—we, the world, life's promise—will be waiting for you.

## A Witness to War's Human Ethos: Whitman's *Memoranda*

Twenty years after first publishing *Song of Myself*, Whitman assembled his *Memoranda During the War*. As we will see, a comparable summons to bear witness persisted from the former text to the latter, albeit in a different register as Whitman turns from enraptured poetry to a more somber prose.

In chapter 2, I noted how Sebald called some of his works "stories." In chapter 3, we saw how Césaire had multiple purposes in mind in titling his poem *Cahier*. His aims appear in the various translations of the title, including *journal* and *notebook*, which each convey literal as well as symbolic meanings. *Memoranda* is the plural form of *memorandum*, or what is commonly called a memo. A memorandum is typically a short piece of writing, a page or two at most, and can serve efficiently many purposes. It can constitute a summary of important facts and decisions in order to facilitate further decision-making. It can contain a brief review of options as well as a recommended course of action. A memorandum can be a response to a problem or to a particular question. It can itself raise questions and highlight relevant issues.

Whitman appears to have selected the term *memoranda* not only because his entries in the book are short, but because of the word's original Latin meaning: *that which should be remembered*. His motive for publishing his notes from the Civil War seems twofold: to provide a more formal gathering of them for his own edification, and to present his growing reading public a witness of receding times and events so that their import might be passed along to subsequent generations. In this respect, we can justly characterize his *Memoranda* as a work of remembrance. We will see why this designation is more apposite than memoir, or memory-gathering, per se. Ultimately, the book reaches beyond his personal experience and becomes both a poignant requiem and a redemptive celebration of the sort evoked in *Song of Myself*.

However, if *Song of Myself* seems, at times, to explode out of the cosmos as a joyful, serious, unrestrained testament to democratic possibilities, the tone of the *Memoranda* is at once measured and modest (cf. Coviello, pp. xvii–xxx). Where in *Song* the poet plunges into language, playfully and boldly, seemingly convinced of its boundless affordances—not unlike his image of the United States—in his memoranda he doubts whether language—or, at any rate, his grasp of it—can do justice to what he witnesses. The devastations of war, illuminated in what follows, challenge Whitman's capacity to respond artfully and meaningfully. He feels the bite of Sebald's concerns about wrongful trespass and cannot wield language—as aspect of which was letting it wield him, as we saw in *Song*—in the same manner as in the poem. He experiences why, for the witness, the work of remembrance entails unanticipated ethical and communicative involvements.

*Heeding a Summons*

In his brief introductory remarks to the book, Whitman reports that during the three years he spent in hospitals and at field sites he carried the following:

> little notebooks for impromptu jottings in pencil to refresh my memory of names and circumstances, and what was specially wanted [by the wounded or ill men]. In these I brief'd[18] cases, persons, sights, occurrences in camp, by the bedside, and not seldom by the corpses of the dead. Of the present Volume most of its pages are *verbatim* renderings of such pencillings on the spot. . . . I have perhaps forty such little note-books left, forming a special history of those years, for myself alone, full of associations never to be possibly said or sung. (p. 3)[19]

His "jottings" as they appear in the book are organized into a total of 91 sections, which range in length from a few sentences to up to four pages. Each section has a title Whitman created, some of them literal, others thematic: "Washington, January, '63," "Fifty Hours Left Wounded on the Field," "Letter Writing," "Spiritual Characters Among the Soldiers," "October 3," "Female Nurses for Soldiers," "A Connecticut Case," "An Incident," "A Glimpse of War's Hell-Scenes," "December 23 to 31," "Boys in the Army." His first entry is from a visit to a thrown-together field hospital of the Army of the Potomac opposite Fredericksburg, Virginia, on December 21, 1862, mere days after a shattering defeat there at the hands of Confederate forces. His final entry derives from a visit on December 10, 1865, to one of the last functioning hospitals in Washington, DC, some seven months after the South's surrender.

Over the course of these three years, Whitman reports, he visited the hospitals that sprang up all over Washington, DC, and surrounding environs over 600 times. (Aside from publishing various articles in newspapers and working several intermittent jobs during those years, Whitman was free from attachments to pursue his unusual calling.) He encountered personally, he writes, thousands of wounded and ill soldiers. These figures attest to the temporal requirements of bearing witness as discussed in chapter 1: the endeavor cannot be rushed. In Whitman's case, the numbers also stagger the imagination given *what* he witnessed. He observed seemingly every form of destruction that war can do to the human body and spirit. The body has no chance against bullets, cannon shot, or saber and bayonet thrusts, and the battles of the Civil War were terrible with the amount of shot and shell flying around, flaying men left and right (see, for example, Whitman's account on pp. 24–27). In Whitman's day, the body also had little chance against diseases such as typhoid and dysentery that often spread like fire through the ranks. And Whitman saw again and again how a traumatized body can break the spirit's resolve to keep a grip on life. He sat beside men who were dying before his eyes, their spirits first, their bodies second.

To sustain himself in his fraught witness—recall his reference above to needing a "cane"—Whitman practiced, if not in so many words, what philosophers have called exercises of the self, or modes of self-care and ethical self-cultivation (see, among other sources, Cooper, 2012; Foucault, 2005; and Hadot, 1995). He slowly but surely began to follow a consistent pattern in his visits, even as his actual schedule depended on circumstance. His sojourns with the hospitalized soldiers "varied from an hour or two, to all day or night; for with dear or critical cases I always watch'd all night. Sometimes I took up my quarters in the Hospital, and slept or watch'd there several nights in succession" (p. 101). He pursued a disciplined routine: "My habit, when practicable, was to prepare for starting out on one of those daily or nightly tours, of from a couple to four or five hours, by fortifying myself with previous rest, the bath, clean clothes, a good meal, and as cheerful an appearance as possible" (30; cf. Morris, 2000, pp. 104).

Then, to restore himself after his often heart-rendering witnesses, he took walks that lasted hours and can be understood as part of his existential "care of the self." Here is his description of an October evening in 1863.

> To-night, after leaving the Hospital, at 10 o'cl'k (I had been on self-imposed duty some five hours, pretty closely confined), I wander'd a long time around Washington. The night was

> sweet, very clear, sufficiently cool, a voluptuous half-moon slightly golden, the space near it of a transparent tinge. I walk'd . . . The sky, the planets, the constellations all so bright, so calm, so expressively silent, so soothing, after those Hospital scenes. I wander'd to and fro till the moist moon set, long after midnight. (p. 47)

The longer his singular witness continued, the more heavily his visits weighed on him (more on this below). On his solitary meanderings he would find himself willy-nilly pondering the men he had just supported, "some of them personally so dear to me . . . lying in their cots" (p. 78).

Many wounded men became "dear" to him precisely because of his endless investment in being what he calls a "sustainer of spirit and body . . . in time of need" (101). He experienced an intimacy that surprised him as much as it did the men, which perhaps helps account for why he called this period "the greatest privilege and satisfaction" in his life (p. 101). Importantly, he was not on regular hospital staff. He had no titles, no surgeon's or nurse's gown. He had no official role of any sort. He had no authority. Nobody introduced him to the men. He was generally tolerated by the staff as he learned to keep out of their professional way, and he also learned to be on the alert if they solicited his aid, which was not uncommon. When entering a ward for the first time, he would wander slowly through, taking in each man on a cot on both sides of the aisle. He would heed his intuitions and his precognitive emotional and aesthetic stirrings, evidently always operating full bore, and he would find himself approaching a man to ask him how he was faring and if he might do anything for him. In time, human connections became much easier and more natural when the men on a ward became familiar with him. They would often call him over the minute he showed up to converse or to ask for assistance. The latter might be to help them readjust their position on their cots, to help them clean up, to fetch a nurse or surgeon, to write a letter for them,[20] or simply to talk and pass some time. Sometimes a group would ask him to read out loud to them. "They were very fond of it," Whitman points out, "and liked declamatory poetical pieces" (p. 55). All in all, Whitman reports, he was "well used" by the men (p. 10).

With respect to material items some of the men requested, this witness found himself caught off-guard at the start. Many of the men came directly from the battle lines with nothing but the tattered uniforms they wore. They had lost their personal possessions in the fighting or in the

Walt Whitman | 137

tumble and rumble of being carted roughly all the way to hospital. Some, alas, had their goods stolen along the way or in the hospitals themselves. In response, Whitman leapt into action. Along with a portion of his own funds from his part-time employment, he began soliciting financial support from people he would meet in Washington who were seeking ways to help. He would do the same with friends and acquaintances from elsewhere. Some of these benefactors—"good women and men in Boston, Salem, Providence, Brooklyn, and New York" (p. 64)—supported his efforts for years. In due course he had a regular budget to work with, and he spent the lot. "I bestow'd," he remarks, "as almoner for others, many, many thousands of dollars" (p. 64). He would procure and bring to the wards paper and pencils—"the men like to have a pencil, and something to write in" (p. 54)—stamped envelopes, newspapers, books, pipes and tobacco, fruits, candies, horseradish, biscuits, pickles, fruit syrups with ice water, tea, combs, toothbrushes, soap, brandy, items of new clothing, and small amounts of cash. "The wounded men often come up broke, and it helps their spirits to have even the small sum I give them" (p. 12, and see p. 64). Whitman would drop by local banks or shops beforehand and obtain coins and bills of small denomination. He would vary the gifts from 10 to 50 cents (not of insignificant purchasing power at that time) depending in part on how badly beaten up by their wounds the men were, physically and/or spiritually. He writes that he would use "tact and discretion" (p. 64) about the actual distribution since this was done in the public setting of the wards.

*A Face-to-Face Witness*

Whitman's memoranda interlace gift-giving with his countless bedside vigils, as the following entries indicate.

> To-day, Sunday afternoon and till nine in the evening, visited Campbell Hospital; attended specially to one case in Ward 1; very sick with pleurisy and typhoid fever; young man, farmer's son, D. F. Russell, Company E, Sixtieth New York; downhearted and feeble; a long time before he would take any interest; wrote a letter home to his mother, in Malone, Franklin County, N.Y., at his request; gave him some fruit and one or two other gifts; envelop'd and directed his letter, etc. Then went thoroughly through Ward 6; observ'd every case in the Ward, without, I

think, missing one; gave perhaps from twenty to thirty persons, each one some little gift, such as oranges, apples, sweet crackers, figs, etc. (p. 11)

*   *   *   *   *   *

Charles Miller, bed No. 19, Company D, Fifty-third Pennsylvania, is only sixteen years of age, very bright, courageous boy, left leg amputated below the knee; next bed to him, another young lad very sick; gave each appropriate gifts. In the bed above, also, amputation of the left leg; gave him a little jar of raspberries; bed No. 1, this Ward, gave a small sum; also to a soldier on crutches, sitting on his bed near. (p. 12; see also Morris, 2000, p. 105)

At another point Whitman describes a young soldier, very ill and depressed by his wounds, who declined gifts of money or anything else. When Whitman asked him one final time if there truly wasn't anything he could do, the youth replied that "he had a hankering for a good home-made rice pudding—thought he would relish it better than anything. . . . I soon procured B. his rice-pudding. A Washington lady, (Mrs. O'C.), hearing his wish, made the pudding herself, and I took it up to him the next day. He subsequently told me he lived upon it for three or four days" (p. 20).

In time, as Whitman became familiar with the men and refined his ability to approach them gently and attentively, he came to see that he was providing, or offering, something more than material gifts. "In my visits to the Hospitals," he remarks on a summer day in 1863, "I found it was in the simple matter of Personal Presence, and emanating ordinary cheer and magnetism, that I succeeded and help'd more than by medical nursing, or delicacies, or gifts of money, or anything else" (p. 30). A year later, he writes: "I learn'd one thing conclusively—that beneath all the ostensible greed and heartlessness of our times there is no end to the generous benevolence of men and women in the United States, when once sure of their object. Another thing became clear to me—while cash is not amiss to bring up the rear, tact and magnetic sympathy and unction are, and ever will be, sovereign still" (p. 65). Whitman could be describing Sebald's narrator, who brings his own "presence" to bear in his innumerable encounters with people troubled or damaged by events. As we saw, the narrator is a highly attentive listener, never in a rush, always open to what is there. People entrust him with things: photo albums, writings, other objects—in a word, with their memories. Both Sebald's narrator and Whitman cultivate layers of pertinent knowledge gained not only through personal study but through the experience of bearing witness itself.

Whitman states explicitly that by "getting experience" (p. 11) from each successive visit, he became better prepared, ethically speaking, for his witness-vigils.

> Dotting a Ward here and there are always cases of poor fellows, long-suffering under obstinate wounds, or weak and disharten'd from typhoid fever, or the like; mark'd cases, needing special and sympathetic nourishment. These I sit down and either talk to, or silently cheer them up. They always like it hugely (and so do I). Each case has its peculiarities, and needs some new adaptation. I have learnt to thus conform—learnt a good deal of hospital wisdom. Some of the poor young chaps, away from home for the first time in their lives, hunger and thirst for affection. This is sometimes the only thing that will reach their condition. (pp. 53–54)[21]

The witness's use of "magnetic" in the previous quotations evokes how his presence allowed the men to leave behind, for a time, their fears, their anguish, and their hurt. Like a magnet, he drew them out of themselves.[22] Put differently, his sympathetic orientation created a space for at least a provisional measure, or moment, of renewal and hope for the men. They often responded by abandoning their reserve and giving voice to their worries, or by letting out pent-up emotions and traumatic images from their battlefield experience. Whitman received it all, without overt judgment, without approval or disapproval.[23]

It appears that Whitman's witness in *Song of Myself* some years before had helped teach him this posture. He had learned to heed the everyday, seemingly ordinary lives of fellow Americans—and he found them extraordinary. He found it essential, somehow, to mark their reality, to acknowledge and affirm it. Put another way, he found himself collapsing the ordinary-extraordinary binary when it comes to reckoning meaning in the world. "All truths wait in all things," he writes in the poem,

> They neither hasten their own delivery nor resist it.
> They do not need the obstetric forceps of the surgeon,
> The insignificant is as big to me as any,
> What is less or more than a touch. (30)

Rather than digging for truths of life, the poet-witness suggests, there are times when it is better to prepare oneself to be able to receive them. This orientation influences how he responds to everyday life in the military hospitals, which with its emerging routines and habitudes mirrors an aspect of life on the street, and yet is categorically different. Indeed, in a stark sense the hospital scene is well *out* of the everyday, like war itself. It can only be described as frightening if not overwhelming to be in rooms filled with people maimed by battle.[24] For Whitman, however, the men in those rooms, in their simple (not simplistic) vulnerability and tenacity, embodied a redemptive beauty that mirrors the American prospect he portrays in his poem. I return to this point below.

As noted in previous chapters, ethical self-cultivation is a fundamental, ongoing aspect of bearing witness. Whitman embraces this task. His memoranda show him becoming increasingly attuned to the emotional and spiritual condition of the men. As he absorbs one story after another from the soldiers about their personal experience, his sensibility evolves such that he can draw that much more on the moral imagination expressed in *Song of Myself*. In the lines of that poem, as we saw, he allies himself with everyone—benefactors, thieves, prostitutes, boatmen, farmers, slaves, carpenters, indigenous people, those with venereal disease—not by presuming to stand in their shoes but by heeding their reality and the reality of their lived experience. As the months of his hospital visits roll by, he fashions an acute sense of the terrible travails the men encountered on the field of battle. He works consciously at refining his speaking and his moment-by-moment comportment when in their presence.

As with the hospital vignettes we have seen, it would be hard to exaggerate the cruelties of war the soldiers conveyed to him and which he saw with his own eyes in the field. The very first memo in the book instantly confronts the reader with what is to come. He reports visiting a banged-up mansion converted into a hospital near the site of the Battle of Fredericksburg. "Out doors," he writes, "at the foot of a tree, within ten yards of the front of the house, I notice a heap of amputated feet, legs, arms, hands, etc., a full load for a one-horse cart. Several dead bodies lie near, each covered with its brown woolen blanket. . . . [T]oward the river, are fresh graves, mostly of officers, their names on pieces of barrel-staves or broken board, stuck in the dirt" (p. 8). He continues,

> The large mansion is quite crowded, upstairs and down, everything impromptu, no system, all bad enough, but I have no

doubt the best that can be done; all the wounds pretty bad, some frightful, the men in their old clothes, unclean and bloody. . . . I went through the rooms, downstairs and up. Some of the men were dying. I had nothing to give at that visit, but wrote a few letters to folks home, mothers, etc. Also talk'd to three or four, who seem'd most susceptible to it, and needing it. (pp. 8–9)

Whitman proceeds to share details of the actual battle as he learned of it, a move he makes several times in the book. For example, he describes the carnage at the Battle of Chancellorsville (April 30 to May 6, 1863), how the trees and grasses on the battlefield caught fire and literally burned to death many wounded soldiers unable to crawl away from the flames (p. 9). He himself tends to several badly burned men. He meets wounded men who had been lying helpless between the battle lines for hours on end (pp. 13–14), sometimes assisted by Rebel soldiers who came upon them, but at others in mortal danger since both sides would often kill wounded men they came upon, a horrifying tit for tat on top of all the other tragedies Whitman touches on that were constitutive of the war and its impact.

He continues his witness near Fredericksburg.

The results of the late battles are exhibited everywhere about here in thousands of cases (hundreds die every day), in the Camp, Brigade, and Division Hospitals. These are merely tents, and sometimes very poor ones, the wounded lying on the ground, lucky if their blankets are spread on layers of pine or hemlock twigs or small leaves. No cots; seldom even a mattress. It is pretty cold. The ground is frozen hard, and there is occasional snow. I go around from one case to another. I do not see that I do much good, but I cannot leave them. Once in a while some youngster holds on to me convulsively, and I do what I can for him; at any rate, stop with him and sit near him for hours, if he wishes it. (pp. 9–10)

After sharing details of the ghastly wounds some men suffered at another battle site, he cannot restrain himself.

Then the camp of the wounded—O heavens, what scene is this?—is this indeed *humanity*—these butchers' shambles? . . .

> There they lie . . . in an open space in the woods, from 500 to 600 poor fellows—the groans and screams—the odor of blood, mixed with the fresh scent of the night, the grass, the trees . . . O well is it that their mothers, their sisters cannot see them—cannot conceive, and never conceiv'd, these things. (24)

One final instance among many others: one soggy night in May 1863, he goes down to the Potomac River outside of Washington, DC, and watches boat after boat maneuver its way slowly up to the docks and unload its groaning, supine wounded. The hospital transport cannot keep up, and the men end up lying all around the docks and shoreline, in a pouring rain. The boats keep floating in from the dark, as if they had just crossed the River Styx. "[A]s I write," Whitman relates, "hundreds more [wounded] are expected, and to-morrow and the next day more, and so on for many days" (p. 22).

As mentioned previously, like so many of his contemporaries Whitman was shocked by the scale and ferocity of the fighting. Moreover, given his passionate, visceral sense of solidarity with the soldiers, attending to them exacted everything he had to give, and then some. In *Song of Myself*, he had placed himself, imaginatively, right alongside others as they went about their daily affairs. In the midst of his hospital visits, he discovers that "I sometimes put myself in fancy in the cot, with typhoid, or under the knife" (in Morris, 2000, p. 120). The costs of such sensitivity can be found in his letters home and to friends, such as in the following.

> It is lucky that I like Washington in many respects. . . . for every day of my life I see enough to make one's heart ache with sympathy and anguish here in the hospitals, and I do not know as I could stand it if it was not counterbalanced outside. It is curious, when I am present at the most appalling things—deaths, operations, sickening wounds (perhaps full of maggots)—I do not fail . . . but keep singularly cool; but often hours afterwards, perhaps when I am home or out walking alone, I feel sick and actually tremble when I recall the thing and have it in my mind again before me. (In Morris, 2000, pp. 143–144)

He mentions in another instance that he sometimes finds himself bustling about mindlessly just to keep himself from weeping and breaking down.

The actual care-taking he enacted is one thing, with respect to drawing on his spiritual reserves. But it is another thing to try to picture what it must have felt like for him to endure hundreds of farewells to soldiers, some of whom he had become very close to, as they recovered and went back to their regiments, or as they partly recovered and were sent home, or as they died under his very eyes (cf. Morris, 2000, p. 132).[25]

Through the vicissitudes of his witness, Whitman begins more and more to conclude that the truth of the war resides, quite literally, on the surface of life, including in the hospital wards he comes to know well. His summons is precisely to bear witness there. One of the achievements of the *Memoranda* is how Whitman juxtaposes seamlessly the physical violence the war inflicted on the men with the physical intimacy and comfort his witness brought to them. As noted at the start of the chapter, Whitman finds himself time and again holding the hand of a soldier, or gently hugging him, or kissing him upon arriving at bed side or upon departing, as if he would deliberately counter the physical violence of war.[26]

In the same moment, Whitman deploys his rich, poetic voice to offer consolation, hope, and a measure of peace. His "personal presence" as witness, to recall his term of art, is both visceral and spiritual.

> I talk with him often [a soldier from Maine suffering badly from dysentery and typhoid fever]—he thinks he will die—looks like it indeed. I write a letter for him home. . . . I let him talk to me a little, but not much, advise him to keep very quiet—do most of the talking myself—stay quite a while with him, as he holds to my hand—talk to him in a cheering, but slow, low, and measured manner—talk about his furlough, and going home as soon as he is able to travel. (p. 29)

\* \* \* \* \* \*

> I staid to-night a long time by the bed-side of a new patient, a young Baltimorean, aged about 19 years, W. S. P. (2nd Md. Southern), very feeble, right leg amputated, can't sleep hardly at all—has taken a great deal of morphine. . . . Evidently very intelligent and well bred—very affectionate—held on to my hand, and put it by his face, not willing to let me leave. As I was lingering, soothing him in his pain, he says to me suddenly, "I hardly think you know who I am—I don't wish to impose

upon you—I am a Rebel soldier." I said I did not know that, but it made no difference. . . . Visiting him daily for about two weeks after that, while he lived (death had mark'd him, and he was quite alone), I loved him much, always kiss'd him, and he did me. (pp. 95–96)[27]

Whitman incorporates in the *Memoranda* several-pages-long letters he wrote to parents whose sons had died in the wards. Here is a portion of his letter to the mother of a Pennsylvania soldier, Frank H. Irwin, who died of his wounds combined with illness on May 1, 1865, only weeks after the South capitulated.

I will write you a few lines—as a casual friend that sat by his death bed. . . .

Frank, as far as I saw, had everything requisite in surgical treatment, nursing, &c. He had watches much of the time. He was so good and well-behaved, and affectionate, I myself liked him very much. I was in the habit of coming in afternoons and sitting by him, and soothing him, and he liked to have me—liked to put his arm out and lay his hand on my knee—would keep it so a long while. Toward the last he was more restless and flighty at night—often fancied himself with his regiment—by his talk sometimes seem'd as if his feelings were hurt by being blamed by his officers for something he was entirely innocent of—said, "I never in my life was thought capable of such a thing, and never was." At other times he would fancy himself talking as it seem'd to children or such like, his relatives I suppose, and giving them good advice; would talk to them a long while. All the time he was out of his head not one single bad word or thought or idea escaped him. It was remark'd that many a man's conversation in his senses was not half as good as Frank's delirium.

He was perfectly willing to die—he had become very weak and had suffer'd a good deal, and was perfectly resign'd, poor boy. I do not know his past life, but I feel as if it must have been good. At any rate what I saw of him here, under the most trying circumstances, with a painful wound, and among strangers, I can say that he behaved so brave, so composed, and so sweet and affectionate, it could not be surpass'd. And now like many other noble and good men, after serving his country as a soldier, he has yielded up his young life at the very outset in her service. Such things are gloomy—yet there is a text, "God doeth all things well,"—the meaning of which, after due time, appears to the soul.

  I thought perhaps a few words, though from a stranger, about your son, from one who was with him at the last, might be worth while, for I loved the young man, though I but saw him immediately to lose him. I am merely a friend visiting the Hospitals occasionally to cheer the wounded and sick. (pp. 90–92)

It is not clear how many witness-letters like this Whitman wrote, but it appears to have been many wherein he could put to good use his poetic gifts. Here is one final entry to share, dated August 10, 1863. After identifying himself as "only a friend, visiting the wounded & sick soldiers (not connected with any society—or State)" (p. 165), he writes the following to the parents of New York soldier Erastus Haskell:

I think Erastus was broken down, poor boy, before he came to the hospital here—I believe he came here about July 11th—Somehow I took to him, he was a quiet young man, behaved always correct & decent, said little—I used to sit on the side of his bed—I said once, You don't talk any, Erastus, you leave me to do all the talking—he only answered quietly, I was never much of a talker. The doctor wished every one to cheer him up very lively—I was always pleasant & cheerful with him, but did not feel to be very lively—Only once I tried to tell him some amusing narratives, but after a few moments I stopt, I saw that the effect was not good, & after that I never tried it again—I used to sit by the side of his bed, pretty silent, as that seemed most agreeable to him, & I felt it so too—he was generally opprest for breath, & with the heat, & I would fan him—occasionally he would want a drink—some days he dozed a good deal—sometimes when I would come in, he woke up, & I would lean down & kiss him, he would reach out his hand & pat my hair & beard a little, very friendly, as I sat on the bed & leaned over him.

  . . . I was very anxious he should be saved, & so were they all—he was well used by the attendants—poor boy, I can see him as I write—he was tanned & had a fine head of hair,

& looked good in the face when he first came, & was in pretty good flesh too—(had his hair cut close about ten or twelve days before he died)—He never complained—but it looked pitiful to see him lying there, with such a look out of his eyes. He had large clear eyes, they seemed to talk better than words—I assure you I was attracted to him much—Many nights I sat in the hospital by his beside till far in the night—The lights would be put out—yet I would sit there silently, hours, late, fanning him—he always liked to have me sit there, but never cared to talk. (167-168)

. . . I write you this letter, because I would do something at least in his memory—his fate was a hard one, to die so—He is one of the thousands of our unknown American young men in the ranks about whom there is no record or fame, no fuss made about their dying so unknown, but I find in them the real precious & royal ones of this land, giving themselves up, aye even their young & precious lives, in their country's cause—Poor dear son, though you were not my son, I felt to love you as a son, what short time I saw you sick & dying here . . . So farewell, dear boy—it was my opportunity to be with you in your last rapid days of death—no chance as I have said to do any thing particular, for nothing could be done—only you did not lay here & die among strangers without having one at hand who loved you dearly, & to whom you gave your dying kiss.

Mr. and Mrs. Haskell, I have thus written rapidly whatever came up about Erastus, & now must close. Though we are strangers & shall probably never see each other, I send you & all Erastus' brothers and sisters my love—Walt Whitman. (pp. 165-168)

A reader's initial response to this letter may be to wonder: What manner of missive is this? What must the youth's parents have felt upon receiving it? It is not the sort of official notice of death, or of being reported missing, that the military sent at the time, whenever possible, to the next of kin. Nor is it from a figure such as a priest or rabbi with an established role in comforting the bereaved.[28] It lacks the authority Whitman lacked in the hospital wards and near the fields of battle. It is "unauthorized." And yet, the voice of its author, with his ongoing moral witness, reverberates from start to finish. Perhaps the dead soldiers' mothers and fathers found the letters, at first glance, a bit peculiar, but at second glance consoling. It was commonplace in the Civil War for parents, wives, brothers and sisters, other relatives, and sweethearts to never learn what had happened to their men. The number of gravesites dedicated to unknown soldiers at Civil War monuments is legion. Dog tags bearing soldiers' names and serial numbers had yet to be invented.[29] Moreover, it was rare at the time for concerned people to be able to travel all the way to Washington, DC. Even assuming they could afford to do so, with respect to time and cost, there was no guarantee they would find the hospital or other location where their men were quartered. Whitman reports that there were regular lists of the wounded affixed to walls and fences, but that they were usually quickly out of date. He describes a man who came from a long way up north to find his brother but failed to locate him, only to discover after his arduous return home that the authorities had written to tell him where to go (p. 49).[30]

These circumstances lend gravitas to Whitman's witness-vigils. It is true that the wounded men in the wards benefited from the unique intimacy that is characteristic of soldiers in war, for whom the terrible, terrifying experience often boils down to self-preservation and caring for one's comrades. Memoirs, novels, and films alike feature piercing moments after a battle when the surviving soldiers desperately embrace one another, often in tears, as if to resolve the awful things that happened literally moments before (cf. Hynes, 1997; Smith, 2007). But Whitman learned how a deep part of the wounded men was alone and isolated, especially the enormous number of them who were barely out of adolescence. They were certainly comforted by letters from home (if they received any at all) but lacked actual familiar companionship. As suggested previously, Whitman seems to have felt summoned to counter the physical violence of the battlefield the men knew all too well with reminders of the physical calm, pleasure, and happiness from a loving touch.

In the letters Whitman sends to parents he refers to himself as "a casual friend," "merely a friend visiting the Hospitals occasionally to cheer the wounded and sick," "a stranger," "a soldier's missionary" (a term he inscribed on the cover of one of his notebooks), "I am only a friend, visiting the wounded & sick soldiers (not connected with any society—or State)." I noted previously his self-description as a "sustainer of spirit and body . . . in time of need" (101). Whitman appears to have treasured his unofficial status. As he declares: "Not connected with any society—or State," words which may have confused but also reassured some recipients. He was not a representative of authority, including the Union itself, although he passionately esteems the latter. When in the presence of the men, and in his letters, he is not partisan politically or in any other manner.

These facts raise the question, again, of what term is most appropriate to characterize Whitman's mode of bearing witness. I have experimented with images such as witness-poet, witness-vigil, and witness-letter-writer. Whitman's conduct combines the doings of a nurse, pastor, teacher, parent, brother, uncle, companion, confidant, comrade, and poet. He refers at one point to his "ministerings" (p. 101) in the wards, a term he secularizes yet also enchants. He and the men seem to share "the password" to which he had referred in *Song of Myself*. After some unsurprising, initial awkwardness, they appear to be at home together. The *Memoranda* calls to mind the figure of Everyman, a late Medieval term from a play by that name for a person who embodies in a luminous manner familiar human capacities, limitations, strengths, and weaknesses, and who aspires to be a good human being. Perhaps that term of art casts a special light on Whitman's sustained witness to the people of his country.

## Conclusion: An Education in Remembrance

A witness is not born as such. Rather, a person arrives in this orientation through a summons, or call, that leads to a transformation from spectator to witness. I have noted thus far a number of metamorphoses Whitman undergoes as he slowly transitions into his singular place in the lives of the wounded and ill. His sensitive attention to emotion, mood, gesture, and touch slowly leads him to a realization mentioned previously: that the truth of the war resides not in official summaries or histories, however valuable they are for comprehending the war's causes and consequences. The truth emerges elsewhere through a person's moral capacity to heed others' experience.

"We already talk of Histories of the War," Whitman writes in an entry dated May 12, 1863, ". . . yes—technical histories of some things, statistics, official reports, and so on—but shall we ever get histories of the *real* things?" (p. 22).[31] Who can grasp, he asks at the close of his introduction to the book, the full meaning of how the war became "an unending, universal mourning-wail of women, parents, orphans"?

—the marrow of the tragedy concentrated in those Hospitals—(it seem'd sometimes as if the whole interest of the land, North and South, was one vast Hospital, and all the rest of the affair but flanges)—those forming the Untold and Unwritten History of the War—infinitely greater (like Life's) than the few scraps and distortions that are ever told or written. Think how much, and of importance, will be—how much, civic and military, has already been—buried in the grave, in eternal darkness! (pp. 7–8)

Whitman reiterates the point behind his detailed, often grim accounts of soldiers in battle and in hospital: "Multiply [them] by scores, aye hundreds—varify [sic] it in all the forms that different circumstances, individuals, places, &c., could afford . . . and you have an inkling of this War" (pp. 63–64). "[The war's] interior history will not only never be written," he contends, "its practicality, minutia of deeds and passions, will never be even suggested" (p. 7). Here, in a nutshell, resides Whitman's office as witness. He *will* write directly of that "interior," thereby rebutting his own claims. As touched on previously, he confronts the limits of language in his attempt to do justice to the forms of violence, loss, pain, and suffering he witnesses day after day. Nonetheless, he hopes, "[t]he present Memoranda may furnish a few stray glimpses into that life, and into those lurid interiors of the period, never to be fully convey'd to the future" (7). Perhaps the book succeeds, in its moving way, because Whitman came to know the war so intimately that he recognized its ultimate inexpressibility (cf. Coviello, 2004, p. xxix).

Whitman is neither a historian nor an archivist. As we have seen, his affecting prose in the volume is a mere shimmer away from the poetic form of *Song of Myself*, even while differing markedly from it in tone and prospect. In figurative terms, he sketches, paints, draws, evokes, echoes, recalls, and sings. Although sobered by the war's realities, his memos instantiate the democratic imagination in his poem. On the one hand, they do so in a deeply personal sense. As Mark Edmundson (2019) suggestively writes: "While he was in Washington at what he called 'my hospitals' . . . Whitman effectively completed 'Song of Myself.' He became a version of the person his poem prophesied. He engaged his soul, 'clear and sweet,' as he called it. His soul became his mode of connection with the sick and wounded and dying men. His imagination allowed him to see who they were, what they were feeling, and how he could best help them."[32]

On the other hand, Whitman's witness in *Memoranda* vindicates the political and cultural experiment that, in his view, is the United States. His daily, face-to-face encounters with the wounded and the ill opened his eyes that had been darkened by the shock of the war ("Now I wash the gum from your eyes" [46]). He did not read into their circumstances his prior democratic commitments. Rather, their faces and their fates read him, poetically speaking, and, in discerning the eros of his soul, gave him a response upon which he could rely. "Before I went down to the Field, and among the hospitals," he remarks, "I had my hours of doubt about These States; but not since. The bulk of the Army, to me, develop'd, transcended, in personal qualities—and, radically, in moral ones—all that the most enthusiastic Democratic-Republican ever fancied, idealized in loftiest dreams. And curious as it may seem, the War, to me, *proved* Humanity, and proved America" (pp. 106–107).

For Whitman, the "proof" resides not in heroic deeds but in the "quiet testimony" (Goldberg, 2013) of the soldiers' simple willingness to rise each day and carry on through thick and thin. He discerns in that acceptance the expression of "a primal hardpan" (p. 109) of commitment to the democratic experiment that had begun with the very birth of the nation, and that had survived the war "like a ship a storm" (p. 123). The "mystic chords of memory" that bound the nation, which President Lincoln named and appealed to in his First Inaugural Address, were not entirely cut. The song would go on. Whitman describes going out one evening in February, 1864, to watch a regiment of soldiers voicelessly making their way toward the battle lines: "It may have been odd, but I *never before* so realized the majesty and reality of the American common people proper. It fell upon me like a great awe" (pp. 50–51, my emphasis). This remark comes from a poet who, decades before, had marvelously expressed his awe in *Song of Myself*. Now, he witnesses something equally compelling to him.

Whitman's newly renewed faith in the nation is not rose-colored (and in his later years it seems to have ebbed). He fully acknowledges what he calls "the corruption and wickedness of my lands and days" (p. 107). He refers to the graft, greed, violence, prejudice, dissembling political speech, and more, which constitute a perennial affront and challenge to democratic-minded citizens.[33] But Whitman's distinctive witness, which in his experience and wordsmithing extends from *Song of Myself* through *Memoranda*, has given him a singular vantage point. The American experiment has survived, however battered and however permanent will be the task of reconstructing it in the face of new trials. The poet has shown readers how to walk alongside him in a sober-minded manner, and what it would be like to align themselves with his moral commitment to fellow citizens. He has enacted how Sebald's narrator mourned for an unknown writer buried decades before. In a searing act of remembrance, the narrator sees that *he* has lost her, *he* is her writer-descendant, that she is *part* of him (see above, p. 49). Whitman refers to the unknown and unnamed lost soldiers as "our hardy darlings" (p. 26): "the dead, the dead, the dead—*our* dead, of South and North, ours all, (all, all, all, finally dear to me) . . . the land entire is saturated, perfumed with their impalpable ashes' exhalation in Nature's chemistry distill'd, and shall be so forever, and every grain of wheat and ear of corn, and every flower that grows, and every breath we draw" (pp. 102–103).

To recur to a previous theme, Whitman as poet-witness loves. This hard-to-characterize love is neither sentimental nor possessive. It is not egoistic, though also not selfless. It is not the work solely *of* a self, but the work *on* the self that occurs through a tensile receptivity that is at once unguarded yet also reflective and contemplative. This love helps constitute the "I" and the "You" that bookend *Song of Myself*. It infuses the witness-memo-writer's profound feeling for remembrance as an active calling into the present the voices of the past, which become vivid and informing the moment one truly listens. This radical love, which Etty Hillesum also discovered, is generous down to its last gesture.

> To a drudge of the cottonfields or emptier of privies I lean. . . .
>   on his right cheek I put the family kiss,
> And in my soul I swear I never will deny him. . . .
> O despairer, here is my neck,
> By God! you shall not go down! Hang your whole weight
>   upon me. (40)

Chapter 5

# Bearing Witness and Education

Here is the time for the sayable, here is its homeland.
Speak and bear witness.
More than ever the Things that we might experience are vanishing . . .

—Rainer Maria Rilke, "Ninth Duino Elegy"

Rilke's prescient words in his famous elegy mark our contemporary world, and are likely to continue to do so for some time. Speed, acceleration, and unprecedented as well as unmanageable overstimulation, all consequences of today's technology, characterize the daily lives of countless human beings. People are learning to be more alert to "the latest thing," but it's not clear they are learning to be more attentive. Attentiveness and alertness are not synonyms. Alertness is instantaneous. Attentiveness is not. Attentiveness differs from "attention" as in "the attention economy" manufactured by contemporary media. Attentiveness necessarily unfolds over time. It requires patience and composure. In our era, it appears that long-honored human practices of untimed attentiveness to the world, undistracted solitude (not to be confused with being solitary), slow, careful reading and thinking, and taking the long way around for the very sake of it, are more and more being elbowed aside by the technology-produced insistence that there is so much to see and do that no-thing can wait. No "Thing" is worth it. Thus, for Rilke, these Things are in danger of "vanishing." The capitalized term reflects the fact Rilke wrote in German, where all nouns are capitalized. However, the effect in English (where in the translated poem all other nouns, except Thing, are lowercase) conjures the existential threat he sees in becoming unmoored from, or failing to reconstruct, all those slowly cultivated, and slowly enacted, cultural and spiritual practices that have helped people feel they *inhabit* the world: that the passing moment can be full rather than merely fleeting. The latest "thing," as the lowercase symbolizes, bears no resemblance to these Things.

Rilke is not a prophet of doom, nor is he a wistful moralizer pooh-poohing the pleasures many people appear to find in speed-driven contemporary life (though Aldous Huxley hauntingly portrays a mindless future society built entirely around pleasure in his novel *Brave New World*). In the epigram above, Rilke is mainly speaking to himself, defining the necessary task, as he sees it, of the witness-poet. It is a task of critical (versus nostalgic) preservation and remembrance. I share the poet's concern that one of the Things endangered in our time may be remembrance itself. This fact is why I concluded chapter 1 by spotlighting several ways in which witnesses can serve as educators, if not in a direct or formal sense of the term. Among other consequences of engaging them, witnesses can fuel both historical consciousness and a sense of remembrance.

## The Second Order Witness, Historical Consciousness, and Remembrance

As Sebald, Césaire, and Whitman make clear, remembrance differs from memory. It issues, in part, from historical consciousness, a term that denotes something more than knowledge of historical facts, vital as that always is. As the epigram to this book by the artist Paul Klee suggests, historical consciousness means seeing oneself as a being in time, living in the present moment but connected to the past and future. It is to approach witnesses such as those featured here as contemporaries, who in turn render contemporary the sufferings and joys of people from other eras. Historical consciousness complements the chronological sequence of events established by historians with a vertical or nonchronological sense of time shared by every human being who ever lived, who lives now, and who will live.

Bruce Snider (2016) captures this truth in his poem titled "The Average Human," which is prefaced by the following words:

> *breath contains approximately 1044 molecules, which, once exhaled, in time spread evenly through the atmosphere*

Here is his poem.

> so today I took
> in the last breaths of James
> Baldwin Marie Curie Genghis
> Khan my great great grandmother's
> breath entering me beside the breath
> of a Viking slave boy immolated
> on the flames of his master's
> burning corpse. I inhaled
> African queens Chinese
> emperors the homeless
> man with the bright blue
> coat down the street. Oxygen
> is the third most plentiful
> element in the universe, moving
> through us like Virgil through
> the underworld. How long
> have I tasted the girl
> drowned among cattails near
> the murky shore? In ancient Egypt
> a priestess unloosed organs
> and packed a corpse with
> salt but not before a breath
> escaped that two thousand years
> later entered me or at least
> atoms of it, a molecule. Plato
> theorized atoms in 400 BC
> and this morning outside
> Athens I took in his last breath,
> my lungs damp crypts
> where Charon's oars dipped
> into the black waters of the River
> Styx, not knowing who would
> pay the ferryman and
> with what coin on what tongue.

Snider's moving image of connectedness—as if all humans shared a single, long breath—evokes Whitman's opening lines of *Song of Myself*:

"I celebrate myself, / And what I assume you shall assume, / For every atom belonging to me as good belongs to you (1). Snider's portrait of the circulation of breath also echoes Whitman's closing remark about the lost soldiers of the Civil War, whose absorption back into nature, he projects, will be part of "every breath we draw" (2004, p. 103). For Whitman, no-thing (or no-Thing, in Rilke's idiom) is isolated. All are in association. Only humans have the capacity to break things apart. But they can also render things proximal and intact. Historical consciousness contributes to "keeping things whole" (cf. Mark Strand's poem [1990] by that name). It does not elide fractured aspects of the world. On the contrary, it can emerge precisely from awareness of ruptures, discontinuities, difficulties of all kinds. But this consciousness supports people in not being cowed by events. It is another name for the shared nonchronological time as well as the ontological continuity that Whitman and Snider conjure.

Remembrance encompasses historical consciousness while foregrounding its moral significance. Remembrance embodies a sense of solidarity across space and time with people who came before. It keeps alive their voices, strivings, and sufferings, and in so doing helps keep contemporaries ethically alive. I mean that without the vivid presence of the past in consciousness, people can become ethically inert. They can fall prey to the dogma of presentism. This one-dimensional mind-set presumes that what *we're* doing is more important than anything people did in the past, that *we* do things better than they did, and that *we* don't need them—forgetting, in this posture, that the touch of the past is precisely what calls out to us to imagine the touch of the future, *when we are the past*, and thus what we would most want to bequeath to those who come after.

As touched on in previous chapters, remembrance differs from sentimental nostalgia, on the one hand, and fanatical adherence to past precept and example, on the other hand. Remembrance involves respecting the past as making possible the present, but also respecting the present as that which makes possible the future. The past can speak *in* the present *for* a better future, so long as people heed it critically and take it as seriously as their own animating interests and concerns. Put another way, remembrance is not looking backward. It is not looking forward. It is *looking*, feeling the rhythm of continuous human movement, the continuous flow of life in which one can learn to participate meaningfully.

Here, slowness is not a virtue in itself. Rather, it makes heeding others and the world possible in the first place. The verb "to heed" implies more than just noting something. It means registering in consciousness and feeling that which has called out for attention. For the witness, to heed constitutes a dynamic password to truth, in the existential sense that Whitman gives to that term. To heed constitutes a moral orientation that embodies attunement, responsiveness, and action. But the latter qualities may not be overtly visible. They may not alter anything immediately noticeable in the passing moment. All the same, the act of heeding triggers a change: a perhaps incremental deepening or widening of the person's involvement in the world, their concern for the world, and their willingness to step forward, when the occasion arrives, to be a force for good however modest or microscopic the scale may be. Remembrance is agentive even as its underlying impetus resides in feeling, which as we have seen is a more encompassing gestalt than emotion and reason considered separately or as an ensemble.

W. G. Sebald, Aimé Césaire, and Walt Whitman illuminate the educational significance of remembrance as well as of other ethical practices. In this concluding chapter, I will draw out educational lessons from their second-order witnesses. I will review elements of bearing witness that constitute it as a moral and ethical orientation. Along the way, I will clarify questions about it that may have arisen for readers. I invite readers to consider the question of education with respect to their own ongoing experience and to its larger purposes. Readers might also consider their own relationship with bearing witness. As we have seen, this orientation cannot be forced on anyone. It can only come from within when a person feels the touch of the world summoning them to respond (cf. Todd, 2023). But it is not necessary to feel a particular summons—as did Sebald, Césaire, and Whitman—to learn *from* and *with* witnesses about how to conduct a humane life in community with others.

## The Orientation of Bearing Witness Revisited

As emphasized in chapter 1, no single aspect of bearing witness is unique to it. For example, a person may be called by a deep feeling to participate in a significant human practice, such as teaching, doctoring, or social work. As another example, the premium on close attentiveness to other people's experience that is embodied in bearing witness is also characteristic of a range of important moral philosophies, including those that focus on virtue and character. To take still another instance, the posture of waiting for unanticipated insight rather than awaiting predetermined outcomes marks a number of arts-based and aesthetic approaches to inquiry (cf. the influential work of Barone & Eisner, 2011). Each of the elements referred to here, alongside the others featured in the book, take on a distinctive aura when fused in a singular constellation: that is, in the orientation of bearing witness.

*A Moral Orientation*

Sebald, Césaire, and Whitman share a moral outlook as witnesses. Their specific concerns differ, as do the actual steps they take as well as their compositional practices. But they walk side by side with respect to wanting to do justice to people's lives: to their sufferings, predicaments, and prospects. They make the time to do so. They will not be penned in by the clock or the calendar, or by deadlines whether imposed from within or without. They go where their summons leads them to go. They attend scrupulously to seemingly every human encounter they experience. They do the same with every encounter with their own selves in solitude. Their moral and epistemic compasses keep them moving in a critically sympathetic direction. They listen for other people's knowledge. They do not impose on them their own knowledge, even as they draw on every ounce of it in their sense-making. But their intellectual modesty does not prevent them from weighing knowledge, others' and their own, against their enduring commitment to truth. They neither approve nor disapprove. They do not exoticize, romanticize, or sentimentalize others, nor themselves. Precisely for these reasons it is challenging to read them, because in the face of trauma humans are primed to seek consolation and comfort. For these same reasons it is important to read them.

Sebald, Césaire, and Whitman do not presume to occupy a higher moral ground than others. As witnesses, they endeavor to clear ever-fresh moral ground in the face of human greed, indifference, prejudice, violence, and moral opacity. They do not take on a new identity as witnesses, for bearing witness is not an identity but an orientation. The particularities of nationality, class, gender, race and other general categories, alongside the distinguishing elements that constitute their psyches, inform and set certain limits to the substance of their witnesses. But they do not determine them. Put another way, these witnesses focus intently on local singularities and yet in the same breath gesture toward universalities with regards to human conditions, capacities, and possibilities. They do not speak *from* other people's concerns for justice, equity, and peace, but they speak *to* them. Their witnesses merit a place in any curriculum, suitably adjusted for age and preparation, whose aims include expanding and deepening critical sympathy toward others.

*Ethical Self-Cultivation*

An ongoing aspect of bearing witness is the necessity of continuous ethical self-cultivation. With the apparent exception of saints, human beings are limited in their moral imagination and in their ability to be morally responsive and consistent. The witness feels these constraints acutely, given their commitment to render other people's realities justly. It becomes imperative to cultivate the meanings embedded in the moral verbs that mark the witness's orientation: to attend, to be mindful, to be patient, to listen. Moreover, to heed another person's testimony is to take it as a spur to communicating, in turn, with others about it (cf. Simon, 2005, p. 51, *passim*). The witness's summons compels them to render what they have heeded into a form for others who may have no access to or knowledge of the events in question. This necessity echoes the French word for witness, *témoin*, which as mentioned previously also means "baton"—the thin tube that runners in a relay race pass ahead to the next sprinter. In likeness, the witness passes ahead to others their rendering.

Receptivity and responsiveness are two sides of the same ethical coin. They oblige the second-order witness to still the will to know in favor of a will to wait, to linger, to loaf in Whitman's deeply serious sense of the term. The wait may often be fruitless and feel counterproductive, so much so that witnesses may be tempted to abandon the endeavor outright. In such circumstances, they turn to the summons that has beckoned them in the first place. They trust the summons more than they do themselves. In that very commitment, they open themselves to the prospect of continuous ethical self-cultivation. They stay the course even as the course leads them on.

Steadfastness merges with courage for the witness. Bearing witness generates vulnerability precisely because witnesses abandon the desire for control. They cannot predict what they will end up heeding, nor can they be certain they will become capable of composing a just witness. While first-order witnesses are legion in number, it is unaccountable how many second-order witnesses across time remain unwritten. As we have seen, Sebald, Césaire, and Whitman feel keenly the prospect of inflicting harm, through an inadequate account, on people who may already have been harmed by various forces. In the face of such realities, they muster courage and humble confidence. The tremendous value in their testimony resides, in part, in how they make plain the transformations they must undergo as witnesses. They *re-inhabit* the world with an enriched as well as sobered sensibility.

*A Dynamic of Wonder and Concern*

Sebald, Césaire, and Whitman sometimes appear animated by a stark, troubling sense of wonder that works against the grain of what that word typically connotes. Put in broad terms, they wonder how it is that humanity became a species capable of so much destructive violence, as seen in war, slavery, and genocide. They wonder about the presence of what Simone Weil (1983) calls "force," a term of art she deploys for the pitiless reduction of human beings into mere objects, an experience Weil argues can happen to anyone at any time depending on the tides of history. As we saw in previous chapters, the witnesses's commitments compel them to confront despair and hopelessness regarding the human condition. They hear the forbidding epitaph of Shakespeare's Macbeth when he intones that human life is "a tale told by an idiot, full of sound and fury, signifying nothing" (act 5, scene 5).

Each witness climbs out of this abyss, albeit not to a necessarily comfortable or comforting ground. But they do not seek consolation. They do not resort, to the best of their ability, to illusions, delusions, fantasies, and other mechanisms to escape reality. They think and write their way out through careful description. Care-full, being full of care, constitutes the watchword. They care about the suffering and fate of those to whom they bear witness, and they care about a just rendering. They are not spectators, bystanders, or voyeurs. They are *concerned*. Their aesthetic and moral imagination enables them to find illuminating words and formulations. Their fineness in language is as unrushed as their witnesses. Their turns of phrase are often stunningly beautiful if not also inspiring. In-spire: they breath spirit into their writing, and in so doing attest to the truth in that to which they bear witness. That truth encompasses beauty, grace, and love, all of which they encounter alongside the force that can kill.

*The Vicissitudes in Communicating a Witness*

Despite or perhaps because of their artful composing, Sebald, Césaire, and Whitman continuously confront the limits of language. In a splendidly paradoxical way, some of their most striking expressions are about those very limits. They do not transcend the latter, but they show that they are not set in stone. Witnesses can push boundaries to get as near to truth as they can, even if they never finally arrive. As we have seen, truth as a regulative ideal is built into the summons that leads them to persevere despite self-doubt, confusion, and uncertainty. They suspect and yet also trust in language in a seemingly never-ending dialectic.

Another way to frame these points is to suggest that all three witnesses confront head-on their degrees of freedom as witness-composers. They are aware that talk of freedom of mind and expression seems to inevitably conjure skeptical questions about what that alleged freedom can achieve. C. S. Lewis (1976) captures the matter succinctly: "Five senses; an incurably abstract intellect, a haphazardly selective memory, a set of preconceptions and assumptions so numerous that I can never examine more than a minority of them—never become even conscious of them all. How much of total reality can such an apparatus let through?" (pp. 74–75). In brief, it sometimes appears all too easy to fall into a rabbit hole of epistemic skepticism, and the witnesses I've touched on here know all about that prospect.

Once again, an image of climbing out comes to mind. In this case, the integrity, the frankness, and the vulnerability in the witness's offering puts the onus on the skeptic to refute its reality and efficacy. Whitman boldly writes, as we saw in chapter 4: "With the hush of my lips I confound the topmost skeptic" (25). His song-poem is itself the vertical finger on his lips. It is the "confounder" of the skeptic who would deny truth and mock all attempts to move toward it. Whitman makes no claims to attaining the truth of human experience, but he shows it is no chimera as the skeptic would have it.

The three witnesses vindicate the value of heeding a summons and finding the right approach to expressing its significance. They compose the most fine-grained accounts of which they are capable. They give form to what Rilke calls the Things that matter. They do not invent the latter. Rather, they enunciate their names, as does Rilke in his own witness:

> Perhaps we are *here* in order to say: house,
> bridge, fountain, gate, pitcher, fruit-tree, window—
> . . . But to *say* them, you must understand,
> oh to say them *more* than the Things themselves
> ever dreamed of existing. ("Ninth Duino Elegy")

For Rilke, names and the reality they denote take on a sacral quality when contrasted with the force that can vanquish them. Sebald, Césaire, and Whitman, on their part, let names come forth again in the fullness of their reality, uniqueness, and dignity. They perceive the aesthetic and moral aura, which is usually invisible to the casual observer, that can surround a name. They regard names in an ethical light, reminiscent of how Césaire's memory of the poverty-stricken black man on the tram sparked his "second sight" as a witness who had hitherto conducted himself as a voyeuristic spectator.

Consider once more what we witnessed in previous chapters: Sebald's meticulous specificity, wherein he rarely says *trees* but instead deliberately names singular species; his acute attention to ways of approaching his teacher's name (Paul); Césaire's sharp focus on both harsh and beautiful particularities associated with names and nature; and Whitman's lengthy trains of verbal images of human and natural diversity, as if he were summoned to be another Adam vouching for their reality through enunciating their names. These witnesses work against the variously numbing, distorting, and corrupting effects that descriptions of others can have when uninformed by an underlying commitment to truth and justice. That commitment need not become didactic or preachy. It is more like the ethos of a communication: how it can resound with care, or its opposite as the case may be.

## Remembrance Reconsidered

The wondrous Jorge Luis Borges composed a parable titled "The Witness" ("El Testigo") for his collection *A Personal Anthology* (1968).[1] In it, he characterizes a witness as a person who is the very last to see or participate in a cultural practice before it disappears in the tide of historical change. His story brings to a head the pathos and the necessity of remembrance.

The tale is set in England, before the Middle Ages when Christianity was in the process of replacing previous Druid and other animist belief systems. Borges's narrator begins by describing an old, impoverished man on his last legs, who is stretched out on the straw in a stable that sits near a newly completed stone church. Lying in the midst of the stable's animal odors, the man "meekly seeks death like someone seeking sleep." As the day passes, shadows and light play across the floor and walls of the stable. Outside are tilled fields, a ditch filled with dead autumn leaves, and the track of a wolf in the mud where the forest begins. "The man sleeps and dreams, forgotten." The bells calling to prayer awaken him. The man has become accustomed to these bells, but they were not heard when he was a boy. In his childhood, "he had seen the face of Woden, had seen holy dread and exultation, had seen the rude wooden idol weighed down with Roman coins and heavy vestments, seen the sacrifice of horses, dogs, and prisoners." But before the next morning, the narrator tells us, the old man would be dead, and with him would perish, "never to return, the last firsthand images of the pagan rites. The world would be poorer when this Saxon was no more."

The narrator steps back from his tale. He says to himself and to us: "We may well be astonished by space-filling acts which come to an end when someone dies, and yet something, or an infinite number of things, die in each death"—unless, he adds, there is what the theosophists conjecture is "a universal memory." He thinks of the day long ago when "the last eyes to see Christ" closed for the final time. He sees in his mind's eye the passing of the last person to have fought in the battle of Junin (in 1824). He pictures how the love of Helen of Troy "died with the death of some one man." "What will die with me when I die?" the narrator asks. "What pathetic or frail form will the world lose?" He wonders: perhaps it will lose the memory he has of the voice of Macedonio Fernandez (an influential teacher in his youth). It will lose an apparently trivial image he has long held in mind of a horse standing in the vacant space of an intersection of two streets in his native Buenos Aires. And it will lose the fact that he knows there is a bar of sulfur in the drawer of his mahogany desk.

Borges evokes a poignant image of endless disappearance as each human being passes away, taking with them into oblivion the vast, unique constellation of events, actions, feelings, hopes, fears, loves, hates, thoughts, and more that accumulate over a life. Moreover, some people—like the imagined old Saxon—take with them the last living touch of cultures and ways of life that may have endured for centuries, so that their disappearance relegates all who follow to secondhand knowledge. Borges's story can also conjure a mixture of unsettlement and sadness in the reader, as in the question: Who will be the last person to mention my name?[2]

However, the parable can also trigger a sense of remembrance, not so much of an individual human being, per se, but of what can outlast personal knowledge of them: namely, what they stood for, what they loved, what they sought to create and to bring to the world, however modest the scale may have been. Secondhand knowledge need not become second best. In this light, consider the following remark from Etty Hillesum, whose witness began this book.

> Living and dying, sorrow and joy, the blisters on my feet and the jasmine behind the house, the persecution, the unspeakable horrors. . . . I wish I could live for a long time so that one day I may know how to explain it [all], and if I am not granted that wish, well, then somebody else will perhaps do it, carry on from where my life has been cut short. And that is why I must try to live a good and faithful life to my last breath: so that those who come after me do not have to start all over again. (1997, p. 154)

In fact, every generation of human beings in the world *does* have to start again, in a manner of speaking, because traditions, the dynamics of individual and cultural interaction, and the force of events constantly change. This fact demands ever-fresh responsiveness, particularly from a moral and ethical point of view as persons encounter new people, new forms of life, and new challenges.

However, through remembrance and sustaining the touch of the past, the reality need not be a case of starting *all over* again, as if prior moral knowledge retains no value. Instead, each new start can be deeply informed, in the very wisest of ways, by witnesses such as Hillesum, Baldwin, Alexievich, and those featured in this book. They have bequeathed to people the very possibility of beginning again, rather than remaining trapped in existential or moral ruts with the hopelessness, despair, and cynicism that can breed in them.

## Bearing Witness and Education: Questions and Replies

People only sustain what they care for. To care for what witnesses can teach means absorbing them into educational work in schools, universities, and other organized settings. The witnesses addressed here are eminently suitable for university and, with appropriate preparation, for the higher grades in secondary school. Whitman's *Song of Myself*, for example, has for generations been taught in schools. His witness, and those of Sebald and Césaire, could figure into educational foundations courses for teachers, courses in literature, philosophy, and other fields, and first-year seminars for undergraduates encountering large ideas for perhaps the first time in their lives. Witnesses would complement historical accounts of a given event. The works would also be ideal for faculty reading groups in schools and universities, as well as for freestanding adult reading groups. Such settings could be where people address the realities of war and peace, the Atlantic slave trade and its aftermath, the Holocaust and its aftermath, the question of democracy and its viability, and more. Or people could "simply" be interested in reading outstanding provocations to ethical thought and practice.

The potential themes in this engagement are timely as well as wide-ranging. They encompass the aspects of bearing witness reviewed above, including notions of remembrance and of ethical self-cultivation as persons who can make a difference in others' lives. Consider also the following questions that can figure into inquiry. All of them have arisen in courses I've taught on bearing witness.

*What Renders a Witness Trustworthy?*

A provocative version of this question would be to ask: Can a witness deliberately lead readers astray, and still be called a witness? At first glance, the answer appears to be: of course. Anyone can be disingenuous with anybody. Witnesses are not saints but fallible, sometimes inconstant and inconsistent testifiers.

At second glance, however, the question brings us to an ethical boundary beyond which the integrity, or role, of the witness seems to morph into something else. As we have seen, Sebald, Césaire, and Whitman are not stenographers recording direct observations. Put another way, they are not video cameras. Though they undertake careful study of facts, they may phrase things incorrectly or inadvertently leave out pertinent details. Moreover, they deploy fictional motifs in their attempts to render the truth in what they've witnessed. This paradoxical position can result, as they well know, in a distorted account and thereby undermine what they most want to express. It can call into question their trustworthiness.

As argued previously, I believe all three witnesses are keenly aware of the question of trust. They echo Socrates's deep worry, enunciated at a dramatic point in Plato's *Republic* (1992), that if he and his fellow interlocutors continue with their inquiry into justice, his own ignorance about the matter may confuse them if not warp their thinking. He regards this prospect as extremely dangerous given the fragility yet also necessity of trying to conceive justice. "[T]o speak, as I'm doing," Socrates remarks, "at a time when one is unsure of oneself and searching for the truth, is a frightening and insecure thing to do. I'm not afraid of being laughed at—that would be childish indeed. But I am afraid that, if I slip from the truth, just where it's most important not to, I'll not only fall myself but drag my friends down as well" (p. 124 [450e–451a]). For Socrates, inquiry into fundamental matters is risky and fraught with ways of going awry. Dialogue itself, without the appropriate mindfulness, can have potentially damaging effects on participants' subsequent thought and action.

Such is the attitude toward bearing witness enacted, if not in so many words, by Sebald, Césaire, and Whitman. They take numerous steps, often subtle and hard to detect, to address the issue of trust. They know their witnesses may fall short morally, thereby wounding already wounded people a second time, and perhaps confusing readers. At the same time, there is a very real sense in which they write first and last for themselves, not for others. That is, they cede priority in their endeavors to resolving as best they can the summons that has beckoned them. But this very commitment leads them to respect the facts of the case, to devote the time necessary to heed the experience of the people in question, and to compose their witness as justly as possible.

In other words, they assume epistemic responsibility alongside their sense of ethical responsibility. The fictional motifs they deploy are not fanciful but undertaken with profound seriousness. They may be dubbed playful, but only in the sense in which play can constitute a mode of activity in which the moral stakes are high and in which the player's own humanity is implicated. As emphasized above, the witness does not compete with historians but complements their efforts. The truths uncovered by the one can fuse with those disclosed by the other into powerful if always incomplete portraits of human experience in times of stress—and in times of joy, depending on the situation. In brief, the historian and the witness, working in tandem (however unintentionally), can contribute educationally to how people reimagine, or establish in the first place, a moral relationship with past, present, and future (more on this point below).

Ruthellen Josselson (2004) and Gert-Jan Van der Heiden (2022) rightly emphasize that the recipients of a witness need to do their own homework. Readers should examine the historical or contemporary contexts in which witnesses move and put forward their testimony. They should also be mindful, not just appreciative, of a witness's rhetorical strategies, since the effects of the latter can be unpredictable (cf. Rorty, 1997). These tasks do not imply a posture of suspicion, in Josselson's and Van der Heiden's view, only prudent caution so that recipients can weigh things judiciously. They urge a dialectic of a deconstructive "hermeneutics of suspicion" (or "demystification") with a reconstructive "hermeneutics of trust" (or retrieval). They show that when the former dominates, judgmentalism if not cynicism about a given text may ensue. They caution fellow critics that to foreground suspicion based on what the latter believe has been neglected or disguised in a text can all too easily morph into misreading or mischaracterizing what *is* said. While a one-sided reliance on the hermeneutics of trust can also be problematic, its chief virtue is positioning witnesses to obtain a hearing on their own grounds, whatever final judgment readers might make.[3]

First- and second-order witnesses may mislead. But so can readers. Because the latter determine whether a witness will be received in the first place, the burden is on them to be just in their own right.

*How Might We Further Link the Work of Witnesses and Historians?*

As discussed throughout this book, witnesses and historians have different if overlapping aims. The witness seeks to heed a summons from the world that addresses them personally. The historian seeks to set the historical record as straight as evidence and their interpretive abilities permit. The witness has no set method bequeathed to them for how to resolve their summons. The historian inherits and adapts creatively an extraordinarily rich legacy of both method and comment on method. Both seek truth, but not the same truth, nor in the same way. The historian seeks the truth of what happened and why. The historian is disposed to be wary of testimony, not because of an a priori mistrust, much less a built-in misanthropy, but because two people involved in the same historical event may put forward disparate factual accounts, and the historian must sort this out.

But the second-order witness can show us why the same two persons, despite their conflicting factual reports, may both speak truly of the lived experience of the event.[4] The witness seeks the truth of experience through careful listening and looking that give rise to vivid description. Readers can *see* the truth of war in Whitman's *Memoranda During the*

*War*; they can *see* the truth of slavery's aftermath in Césaire's *Journal of a Homecoming*; and they can *see* the truth in what it means to have survived the Holocaust and yet, in other ways, to have been destroyed by it, as Sebald shows.

From the point of view of reading and pedagogy, witnesses and historical accounts can complement and complicate one another. In a series of studies, Ann Chinnery (2010, 2013) illuminates the limits of first-order testimonies with respect to engaging students and helping them develop historical consciousness. As she notes, personal testimonies saturate social media, the internet, and the publishing world. Humans today are virtually drowning in testimonies, which often come at them in a spasmodic, speedy manner via technology. Chinnery elucidates how this cultural saturation in testimony can inure students to the voice of the first-order witness to trauma (see also Di Paolantonio, 2009, 2015). It may put them off of that voice: "Here we go again" may be the reaction students have, given the overwhelming cultural environment of highly personal testimony ("look at me!"). Chinnery shows how historical accounts of the events addressed in first order testimonies can sharpen students' awareness that it is not at all "here we go again" but rather "I have never truly seen and felt anything like this." As I will touch on below, with that realization students may themselves become a bit traumatized, or at any rate deeply marked emotionally by their encounter with the truth of human experience when it is under harsh pressure.

Historians and moral witnesses can trigger a sense of solidarity with people in the past, present, and future. *Solidarity* is a familiar term, connoting a mode of relationship, kinship, and comradeship pivoting around shared concerns. From the perspective of bearing witness, the term fuses with remembrance as a state of mind and heart. Put another way, solidarity and remembrance are ways of moving in the world—of orienting oneself toward others and the predicaments of human life. Like names and "Things," their value is not instrumental, as if they are mere "tools" to deploy in pursuing ends, or as if their value depends on the relative success of their "application." José Medina (2013) expresses this theme in a timely manner.

> The past is renewed in and through our interpretative practices; it is rendered present in our lives through interpretations that are always the result of re-descriptions and negotiations from the vantage point of the present informed by our current vision

of the future. For this reason, our past is *incessantly novel*: we make it and remake it, incessantly, in every present. But here an important worry arises: *the worry of instrumentalization*. We can do harm to past subjects by instrumentalizing their struggles, by co-opting their voices and experiences and using them for our own purposes. If forgetting or ignoring past subjects and their struggles can be unjust, we also commit injustices by spoilating past lives. (p. 287)

Consider also James Hatley's (2000) concern starkly expressed in his study of witnessing: "[H]umans show the reprehensible capacity to turn their history, their remembrance of time across the aeons, the generations, into a sort of narcissistic mirror. One eliminates all the strangers, all the disruptions of one's own vision, so that one's history only articulates one's own concerns, one's own needs. One writes the past and the future as a mode of colonization. All the other times are resources for one's own" (p. 63). Hatley's and Medina's remarks call to mind the moral witness's worries about wrongful trespass. They point to how studying moral witnesses and historians, in combination, can help students perceive how they themselves can steer clear of wrongful trespass in engaging the lives of others. Trespass they must, as must witnesses and historians. The alternative is isolation and silence. But they can do so in an emerging spirit of humility as well as of participation—that is, beginning to see themselves as participants in the moral well-being of the world.

*Do Second-Order Witnesses Constitute an Elite?*

Bearing witness differs from other forms of observing, studying, examining, questioning, probing, and so forth, all of which may be perfectly appropriate and warranted in particular contexts, while in others they may be troubling if not hurtful. But as argued here, bearing witness just is an ethical and moral orientation. The moral points to whether a witness's regard for and treatment of others is characterized by respect, concern, fairness, and other related qualities. The ethical points to the witness's willingness and concrete dedication to bettering themselves: for example, becoming more sensitive to others' sufferings rather than less so; becoming more attentive to seemingly ordinary, everyday events and gestures rather than less so; becoming more capable of speaking justly of such things rather than less so; and more along these same lines. This image of a moral and ethical ascent is another way to express the educational value of studying witnesses' work. They provoke readers to move outside of, and higher than, self-complacency and self-comfort. They do not dictate to them or preach at them. Their witnesses, in themselves, call out, invite, and touch recipients who are willing to let their guard down.

However, talk of a moral and ethical ascent may conjure Romantic images of an elite vanguard. Sebald, Césaire, and Whitman are certainly unusual figures. They are well-educated with respect to reading and study (Whitman largely self-taught) and, though hardly well-to-do, could organize the time to undertake their respective witnesses. And yet, countless contemporaries had such affordances but never bore witness; these figures did. Posed differently, while the witnesses mimic various conventional beliefs and biases of their eras, such facts are not interesting in themselves precisely because virtually everyone around them harbored the same conventional beliefs and biases. What *is* interesting is their attempts to step outside of or beyond convention. The three are unusual in their remarkable commitment to heed a summons and to follow it through to a resolution. These aspects are why their works speak to contemporary concerns and hopes, and why, in my view, they will continue to do so to future generations. This prospect contrasts with the fate of the vast majority of works published in a given era, which speak only to their own times (and, to be sure, sometimes invaluably so). As Anna Julia Cooper (2016) remarks, every generation seems to have its "isms" that "have their day and pass away" (p. 88).

If the three figures constitute an elite, it would be in the spirit of what the political theorist Benjamin Barber dubbed "an aristocracy of everyone." His term of art points to democratic conditions which, in principle, would support any person to ascend morally and ethically as individuals and as citizens—and, indeed, to bear witness if summoned to do so. Robert Harvey echoes this point is describing what he calls "witnessness": "the state, condition or potential for being a witness" (2010, p. x). Harvey admires well-known witnesses such as James Baldwin, but argues that the role is accessible to anyone with the mind-set and tenacity to enact it. In so arguing, he calls to mind Plato's familiar claim that education does not mean pouring knowledge into people, but rather what Plato calls "turning the soul" toward high and worthy moral aims. Plato contends that this capacity "to reach for the Good" is universal, though it requires education to be fully unleashed and developed. His point mirrors why bearing witness has its own built-in educational requirements which, as we have seen, include learning to cultivate oneself ethically and learning as much as possible about the circumstances of those to whom one is attending.

*Bearing Witness and Degrees of Activism*

Bearing witness is not a synonym with political activism in the familiar sense of that term. Certainly, in other realms of their lives, witnesses can be activists. Césaire is a case in point. Though he composed his *Cahier* before running for political office, he continued to refine it over the years, ever-expanding his witness even while serving as a mayor and later parliamentarian. Whitman, on his part, held several jobs as a journalist and often enunciated strong political positions (such as his opposition to slavery). But most of the witnesses mentioned in this book, ranging from Svetlana Alexievich and James Baldwin to Etty Hillesum and W. G. Sebald, did not lead causes, organize political action, or run for office.

Consider Baldwin's testimony in Raoul Peck's documentary, *I Am Not Your Negro* (produced in 2016). Baldwin explicitly describes his role in the civil rights movement of the 1950s and '60s to be that of a witness. In a narrative recollection of a journey he once undertook with the activist Medgar Evers, Baldwin describes how his witness is complementary to, yet distinct from, the work of the Black Panthers, the NAACP, and Martin Luther King Jr.

> As a member of the NAACP, Medgar was investigating the murder of a black man, which had occurred months before, had shown me letters from black people asking him to do this, and he had asked me to come with him. I was terribly frightened, but perhaps that fieldtrip will help us define what I mean by the word "witness." I was to discover that the line which separates a witness from an actor is a very thin line indeed. Nevertheless, the line is real. . . . I did not have to deal with the criminal state of Mississippi, hour by hour and day by day, to say nothing of night after night. I did not have to sweat cold sweat after decisions involving hundreds of thousands of lives. I was not responsible for raising money, or deciding how to use it. I was not responsible for strategy controlling prayer-meetings, marches, petitions, voting registration drives. . . . I was never in town to stay. This was sometimes hard on my morale, but I had to accept, as time wore on, that part of my responsibility,

as a witness, was to move as largely and as freely as possible. To write the story, and to get it out. (Peck, 2016, 20:35–23:05; for extended commentary, see Glaude [2020, pp. 29–55])

"To get it out" evokes the impulse that drove other witnesses whom we have met in these pages. Baldwin's orientation calls to mind Whitman's declaration in *Song of Myself*: "I witness and I wait" (4). Whitman's passion for democracy does not lead him to organize a movement or form a political party. Rather, it spurs him to dive ever deeper into the possibilities of poetry for conveying ideas, feelings, and commitments that he sees as constitutive of a democratic orientation.

Could Baldwin and Whitman have sustained their witnesses had they thrown themselves, like Césaire, into political leadership and direct action? The answer is: perhaps. Perhaps they could have marshaled the extraordinary energy it would have taken to undertake both endeavors and to enact them responsibly. Perhaps they could have maintained the distance indispensable to bearing witness alongside the need for proximity. But the central point is that the world needs both witnesses and political activists in the fullness of what each can uniquely bring forward. The one can support the aims of the other.

This state of affairs resembles the relationship between philosophy and action. Karl Marx famously declared that the purpose of philosophy is not just to understand the world, but to help change it. I do not hear him stating that all philosophers, much less all thoughtful people, must therefore become public activists—a forcing that would contradict the very idea of social justice. Marx's own experience as a scholar showed him that understanding the world is in and of itself an enormous, never-ending undertaking. Philosophers and witnesses can help a great deal here given how well-positioned they are for this task. For witnesses, their distance from and yet also self-chosen nearness to human affairs provides them a distinctive perspective of great value to any project of justice. They can help, indirectly, generate an ethical rationale or warrant for a given course of action. They can conjure images of justice that can inspire and sustain people. As crucially as anything, they—alongside artists of all stripes and persuasions—can trigger a living sense of remembrance without which any movement toward justice may be ephemeral. Thus, while witnesses do not generate blueprints for action, they do illuminate what it means *to engage the world with care*, in whatever humans do and despite their many limitations as the creatures they are.

Roger Simon's work on what he and his colleagues (2005, pp. 104–131) call "witness as study" nicely captures the ways in which careful reading and discussion of witnesses can fuel moral and political imagination which can, in turn, trigger action however modest the scale may be (it is worth keeping in view that a democratic way of life constitutes, in large part, a myriad of modest, that is, quite local, non-overtly-political interactions that keep communication between people alive). There are other valuable consequences of reading witnesses, including a deepened appreciation for artful writing and how it can influence human sensibilities, a renewal of personal hope, and an inspiration to bear witness oneself. Precisely because there is always much ethical work to do in the world, all of these potential educational consequences are valuable.

Simon and colleagues pair the idea of witness as study with what they call "witness as obligation." They argue that there is always a further step readers can take, namely (as indicated earlier), to fuse self-transformation with concrete action. Again, such action can take many forms. For example, Elizabeth Dutro (2011, 2013) makes use of the concept witness to illuminate moments when it can be timely, if not indispensable in her view, for a teacher to share testimony about a personal life trauma when offering support to a student experiencing a trauma of their own. In such instances, which Dutro characterizes as "critical witnessing," teacher and student can become witnesses to one another's testimony, with potentially generative consequences for both to become more at home in the classroom. Dutro emphasizes how important such moments can be in working with children from disadvantaged backgrounds who may be facing trying circumstances. At the same time, she cautions teachers to be mindful of not crossing a line: neither forcing their own experiences on students nor prying inappropriately into a student's personal life, and while also being mindful of issues of teacher authority and power.[5]

Michal Givoni (2014) suggests that an orientation of bearing witness can "re-enchant" practitioners in fields such as medicine that, to some, have become increasingly impersonal and rationalistic in their approach to people. She examines how the international organization, Doctors Without Borders, has revitalized the idealism and sense of hope of many doctors who feel alienated from contemporary institutionalized medicine. Givoni dubs their volunteer medical work "humanitarian witnessing." They serve willingly—not unlike, in a way, Walt Whitman—in parts of the world riven by war, drought, and other calamities. "Witnessing," she writes, becomes "translated into a multilayered set of practices designed to create a sense of proximity with otherwise distant suffering, such as providing effective assistance on the spot, observing the plight of the victims firsthand, getting to know their culture and their cause, and conveying one's personal impressions upon one's return" (134). "Witnessing in this straightforward and politically unassuming version," she goes on to say, "functioned as an antidote to the mounting legitimacy crisis of the medical profession and provided a conduit for the re-enchantment of physicians. It offered a replicable trajectory of self-making that could, to quote a declaration by [the organization's] founders, 'put in practice the idealism that lies dormant deep inside every physician, and without which a physician risks being nothing but a merchant'" (p. 134).[6]

Dutro's work and the work of the many idealistic, inspired practitioners in Doctors Without Borders disclose ways in which the idea of bearing witness emerges as a response to trauma. In turn, these responses evoke the witness of figures such as Sebald, Césaire, and Whitman, though the latter are typically far more systematic and longitudinal in nature and, as we have seen, issue in truly powerful, universal attestations. In this respect, it is important to retain the critical edge in the idea of bearing witness as portrayed in this book. There are limits to what the concept can contain, beyond which it loses its distinctive focus and value. Bearing witness is not a matter of choice, as such, but depends crucially on a summons from the world. Nor is the orientation synonymous with every endeavor that centers on moral concern and justice. There are countless occasions when other valuable concepts will be far more to the point (including "concern" and "justice" themselves).

All the same, it seems to me there are numerous forms of bearing witness—in prose, speech, film, poetry, painting, and more—that can embody the inductively derived criteria of bearing witness examined in chapter 1, if (again) often in a less extended or systematic manner. The criteria include (1) heeding what has summoned the witness, (2) immersing themselves in others' lives and firsthand testimony, (3) devoting whatever time is necessary to realize (make real) one's witness, (4) studying intensively the circumstances involved, (5) working continuously on their ethical capacities to heed the reality of others, and, finally, (6) rendering their witness in an accessible and compelling form.

*The Psychological Delicacy and Risks in Teaching Moral Witnesses*

To teach witnesses in educational settings will call on participants' patience, tenacity, and faith that the endeavor is worthwhile. Part of this commitment will entail heeding possible emotional and other psychological vulnerabilities on the part of students.[7] First-order testimony from those who suffered in concentration camps, under conditions of slavery, or on fields of war, as well as second-order witnessing of the same events, can potentially trouble and disturb students. As Simon and colleagues write, such testimony can constitute a "difficult inheritance" (2005, pp. 104–131, *passim*) precisely because it can be challenging to face up to the realities of others' suffering. Moreover, it can be hard to entertain the fact that people just like oneself, and in similar uncoerced circumstances, let such suffering occur in the first place, either through indifference, moral weakness, ignorance, or some other factor. Students may discover how easy it is to be both implicated in unjust events and yet also oblivious to them. These experiences can generate strong, unanticipated emotions that may negate or at any rate throw off track the educational purposes behind such an engagement.

As part of the important, inaugurating work on bearing witness that Laub and Felman (1992) undertook, Felman describes at length a course she taught that featured extensive first-order testimony from Holocaust survivors. In visceral, sometimes excruciating detail, she describes how anguished, heartbroken, confused, and angry some students became in response to this testimony. Their anger was variously targeted toward humanity itself for breeding such appalling cruelty, and toward their teacher for compelling them to face up to it. It bears noting that, at the time of Felman's teaching, the internet was in a nascent state and had yet to appear with its incessant bombardment of shallow, ultimately numbing scenes of horrors across history. Many of Felman's students were encountering Holocaust testimony for the first time. However, even in today's flooded visual environment, students can be strongly affected by sustained, educational involvements with witnesses that combine slow, in-depth reading alongside other media. There have been heavy hearts and occasional tears in classes I have taught on the subject.

*Pedagogical sensitivity* will be key watchwords here, alongside considering students' age and background experience. Teachers and discussion leaders can facilitate matters by providing historical background and speaking directly about both the meanings and the challenges in reading witnesses. As we have seen, the recipient of a witness cannot remain passive. They are called on to respond. But this beckoning does not necessitate putting on their shoulders the full weight of others' trauma and loss, as if they must become like the figure Atlas in ancient myth who was required by the gods to carry the whole earth on his back. As outlined in the

Preface and in chapter 1, part of engaging a witness is learning how to read them, since the forms they deploy differ from reading journalists, historians, research articles, blogs, and more. Second-order witnesses themselves indirectly show readers how to read them and, thereby, come in touch with the moral and ethical power in bearing witness. An attentive teacher can draw this "showing" out from the texts, and thereby help position students to feel genuinely the touch of the past but not to be sundered emotionally by that encounter.

Despite the potential risks in heeding moral witnesses, it remains important to press ahead with the task. For one thing, as Megan Boler (1999), Mark Jonas (2010), Avi Mintz (2012, 2013, 2017), and others have persuasively argued, pain or suffering accompanies the process of education (as contrasted with socialization and enculturation, which carry their own difficulties and intermittent sufferings). No education is possible without the friction that the encounter with new ideas, new ways of thinking, and hitherto unknown facts can generate. This encounter often necessitates suffering, or pains of a kind, as learners have to abandon previous assumptions and understandings, live with uncertainty, and undertake the work of reading carefully, listening acutely, writing competently, and more.

To be sure, dedicated teachers do not want such pains of learning to be debilitating. But they also refuse to patronize students and deny them the powerful forms of growth and personal realization that genuine educational experiences can provide. As I have sought to illustrate here, to study witnesses can help students deepen their understanding of what it is to be a human being: to be prone to mistakes and moral failures, to become aware of what it is to harm others and to be harmed, to grasp what it means to truly attend to others, and so much more. All of this can give rise to a richer and more complex moral understanding of themselves and of the world.

For another thing, if students are to be positioned to make a positive difference in the affairs of life, then an education that features moral witnesses becomes all the more important. There is both insight and inspiration to be gained from the tremendous effort moral witnesses put into heeding the summons that compels them. They shed ethical light on paths toward the truth of life and toward the sense of moral responsibility that witnesses themselves feel so deeply. They show how vital it is to resist the all-too-human temptation, in the face of historical and contemporary injustices, to say: "I was not there" or "I didn't contribute to it." For Sebald, Césaire, and Whitman, to withdraw to such a posture is to give the perpetrators of injustice the victory they seek: that people remain indifferent and silent, with their backs turned.

## Conclusion: Bearing Witness and Participation Across Time and Space

Responsibility is not blame or guilt. It is participation. It is solidarity. It is walking alongside. It is listening and, when the time calls for it, speaking and acting. Put another way, responsibility is remembrance. As framed here, remembrance is not synonymous with memory. Rather, it forms part of how a person moves in the world: what they notice, and the significance they attach to it. Remembrance fuels perceptual transition from regarding things as objects to seeing them as Things, to recall Rilke's poetic term of art for how a person can more fully inhabit and respond to the world. Remembrance is nothing "heavy" as such. On the contrary, it is gratitude for the capacity to care in the face of events marked by carelessness, as well as for the capacity to note moments where care sparkles, including in the most fleeting of gestures and touches.

As discussed above, formal education can cultivate and refine people's sense of remembrance, including through engagement with witnesses in the company of teachers and peers. That process can complement, and sometimes counterbalance, life's own day by day, moment by moment tuition. Whitman evokes what the outcome might look like when he considers the countless influences across time and space that have brought him into the world, beginning from the very birth of the cosmos.

> Rise after rise bow the phantoms behind me,
> Afar down I see the huge first Nothing . . .
> I know I was even there. . . . I waited unseen . . .
> Long I was hugged close. . . . long long.
> Immense have been the preparations for me,
> Faithful and friendly the arms that have helped me.
> Cycles ferried my cradle, rowing and rowing like cheerful boatmen;
> For room to me stars kept aside in their own rings,
> They sent influences to look after what was to hold me.

> Before I was born out of my mother generations guided me . . .
> All forces have been steadily employed to complete and
>   delight me,
> Now I stand on this spot with my soul. (44)

Whitman's vast witness here to time and space, in which he discovers himself to be at home, echoes Bruce Snider's image of breath passed forward, and then forward again. Both poets conjure the idea of remembrance as itself a way of moving in time and space. This emerging sensibility holds in presence the reality that past, present, and future are all one.

For millennia, people have inherited many Things from the past: hopes, aspirations, ideas, ways of seeing and feeling, culture itself. These Things have been dynamic; people have transformed them through their own singular and generational experience. They bequeath Things in turn to those who come after. However, as touched on at the start of the chapter, long-standing cultural rhythms appear to be unusually precarious in our time. The unique, rapidly changing relationship between today's technology and social and political life, to which should be added the fraught reality of climate change, can feel like a sudden break in human continuity. It can make the appeal to remembrance, so constitutive of the witness's endeavor, seem like an elegiac swan song.

That would be a false interpretation, though of the three witnesses I have attended to Sebald comes the closest to embodying it, albeit not fully. He regrets what he judges to be the incessant commodification of cultural values and achievements, where history is converted into theme parks, knick-knacks, and numbingly homogeneous representations in films and elsewhere, and where self-commodification—"marketing'" oneself in a market-driven cultural ethos—displaces holistic self-formation, a crucial element of which is regard for others and nature. Sebald worries about a deepening alienation between humanity and nature, materialized visibly in the continued destruction of the natural environment. At one point, as mentioned in chapter 2, he quotes a pained remark by Johann Wolfgang von Goethe: "Our world is a cracked bell that no longer sounds" (in Sebald, 1996, p. 220).

Césaire and Whitman are also mindful of cultural and human loss. Césaire feels the fragility of historical consciousness, how easy it is to dissolve a vivid link with inheritances from the past, which include important philosophical questions alongside particular ideas, values, and practices. For Césaire, this vivid link constitutes another term for remembrance, which as we have seen is dynamic in its appeal to persons to see themselves in time and space. Whitman is not complacent about social changes he pictures occurring around him. He sees at play the substitution of economic and business interests for the interests of democracy itself. In the lines between his lines, he laments the erosion of the artisanal, community-based life he had seen all around him as a boy and youth. As noted in chapter 4, he is at times anguished by what he sees as the political and economic corruptions of his time.

Such concerns have been amplified, in ever-changing ways, in contemporary discourses in the academy, in journalism, and across various media. The issues remain uncertain, unresolved, and tense, in part because they are *so very present*. They press on people in ways that make it difficult to gain reflective distance. Here moral witnesses come into their own once more. Whatever their personal fears and anxieties may have been, Sebald, Césaire, and Whitman point in their witnesses to inextinguishable features of an underlying human quest for meaning in conjunction with justice. However thwarted that quest has often been, its sheer persistence enchants if not amazes. It is the very sine qua non of bearing witness, just as it is the sine qua non of education itself. All three witnesses attest to having been moved, in their singular ways, by a profound educational experience expressed by another moral witness, James Baldwin: "You think your pain and your heartbreak are unprecedented in the history of the world, but then you read. It was books that taught me that the things that tormented me most were the very things that connected me with all the people who were alive, or who had ever been alive" (1964).

Education is inconceivable in an ethos of cynicism, jadedness, or hopelessness. It presumes belief in humane, thoughtful, and beneficent growth, for both individuals and communities. I read all three witnesses as claiming education is also justified by the outcome of the careful, concerned modes of attending they enact. For them, as I have sought to show, the world discloses endless testimony regarding the reality of justice, beauty, and truth, however threatened and vulnerable they remain. To see what they see does not require comparable acts of bearing witness, as such. It requires participation, a stepping into the turbulent stream of life rather than remaining on barren shores of resignation or entrenchment. No hurrahs here, the witness avers, only heeding what is always there.

# Acknowledgments

As countless authors have attested, composing a book occurs in solitude, but it is not a solitary undertaking. Many persons have affected my approach to bearing witness. I lack the space to name them all here, but the influence of the following individuals has been pronounced: the students in several courses I have taught on the topic for their moving, enlightening responses to the figures whom we studied; Rebecca Sullivan and Yuval Dwek, who each cotaught with me in a particular iteration of the course, and whose insights and sensitive appreciations continue to enhance my thinking; Yuval Dwek for putting forward many generative questions and suggestions regarding the book (which resulted, for example, in the creation of its preface); Simón Ganitsky for his exceptionally fine-grained reading of the manuscript and his wide-ranging insights, of which I have freely availed myself; Vik Joshi for a yearlong, systematic conversation on bearing witness with respect to W. G. Sebald and the practice of teaching; Erina Iwasaki and John Keenan for generously reading the entire manuscript and offering heartening responses; Kirsten Welch for outstanding bibliographic assistance and rewarding philosophical conversation; audiences where I have presented on themes in this book, including the Philosophy of Education Society; the American Educational Research Association; and my own institution, Teachers College, Columbia University; and three anonymous reviewers for SUNY Press who provided timely and trenchant criticism. My other intellectual debts can be found in the footnotes and references.

I also thank the superb writer (and my dear friend) Caroline Heller, for both lengthy, informing conversations about bearing witness, and for introducing me to the work of W. G. Sebald by inviting me to join her at what became his last public reading in the United States—at the famed

92nd Street YMCA in New York City—on October 15, 2001, only weeks before his death in a car accident. I have taken inspiration from Ruth Jean Simmons, former president of Smith College, Brown University, and Prairie View A&M University. We discussed her excellent, unpublished dissertation (completed in 1973) on Aimé Césaire's poetics, which in many respects anticipates central themes scholars would take up in more recent years.

I am grateful to my editor at SUNY Press, Richard Carlin, for his support and encouragement of this project. I also much appreciate the professionalism of Diane Ganeles and others at the Press, who have rendered the whole process of publication rewarding.

Last, but hardly least, my sincere gratitude to Rachel Wahl for composing such an elegant foreword to this book. Her first-rate scholarship and her moral vision walk hand in hand, in a spirit Ivan Doig captures in his novel, *The Whistling Season*: "*Lux desiderium universitatis*: Light is the desire of the universe."

Portions of various chapters have been published previously and have been reworked here with kind permission from the publishers:

Some elements in chapter 1 appeared in earlier form in Hansen, David T. 2017. "Bearing Witness to Teaching and Teachers." *Journal of Curriculum Studies*, 49 (1): 7–23; Hansen, David T. 2017. "Among School Teachers: Bearing Witness as an Orientation in Educational Inquiry." *Educational Theory*, 67 (1): 9–30; Hansen, D. T. 2021. *Reimagining the Call to Teach: A Witness to Teaching and Teachers* (New York: Teachers College Press); and Hansen, David T. and Sullivan, Rebecca. 2022. "What Renders a Witness Trustworthy? Existential and Curricular Notes on a Mode of Educational Inquiry." *Studies in Philosophy and Education* 41 (2): 151"172. Some elements in chapter 2 appeared in Hansen, David T. 2012. "W. G. Sebald and the tasks of ethical and moral remembrance." *Philosophy of Education* 2012: 125–133. Finally, a portion of chapter 4 appeared in Hansen, David T. and Dwek, Yuval. 2023. "Cultivating Cosmopolitan and Democratic Imagination in Education: The Voice of the Poet." In Julian Culp, Johannes Drerup, and Douglas Yacek (Eds.), *The Cambridge Handbook of Democratic Education*: 395–415.

# Notes

## Chapter 1

1. See Roger I. Simon's (2005) pioneering studies of bearing witness for further discussion of the differences and similarities between the first- and second-order witness.

2. In their influential study of first order witnessing to the Holocaust, Dori Laub and Shoshana Feldman (1992, pp. 75–76, *passim*) conceive a different typology of bearing witness. They refer to three "levels": (1) the survivor who attests to personal experience of trauma; (2) a sympathetic confidant, who may have specially trained skills, who listens and supports the survivor through the ordeal of surfacing horrible memories; and (3) the third-level witness who contemplates the intimate interaction of first- and second-level witnesses and attempts to share with them, and possibly others, whatever insights they have gained about the process as well as lessons that might apply to humanity as a whole.

3. It is incalculable how many scholars and commentators deploy the terms *witness* and *bearing witness*. However, in almost all cases they are words rather than *concepts*. Formal conceptualizations of the term are comparatively rare. The most illuminating and systematic of these include Felman and Laub, 1992; Givoni, 2016; Hatley, 2000; Kramer and Weigel, 2017; Oliver, 2001; Simon, 2005; and Wieviorka, 2006. While I have learned from these important studies, none of them frames bearing witness in the manner that follows. This framework constitutes not a distillation, as such, but an inductive, fresh path influenced directly by my reading of Sebald, Césaire, Whitman, and other witnesses, as well as by my extensive witness of persons in war and of teachers' work and testimony, as touched on in the Preface.

4. This notion of heeding a summons, which I will further elucidate as we proceed, constitutes what I understand to be a key motivation for the witness. As such, the idea differs from Avishai Margalit's conception (2002, especially chapter 5) of what he calls "a moral witness," which, in his view, denotes a person animated

from the start by overt, pre-established, and clearly enunciated moral purposes. In my view, Sebald, Césaire, and Whitman *become* moral witnesses—persons profoundly concerned about others—precisely through tethering themselves to what has called or summoned them.

5. As we will see in chapter 4, the poet Walt Whitman ascribes to the terms *loaf* and *loafer*, which are typically associated with laziness, a strongly positive association of waiting and lingering. As he remarks in the opening lines of his "Song of Myself": "I loafe [sic] and invite my soul, / I lean and loafe at my ease." Michel de Montaigne, the 16th-century essayist who many critics argue invented the very form of the essay, inserts as his first text in his collected works a short piece simply titled "On Idleness." But he is anything but idle, in the usual sense of that term associated with boredom and lassitude. Idleness becomes a mode of sustained self-scrutiny alongside ever-deepening attentiveness to the passing moments of his life and times. He does not seek to "produce," but to respond.

6. For further discussion of these dimensions of witnessing and their bearing on trust, see Hansen and Sullivan (2022).

7. Giorgio Agamben (2002) elucidates a perspective on what can be summarized as the "impossibility" of bearing witness to what transpired in the Nazi extermination camps, based on his view of the limitations of language and of comprehension in the face of the sheer, impenetrable reality of the event. For sympathetic commentary in a context of educational practice, see Marie Hallender's study (2012). The witnesses I am addressing here *feel* as well as think the truth that no witness can ever be morally complete, much less perfect, but that the endeavor remains warranted and can yield a meaningful, generative issue.

8. Whitman's injunction here echoes countless other poets' attempts to ward off being read in a reductionist manner. For example, the 17th-century poet-philosopher-playwright Sor Juana Inés de la Cruz (2016) writes of her chagrin at how her fervid fans reduce her and her work into a caricature.

> I am not she of whom you think,
> unless over there you give me
> another being through your plumes,
> on your lips, another breath;
> as though a stranger to myself,
> among your quills I wander,
> not as I am, but as you see
> and what you wished to imagine. ("Ballad 51," lines 13–20, p. 156)

9. The wide-ranging literature on Césaire, in both French and English, cuts across many subfields in literary analysis, Caribbean studies, Black Diaspora studies, and more. The literature features considerable debate regarding Césaire's fundamental artistic, cultural, and political views, even while every critic regards

his *Journal of a Homecoming* as one of the great poems of the modern era. There is also a highly diverse literature on Sebald, in multiple languages including English, whose mode of composition in the works examined here has been intensely addressed and has led to an ever-growing stream of works of fiction and other forms of prose he has inspired—just as Césaire's extensive published poetry has had a marked impact on subsequent generations of poets.

The scholarly literature on Whitman is even more pronounced, such that it's unclear whether even the most industrious specialist studying 24/7 could ever come to grips with it all. There are numerous biographies alongside countless books and articles. There is even a journal, *Walt Whitman Quarterly Review*, founded in 1983 on the heels of two previous long-standing reviews of work on him. This journal has published hundreds of articles and bibliographies on Whitman's life and work. My sense from having dipped liberally in this literature is that seemingly every claim over the last 150 years made by a given scholar about Whitman as person and/or as poet has been contested or reconstructed by another. Moreover, the literature reveals what seems to be the fundamental elusiveness of the man Whitman with respect to who he "really" was and what his poems "really" mean (cf. his own testimony touched on previously). I make no claims about these realities, save one: that "Song of Myself" and *Memoranda During the War*—like the works by Sebald and Césaire I take up—shed light in a distinctive, moving manner on the very notion of bearing witness as a moral orientation toward the human condition.

## Chapter 2

1. On a personal note, I had occasion to attend a reading Sebald gave from his writing at the 92nd Street Y in New York City, on October 15, 2001. I remember vividly the deep timbre and steady rhythm of his voice as he read, as well as his subtle, self-deprecating good humor in the discussion he held afterward on the stage with André Aciman and Susan Sontag, both of whom had introduced him and his work to the audience.

2. Page numbers from the three will be noted by the letters *E*, *R*, and *A*, respectively. E: *The Emigrants* (1996), originally published (1992) as *Die Ausgewanderten: Vier lange Erzählungen* (The Emigrants: Four Long Stories); R: *The Rings of Saturn* (1998), originally published (1995) as *Die Ringe Des Saturn: Eine Englische Wallfahrt* (The Rings of Saturn: An English Pilgrimage); A: *Austerlitz* (2001), originally published (2001) under the same title in German. A previous work—titled *Vertigo* (2000), originally published (1990) as *Schwindel. Gefuhle* (Dizziness. Feelings)—marked Sebald's first major foray into his distinctive oeuvre. It features a set of four "studies," as he dubs them, with three modeled after well-known writers, including Franz Kafka.

3. Sebald based some of his fictionalized characters on living people, including members of his extended family as well as individuals who are Jewish. He did not always consult with them, or acknowledge them in his works, and several have reported being angry that Sebald incorporated aspects of their personalities and actual doings. This question of artistic license is as old as literature itself, or certainly as old as the novel, a genre in which authors constantly raid the lives of real people for material without ever letting them know. The issue intensifies (and bewilders) in Sebald's case because of his sincere attempt at restitution for what his nation did to the Jews of Europe. In her recent biography of Sebald, Carole Angier (2021) offers no apologia for his malfeasances, or for novelists in general. However, in a nonmoralistic, nuanced, and dignified manner, she vindicates Sebald's oeuvre—namely, how invaluable its sheer existence is—while criticizing some of his decisions. She provides a thoughtful defense of the integrity of both art and of human beings.

4. For biographical details, see Angier's (2021) biography, Deane Blackler's (2007) appreciative study, and Philippa Comber's (2014) memoir of her friendship with Sebald.

5. This same route has since become something of a pilgrimage for a wide array of scholars, writers, artists, and others taken by Sebald's work. See, for example, the documentary entitled *Patience: After Sebald* (2012), and http://www.guardian.co.uk/books/video/2011/jan/25/sebald-suffolk-walk-documentary-video.

6. See also Sebald's set of essays, *Campo Santo* (2005, pp. 13–14), where he refers to the "logically indecipherable laws" of history.

7. Sebald's initial reputation in the English-speaking world hung, in part, on the label of being a "Holocaust writer" despite his avoidance of the term. Scholars have shown that his oeuvre can be read, more broadly, as a sustained meditation on where and how modernity, with all its hopes and dreams of progress, has gone awry. See, for example, J. J. Long's (2007) book-length study, as well as essays in J. J. Long and Anne Whitehead (2004).

8. The name of this town is Sonthofen, where Sebald moved as a child of seven from his birthplace in Wertach (about 10 miles away), and first encountered the teacher after whom he models this chapter. Sebald's Kafkaesque move in denoting the town "S" distances the writing from autobiography, while also jarring the reader's conventional habits of reading.

9. See the published interviews in Schwartz (2007) as well as the in-depth material in Angier (2021).

10. For a rich and wide-ranging discussion of this influence, see Elon (2002).

11. The reader of these books soon notices how often people give or, better, *entrust* things to the narrator: a mother's memoir, a box of photographs, travel diaries, books, an old business card, and more. The reader notes, too, that the narrator seems to be the *listener* for whom many individuals have unknowingly been waiting (for example, A43, R47).

12. Another recurring theme in Sebald's writing is the unexpected, unexplainable coincidences, correspondences, and affinities that ultimately, in his view, connect everything in the cosmos. For discussion, see Friedrichsmeyer (2006). Sebald mirrors this theme here in calling Ferber "Max," which was the name that Sebald's own friends and associates called him and which appears on his gravestone in Framingham Earl, Norfolk (his full name was Winfried Georg Maximilian Sebald). Here in *The Emigrants*, Sebald places himself, symbolically, in the role of a lost son to Luisa Ferber, one who aspires to understand her experience and to remember.

13. For discussion of the ethical relation between names and remembrance, see Margalit (2002, pp. 18–26). To anticipate the next chapter, also consider Aimé Césaire's commitment as poet to be as specific as possible in his oeuvre: "If I name with precision . . . it is because in naming precisely, I believe that one restores an object's personal value . . . it's value as strength, it's strength-value. . . . In naming objects, it's an enchanted world" (in Scharfman, 2010, p. 115). Naming can also be an act of remembrance. At one point in his epic poem, *Journal of a Homecoming*, Césaire explicitly names several slaves as an act against the anonymity imposed by the colonial order (see stanzas 135 and 136).

14. See the essays in the beautifully produced volume edited by Lise Pratt (2007), as well as the comprehensive treatment of Sebald's photos in Clive Scott and Nick Warr (2023); also see Maya Barzilai (2006). Sebald implies that photography stands as a metaphor for the writing process. Truth can "develop"—like a developing print in an old-time darkroom—in a "solution" of careful inquiry and equally careful handling of what one learns (cf. A77).

15. Wittgenstein has in mind understanding another culture. Elsewhere, he deploys comparable language in urging the need to either find or generate "intermediate cases" to help people gain clarity on their use of terms (1953, p. 49e [PI 122]).

16. In an interview, Sebald remarked that he had Wittgenstein's work with children in mind when he penned the story on Bereyter. He mentions, with no further elaboration—perhaps because it becomes plain in the story itself—that Bereyter shared with Wittgenstein the same "moral radicalism" about education (Angier, 2007, pp. 72–73). It bears adding that Sebald himself tried, and failed, to launch a career as a primary school teacher. He served for less than a year in a remote village school in the Alps, not far from where Wittgenstein taught.

17. Claudia Eppert, Mark Clamen, Laura Beres, and Roger Simon lend perspective on this mode of inquiry in their analysis of what they call "witness as study" (in Simon, 2005, 105–131).

18. References to email, social media, cell phones, computers, and other contemporary communications technology are conspicuously absent in the pages of these books.

19. In his appreciative essay on Robert Walser, touched on previously, Sebald (2013) describes Walser as "a clairvoyant of the small" (p. 139)—not to be confused with the insignificant—and he seems to have metabolized this capacity himself.

20. Ironically, and painfully, the narrator's *bildung* (formation as a person) also positions him to turn the *Bildungsroman* (novels of human formation) tradition on its head, with his accounts in *The Emigrants* of the unraveling rather than the building up of lives (cf. Summers-Bremner, 2004, p. 323). For a wide-ranging perspective on Sebald and *bildung*, in a context of curriculum theory and architecture, see Crichlow et al. (2023).

21. Sebald's and Richter's practices intersect in their deliberate use of blurred images of historical events, a tactic that embodies questions about our ethical perspicuity as well claims to know and understand.

22. For an extended response to Sebald's statement, see Baxter, Henitiuk, and Hutchinson (2015).

## Chapter 3

1. Numerous scholars have argued that *Cahier*, with its author's deep intertextual awareness of classical works, merits the label "epic" because of its powerful engagement with universal as well as particular aspects of the human condition. For example, F. Abiola Irele, an extraordinarily learnèd interpreter of Césaire's oeuvre, compares it to writings such as T. S. Eliot's *The Waste Land*, Walt Whitman's *Song of Myself* (see chapter 4), Gerald Manley Hopkins's *The Wreck of the Deutschland*, Samuel Taylor Coleridge's *The Rime of the Ancient Mariner*, and Arthur Rimbaud's *Le Bateau ivre* (*The Drunken Boat*), all of which express what Irele calls "a consciousness wrestling with the vicissitudes of a prior determination and of its progression toward a new mode of awareness and being" (2017, p. 66). A. James Arnold (1981), another accomplished scholar of Césaire's work, writes: "Like the epic of ancient Greece, [*Cahier*] claims to save from oblivion the past as a cultural community. Like the *Aeneid* it conveys a sense of origin and collective destiny. The *Notebook* begins and ends *in medias res*, as epic should do" (p. 168).

2. See Alex Gill's (2011) history of the editions for a sound argument about why the 1939 version is what he calls the "gravitational center" (p. 46) that gives coherence to the others. Arnold (2004, 2008) and Irele (2017, pp. 41–42 and footnote 22, p. 71) have also usefully examined the textual history of the poem.

3. Note the verb *to navel* in the epigram to this chapter, which is a translation of *omphale*, a term denoting the birth-giving "navel of the world." Césaire was doubtless aware of the great 19th-century poet Percy Bysshe Shelley's claim that "the poet is the unacknowledged legislator of the world," by which he meant, among other things, that poets illuminate possibilities that can then be pursued through politics.

4. For studies of Césaire's engagement with Homer alongside his transfiguration of Odyssean motifs, see Davis, 2007; Greenwood, 2010 (who addresses the

poet's relation with the Greek and Roman classics writ large); McConnell, 2013 (who dubs *Cahier* "a Martiniquan Ithaca," mindful of C. P. Cavafy's famous poem "Ithaka"); Nolden, 2015; and Zerba, 2021. With regards to Césaire's close study of Dante, see Allen, 2017, and Davis, 2016. Davis (1997, p. 22) remarks that the "Homeric shadow" anticipates "a central problematic of all literary homecomings: the indeterminate identity of the returning figure . . . and his painful social reintegration into a world whose horizons have been inevitably altered during his period of absence."

5. In a later interview, Césaire suggested the term *notebook* (*cahier*) mirrored his state of mind at the time he commenced writing it. "I had abandoned the idea of writing poems," he states; "all of traditional prosody hampered me a lot, paralyzed me. I wasn't happy. One fine day I said to myself 'After all, let's throw it all overboard.' Then I started to write what was closest to my heart. This is maybe why I took an extremely neutral title: notebook. It became in reality a poem. In other words, I discovered poetry the moment I turned my back on formal poetry" (quoted in Melas, 2016, p. 471).

6. I think here of Saidiya Hartman's (1997) hard-to-classify account of her sojourn in Ghana, where she sought to come to grips with her distant African past in conjunction with her all-too-present America. As with Sebald and Césaire, her writing features factual and fictional motifs in a manner which she variously calls "critical fabulation" (2008, p. 11) and "recombinant narrative" (p. 12). Her article casts helpful light on the dynamics of bearing witness (for discussion, see Hansen & Sullivan, 2021).

7. Michael Hamburger (1982), in his study of truth in poetry, refers to poets who aspire to "an imagery not subservient to argument" and to "a diction determined more by acoustic values than by semantic exigencies" (p. 21). For general discussion of Césaire's style, see Kesteloot (1991, pp. 177ff) and Simmons (1973, pp. 62–81).

8. A classic statement of surrealism is by André Breton (1978), whose work Césaire knew intimately alongside work by other poets inspired by the idea. Scharfman (2010, 115) writes that, for the surrealists, the priority of the poetic image over abstract analysis constitutes "the royal road that leads to an unconscious capable of transcending contradictions. Their research into the deep impulses of being, their renouncing of logic and their call to disalienation of the self through the primacy of desire all resonate with Césaire." This orientation encompasses procedures such as writing with no advance planning or forethought (teachers sometimes ask students to engage in "speed writing," where at a given signal the student starts writing in response to a prompt and does not stop for even a split second), side by side with trusting, in a free associationist manner, the unconscious and the "voice" of intuition. A representative sample of Césaire's poetry in its most intense surrealist mode is his volume *Corps perdu*, published in 1949 with illustrations by Pablo Picasso, whom Césaire first met in 1948.

9. On Césaire's deep knowledge of French poets, including Victor Hugo, Arthur Rimbaud, Isidore Ducasse (Comte de Lautréamont), Charles Baudelaire, and Stephane Mallarmé, see his essay "Poetry and Knowledge" (1990), one of a number of writings where he addresses these influences. For commentary, see, for example, Arnold (1981, pp. 65–70), Eshleman and Smith (1983, pp. 14ff), Irele (2017, passim), and Simmons (1973, pp. 24–33, 182–183). It bears emphasizing that, as can be seen in Césaire's pioneering oeuvre, none of these French writers speak *for* him. But they do speak *to* him just as, figuratively speaking, he replies back even as he moves beyond to his own singular mode of expression. With regards to the point of this chapter and book, Césaire speaks *to* and *with* all who read him and listen to his witness, even if he does not speak *about* their particular circumstances and concerns.

10. Among the helpful sources on this dynamic background are Edwards (2003) and Kesteloot (1991).

11. I mentioned previously that the poem is not an easy or light read (any more than are Sebald's works). Given the racism that continues to mark our era, readers may find Césaire's blunt, seemingly colonial-echoing condemnation hard to bear. "Must we hear this again?" some readers may be feeling. However, the poet's words are not gratuitous. His frankness, his highly detailed *directness*, constitutes a necessary phase in his metamorphosis from spectator to witness, as we will see.

12. Translators of the poem deploy this controversial term to translate the equally controversial French original, *nègre*, which has a comparable history of racism in its use by whites. The poet, as I read him, intends to shock and thereby throw the term's ugly meanings back in the face of colonialism, while also reconstructing the term for aesthetic and political purposes (see the ensuing section).

13. Césaire could be charged in this passage, as was Sebald in some of his pages, with manipulating the lives of real people to put forward a point or perspective. Césaire's parents were not, in fact, as poverty stricken as portrayed here (Arnold, 1981, p. 3; Kesteloot, 2008, pp. 15–16). Elsewhere, Césaire reports that he learned his love of books from his father, who was one of the rare islanders to secure formal education beyond the elementary school level. It remains true, however, that his family was not well off and dwelled with the tensions and anxieties associated with that condition.

14. Scharfman (2000) reminds us that the original French phrase, "*ce qui est à moi*" (literally, "that which is to me" or "for me") differs radically from a formulation the poet might have deployed, *j'ai* (I have). Instead, the poet—the artist who creates—places the world first, so to speak—*ce qui est*—"to signify that the subject was immaterial in its creation" (40). As suggested in chapter 1, the witness waits. The witness uses their will, so to speak, to still the will so that they can listen to and heed the world.

15. Césaire later composed a book on Toussaint (2000b) in which he analyses aspects of the French revolution in conjunction with the realities of

colonialism. The classic account of Toussaint and the revolution he helped lead is by C. L. R. James (1989).

16. In an interview appended to his *Discourse on Colonialism*, Césaire states that he and his confreres adopted *nègre* explicitly as "a term of defiance" (2000a, p. 89) and a mode of counterassimilationism (cf. Davis, 1997, p. 7). Brent Hayes Edwards, in his helpful discussion of the diverse uses of *noir* and *nègre* across time, shows how several of Césaire's precursors in the 1920s and '30s had already begun the project of reconceptualizing the terms (2003, pp. 26–38).

17. These debates were triggered, in part, by an influential and controversial essay by Jean-Paul Sartre titled "Black Orpheus," which he composed as a preface to one of the first widely distributed anthologies of black francophone poets published, in 1948, and edited by the poet and future politician Léopold Sédar Senghor. Sartre enthusiastically praises Césaire and other black poets for what he sees as their radical intervention in the cause of freedom. He interprets negritude as an essentialist "anti-racist racism."

While appreciative of Sartre's luminous analysis, Césaire, Frantz Fanon, and other black writers criticized the famed philosopher for reducing negritude, as they interpreted him, to a passing phase, or passing "song," on the road to the universal liberty of the proletariat. Césaire, a member of the French communist party for a decade, left it in 1955 because it would not recognize racism as of equal moment to the class struggle. For helpful treatments of the still active debates surrounding negritude, which range from treating it as an inherent philosophy of rhythmic life and force (fr. *élan vital*, per Henri Bergson) to picturing it as a nonessentialist and cosmopolitan-minded racial consciousness, see, among others, Arnold (1981), Edwards (2003), Diagne (2010, 2011, pp. 18–44, and 2023), Irele (2017, pp. 49ff, and 2009), and Wilder (2015).

18. As another echo of Sebald's witness—thinking, for example, of his narrator's hospitalization because of spiritual exhaustion—there is evidence that while Césaire was composing the poem he felt considerable personal stress. His close comrade Léopold Sédar Senghor later reported, "The *Cahier d'un retour au pays natal* was delivered in suffering. Its mother nearly lost her life, I mean reason" (in Irele, 2017, p. 18). As noted previously, in struggling to conceive the *Cahier*, Césaire destroyed his earlier work because he could no longer recognize his deepest yearnings in it (cf. Simmons, 1973, p. 225).

19. Arnold (2013) remarks that in this tense moment readers can see how "centuries of dehumanization have produced a masterpiece of caricature" (p. vi). I would add that the poet may be startled—even frightened—by the potentially harmful if not devastating effect of his poetic artistry, an echo of Sebald's unshakeable worries about the effects of prose. Both witnesses bring to mind Plato's pioneering manner of calling into question the possible impact on persons of poetry as well as of rhetoric writ large. Depending on the context, it appears words can exert an educative *and/or* miseducative influence.

20. This claim differs from readings of the poem that suggest the poet projects himself throughout as a prophet (Condé, 1978, p. 41), messiah (McIntosh, 2012), and/or redeemer (Ormerod, 1985, p. 4). In her in-depth study of the influence of Henri Bergson's "life philosophy" (*élan vital*) on the idea of negritude, Donna V. Jones (2010) refers to the poet as a Nietzschean "Black Zarathustra" (p. 178), proclaiming a new moral enlightenment to the world. There are passages that support these qualifiers, such as in stanza 81: "I desire the beautiful egoism/that braves risks." But I discern an abiding strain of modesty, confusion, self-doubt, and self-criticism in the poet's voice, all bound up in the act of witnessing. Like every witness, he cannot assume an Olympian standpoint, and he is the last to judge what he has accomplished. Its measure lies in its reception—which, in the case of *Cahier d'un retour au pays natal*, has been both remarkably varied and lasting.

21. The poet repeats this phrase a remarkable twenty-five times in the poem, twenty of them in the original 1939 version. As mentioned, the poem opens with the words in stanza 1, with the final appearance being in stanza 145. *Au bout du petit matin* are the opening words in sixteen stanzas. The poet truncates the phrase, referring six times to *du petit matin* (foreday morning or first light). As critics have rightly noted (cf. Figueroa, 2009, p. 99), these repetitive if not incantatory terms complicate a purely linear reading of the poem and dramatize that much more the poet's turns and shifts of mind. For Davis (1997), the refrain "reminds us that the speaker is between two worlds, positioned at the margins where cultures intersect and, above all, where lines of identity become blurred" (p. 24). Moreover, Davis adds, the image of early dawn "is also to be understood as the locus of poetic creativity, because it straddles the borderline between the oneiric and the real" (p. 24). As mentioned, I understand the anaphoric phrase as pointing to the transition the poet undergoes from spectator to witness.

22. Césaire would have been familiar with the opening line of the "Internationale," the anthem of socialist and communist parties since the 19th century: "*Debout, les damnés de la terre*"—"Arise and stand tall, you wretched of the earth." Frantz Fanon famously deployed the latter phrase as the title of his influential anticolonial critique, first published in 1961.

23. In an essay he composed in 1941, two years after his return home and in the midst of world war, Césaire stated: "We know that the salvation of the world depends on us also. That the earth has need of any one of its children. The most humble" (in Irele, 2017, p. 19).

24. Irele (2017) characterizes Césaire's ecological dispensation as telluric, that is, earth-rooted and earth-oriented, and considers him a "nature poet" (pp. 29, 51–52, 63–65; see also Allen-Paisant, 2022). René Hénane (2020) has composed a glossary of Césaire's extraordinarily rich vocabulary in his many poems and prose works. Among other things, these writings (including *Cahier*) overflow with voluptuous terms and neologisms pertaining to nature and to humanity's embeddedness in nature. Irele (2017) also provides invaluable notes and perspective—among

the very best in the secondary literature—in his introduction and in his book-length, stanza by stanza examination of Césaire's terminology in *Cahier* (pp. 1–73, 151–293). See also Kesteloot's (2008) blow-by-blow analysis in her text composed for university students, and the detailed studies of the poem by Davis (1997) and Scharfman (1980). Césaire's imaginative investments mirror his concerns about the alienating effects of capitalism, which time and again converts values, and things of value such as nature itself, into commodities to exploit. Sebald's oeuvre is replete with a comparable passion and concern for nature, intermixed with fear of its power and what he regards as its indifference to human hopes. We will also see a profound engagement with nature as part of Walt Whitman's witness.

25. Césaire (2000a) stated: "I'm not going to confine myself to some narrow particularism. But I don't intend either to become lost in a disembodied universalism. . . . I have a different idea of a universal. It is a universal rich with all that is particular, rich with all the particulars there are, the deepening of each particular, the coexistence of them all" (pp. 25–26). For insightful discussion of this outlook, see Hiddleston (2010, 2014), Nesbitt (2000, 2010), and Wilder (2015, 2016). For an extended discussion of cosmopolitanism as itself an educational orientation, see Hansen (2011).

26. This turn is mirrored in the fact that Césaire changed the original name of the student-run journal from the local-sounding *L'Étudiant martiniquais* to the far more encompassing *L'Étudiant noir* (Davis, 1997, p. 10; Scharfman, 2010, p. 111).

27. Césaire has been criticized for composing in French rather than in Creole, the Antillean language that arose over the centuries since the beginning of colonialism and that fuses French and other linguistic elements in a dynamic manner. Césaire was well-aware of this option but, perhaps affected by his intense early education in French (cf. Davis, 1997, pp. 4–5) as well as by his fluency in Latin (cf. Greenwood, 2010, pp. 371–372), found French more stylistically supple for his purposes. He does deploy specific Creole terms in the poem and incorporates, alongside surrealist motifs, what he regarded as the unique ethos of Creole (Simmons, 1973, p. 35). His fellow Antillean poet, Derek Walcott, remarks that *Cahier* is "written tonally in Creole" (in McConnell, 2013, p. 31). Césaire also aspired to reach the widest possible audience, and French served this function well given its continued use in various parts of the world. As touched on previously, it would be wrong to assume Césaire merely "adopted" French in an assimilationist form. Just as he rejected the styles and themes of the previous generation of Antillean poets, whom he regarded as would-be Frenchmen, so he transformed French in his own oeuvre, especially with regard to syntax and vocabulary, a fact that offended some French critics when *Cahier* appeared on the literary scene (a mirror to how previous surrealist poets composing in French scandalized the gatekeepers of linguistic convention). It is no surprise that in the cosmopolitan world of French letters a work focused entirely on Césaire's vocabulary would appear (cf. the reference to Hénane, 2020, above).

28. This image constitutes one of many instances of what Arnold (1981, p. 136) calls Césaire's "corrosive poetics" and what Irele (2009, p. 94) dubs his "poetics of aggression."

29. In an interview he gave decades later, in 1967, Césaire looks back on his poetic career up to that point and remarks: "I don't deny French influences myself. Whether I want to or not, as a poet I express myself in French, and clearly French literature has influenced me. But I want to emphasize very strongly that—while using as a point of departure the elements that French literature gave me—at the same time I have always striven to create a new language, one capable of communicating the African heritage. In other words, for me French was a tool that I wanted to use in developing a new means of expression. I wanted to create an Antillean French, a black French that, while still being French, had a black character" (2000a, p. 83). He adds that "Surrealism provided me with what I had been confusedly searching for. I have accepted it joyfully because in it I have found more of a confirmation than a revelation. It was a weapon that exploded the French language" (p. 83).

30. A classical statement of this dualistic view is Senghor's (in)famous saying: "Emotion is Negro, as reason is Hellenic [*L'émotion est nègre comme la raison hellène*]" (quoted in Diagne, 2011, p. 69). However, Diagne (2011) goes on to demonstrate that Senghor in fact held a much more nuanced, if sometimes inconsistent, view of the matter (cf. pp. 15, 69-71, 122-123, 195-196).

31. In his essay, "Poetry and Knowledge" (1990), Césaire writes the following:

"The barriers are in place [against undiscriminating imagination]; the law of identity, the law of non-contradiction, the logical principle of the excluded middle. Precious barriers. But remarkable limitations as well" (p. li).

32. Spiritual hunger has been a recurring motif across the work, pulsing beneath the affairs of everyday living on the island; see, for example, stanzas 7, 16, and 28.

33. The poet repeats the image of "bitter fraternity" at the close of the poem (173). He refers to the links between a suffering but now reconstituting black being ("my black vibration") and the earth of the island ("the very navel of the world") that the colonizers had abused through establishing plantations, but which has retained the abiding beauty he has evoked previously. The poet also refers to fraternity in stanzas 36 and 41; in the former, he pairs it with liberty.

# Chapter 4

1. Peter Coviello (2004) trenchantly writes: "With a fervor few before him had matched, Whitman believed in an ideal of American coherence, and in the larger possibilities for human experience, both collective and individual, such an

expansive mutuality would surely allow. Through the new form of his poetry, he had endeavored to imagine for the citizens of the nation a mode of belonging that compounded breadth and depth, that was at once intimately experienced—was in fact shaking in its palpable, physical intensity—and unlimited in its reach into and across the vast expanses of the republic. For such a vision of the nation, one could scarcely have imagined a more complete rebuke than the Civil War" (xvii).

2. Dewey (1984, p. 350) dubbed Whitman "the seer of democracy." For discussion of Dewey's remark as well as of Whitman's influence on him, see Garrison (2011).

3. Malcolm Cowley (1986), in his introduction to the Penguin edition of the 1855 poem, argues that "the text of the first edition is the purest text for 'Song of Myself,' since many of the later corrections were also corruptions of the style and concealments of the original meaning" (p. x). He judges that the initial work features "Whitman at his best, Whitman at his freshest in vision and boldest in language, Whitman transformed . . . so that he wanders among familiar objects and finds that each of them has become a miracle" (p. xxxvi).

4. Cowley (1986, pp. xvi–xvii) suggests the poem reads like a "musical progression" and argues that the stanzas, or "sections," as some critics call them, should properly be called "chants." Whitman formally embraced something like this viewpoint in his 1881 version, when he first used the title "Song of Myself" and where he added the words "and sing myself" in the opening line after "I celebrate myself."

5. Paul Zweig (1984, p. 173) and Matt Miller (2010, pp. 140, 180) refer to these many lines of naming and characterizing people as Whitman's "catalogues." Miller suggests that what he also calls these "lists" enact Whitman's democratic outlook because they embody no hierarchies. Zweig suggests that they "don't really list at all but present a succession of 'stills'—daguerreotypes, he might have said—received by a mind out on the open road" (p. 173). For Zweig, Whitman "sees all the dreamed-of fulfillments of religion and literature in the unvarnished, shaggy particulars of the everyday world" (p. 136). The poet rehearses his on-the-ground naming in other works such as his poem, "I Hear America Singing" (published in 1860), where he extols the individuality of American working-class people while conjuring how they constitute a democratic collective. The African American poet Langston Hughes embraces Whitman's vision while emphasizing the inclusion of blacks in his "response" poem, "I, Too, Sing America" (1926).

6. Whitman would have been aware of Plato's allegory of the cave where such images are prominent. In the course of his highly eclectic writing and editing life, Whitman accepted in 1858 a commission from a publisher to help prepare an annotated edition of Plato's dialogues, though it is unclear how far along he took the project (Zweig, 1984, p. 290).

7. The poet refers to being "a tramp" on a "perpetual journey" (46). His movements differ from yet echo those of Sebald's narrator, who wanders through

places sometimes knowing what he seeks, but at others giving himself over, flaneur-style, to what the next crossroads will yield.

8. Whitman follows Michel de Montaigne—whom we met in the previous chapter—in valuing what Montaigne calls, tongue-in-cheek, "idleness," which is anything but that. Rather, for Montaigne it constitutes an intense mode of study and contemplation bound up with self-examination and self-cultivation. Whitman's mode of waiting also echoes arguments on the values in "lingering," a practice we saw in Sebald's and Césaire's witnessing and that I touched on in chapter 1. These postures are not antithetical to concrete action. On the contrary, they can yield perspective and vision to guide action more wisely. This educational outcome is immanent in every accomplished witness, but it must be brought to the surface and catalyzed by its recipients.

9. Like Sebald and Césaire, Whitman had a tremendous interest in etymology and ransacked dictionaries and encyclopedias while writing. He even thought of composing a personal dictionary that would capture his ever-evolving lexicon (Miller, 2010, p. 139).

10. In his parallel poem, "Whoever You Are Holding Me Now in Hand"—where "me" refers to *Leaves of Grass*—the poet explicitly rebukes readers who merely admire his work and seek to mimic it. He urges them instead to *live* what their encounter with it has taught them, whatever that may be. "I am the teacher of athletes," he pens, appealing to all of his readers while signaling to them that they are stronger than they may realize.

> He that by me spreads a wider breast than my own proves the width
>   of my own,
> He most honors my style who learns under it to destroy the teacher. (81)

Like the leaves of grass (he does not call them "blades") that feed much life, the leaves, that is, pages, of the poem might feed readers, but only if they metabolize them within their own life trajectories.

11. Césaire (1990) explicitly applies the notion of a password to the poet's eros: "The poet is that very ancient yet new being, at once very complex and very simple, who at the limit of dream and reality, of day and night, between absence and presence, searches for and receives in the sudden triggering of inner cataclysms the password of connivance and power" (p. lvi). "Connivance" points to these witnesses' commitment to not be bound by conventional method or thought in their endeavors. Gregson Davis (1997) remarks: "The liberation that *Cahier* envisions is ultimately the freedom to examine ready-made identities—fragmentary models of the self—and to re-make them into an integrated whole with the connivance of an engaged reader" (60).

12. Consider these lines from his poem titled "Beginning my Studies," where "studies" constitutes a metaphor for experience. Whitman writes,

> Beginning my studies, the first step pleas'd me so much,
> The mere fact, *consciousness*—these *forms*—the power of motion,
> The least insect or animal—the senses—eyesight;
> The first step, I say, aw'd me and pleas'd me so much,
> I have never gone, and never wish'd to go, any farther,
> But stop and loiter all my life, to sing it in extatic songs.

He later wrote: "We hear of miracles—But what is there that is not a miracle? What may you conceive of or name to me in the future that shall be beyond the least thing around us?" (in Zweig, 1984, p. 177).

13. The poet's shaken condition, as he faces the reality of violence and injustice, calls to mind the emotional and spiritual costs that can accompany bearing witness. We saw how, in chapter 2, Sebald's extraordinary witness in *The Rings of Saturn* opens with the narrator in a hospital, having suffered a moral, psychological, and spiritual collapse from all the hurt and turmoil that he has witnessed. The narrator lacked a cane.

We will encounter below Whitman's response to his many visits to Civil War hospitals. After almost two years of witnessing death nearly every day, he will be on the cusp of a breakdown and will require a six-month spiritual and physical convalescence at home.

14. See also Whitman's affecting poem, "Vigil Strange I Kept on the Field One Night," where he imagines himself a Union soldier during the Civil War keeping watch over a fallen comrade. Martin Buinicki (2011, p. 70) suggests Whitman's impulse to walk alongside others, as I've posed the matter, deepened over time, such that he sought to transform his debilitating illnesses triggered by a stroke in 1873—itself fueled by the deep wear and tear his hospitals visits cost his body and soul—into, in effect, war wounds like those that still troubled many veterans years after the war.

15. Whitman acknowledges that tension is ever-present in human affairs, but he believes it can be generative rather than solely destructive. He later writes, looking back on the American Civil War: "What is any Nation, after all—and what is a human being—but a struggle between conflicting, paradoxical, opposing elements—and they themselves and their most violent contests, important parts of that One Identity, and of its development?" (*Memoranda During the War*, p. 126). I take "One Identity" to refer both to the United States—*e pluribus unum*—and to the singular human being perceived as a whole.

Speaking of "opposing elements," Whitman's attitude toward blacks and other minoritized communities in the nation was inconsistent. On the one hand, he was ardently opposed to slavery and in many written expressions, as we have seen, was enthusiastically egalitarian and unprejudiced, including with respect to Indigenous peoples. On the other hand, he sometimes enunciated racist attitudes toward blacks, just as he had occasionally manifested discriminatory, anti-Irish views in his younger days as a journalist. In brief, Whitman expressed outlooks conventional in his day even as he writes his way beyond them. For discussion, see, inter alia, Wilson (2014).

16. As we saw in the previous chapter, "I accept" constituted a key expression in Césaire's witness in which he, too, experiences a profound sense of love through taking to heart the plenitude of his people, warts and pearls and all. On Whitman's conception of what can be dubbed a cosmopolitan-democratic love, see Nussbaum's (2012) account in a section of her book titled "Accents of Love" where she also comments on other figures such as Plato, Dante, and Emily Bronte.

17. Césaire's notion of "beautiful [versus ugly] egoism" (*Cahier*, 81) comes to mind, wherein the poet takes courage to speak frankly, directly, and truly despite what conventional thinking would have him utter.

18. In his book, Whitman always deploys an apostrophe instead of an *e* in -*ed* endings, and I will retain this form.

19. Whitman refers elsewhere to what he calls his "soil'd and creas'd little livraisons . . . I leave them just as I threw them by during the War, blotch'd here and there with more than one blood-stain, hurriedly written" (pp. 3–4). The flesh and blood materiality of the notebooks in itself forms part of his witness (cf. Buinicki, 2010, p. 54).

The contemporary edition of the *Memoranda* contains facsimiles of two pages from Whitman's notebooks, each of them long lists of names and regiments. The book also includes facsimiles of several of his letters to parents of wounded men as well as seventeen photographs of hospital wards and field settings.

20. "[I] write all sorts of letters for them," Whitman remarks, "(including love letters, very tender ones)" (p. 14). For soldiers who had not heard from home in a long while, Whitman would include in his letters on their behalf a prestamped envelope family members could use to reply (Morris, 2000, p. 127).

21. It is worth noting that Whitman already had hospital experience before the Civil War. For a number of years, while residing in New York City, he enjoyed spending his free time with the streetwise drivers of public coaches that roamed the city's muddy, congested lanes. He relished the rough and tumble of these hours with the drivers while encountering people from all walks of life. However, there were few traffic regulations at the time, and accidents were common with drivers badly injured and sometimes killed. Whitman took to visiting the local hospital where they were cared for, providing comfort and, unbeknownst to him, acquiring knowledge of medicine that later would be very useful (Coviello, 2004, pp. xix–xx; Zweig, 1984, p. 323). Even during his convalescence from the rigors of his wartime witness—he was back in New York during the second half of 1864, recovering from illness and spiritual exhaustion—he devoted his Sundays to visiting a local hospital for soldiers (Morris, 2000, pp. 32–33; Zweig, 1984, p. 172).

22. Whitman's contemporary, Louisa May Alcott—author of *Little Women* (1868) among other works of fiction—volunteered for hospital work in early 1863. She was only able to serve for six weeks before contracting typhoid, which necessitated a long recovery back home in Massachusetts. (Many hospital staff, especially in the early months of the war when things were chaotic and there was scant attention paid to disinfection, fell seriously ill and their mortality rate was high.) With strong encouragement from others, Alcott published the letters she had sent to family and friends while working as a nurse. They came out in a volume she titled *Hospital Sketches* (1960/1863). Whitman knew her book (it is not clear if he met her personally, though we know she admired the creativity in *Leaves of Grass*, cf. Cowley, 1986, p. ix) and it helped solidify his own eventual plan to write of his time during the war.

With respect to face-to-face work in the wards, Alcott refers, in a manner that both moves and surprises her, to the "sympathetic magnetism" (p. 51) of her presence at soldiers' bedsides. She reports how "the gentle tendance" she could bring eased their anxieties. (Alcott's and Whitman's references to magnetism may echo the popularity of mesmerism at the time, namely. the idea that there is an invisible, organic force shared by all living creatures that has generative effects.)

23. Tellingly, Whitman attended to the occasional Confederate soldier brought into a ward in the same way he did the Union wounded, which offended some of the latter who objected to having Rebel survivors in the same room (Alcott, 1960, pp. 33). Whitman also sometimes encountered groups of Southern prisoners being marched through the city. When they came to a rest, he would strike up a conversation with them, just as he frequently did with brigades of Union soldiers passing through on their way to or from the front. Whitman also devoted time to wounded and ill black soldiers who were segregated in separate quarters. His interest in and commitment to the soldiers of the war, in all its existential harshness, was truly ecumenical.

24. "One ward has a long row of officers, some with ugly hurts," Whitman writes on a June day in 1863. "Yesterday was perhaps worse than usual. Amputations are going on. . . . As you pass by, you must be on your guard where you look. I saw the other day a gentleman, a visitor apparently from curiosity, in one of the Wards, stop and turn a moment to look at an awful wound they were probing. He turn'd pale, and in a moment more he had fainted away and fallen on the floor" (p. 31). Mindful of such scenes, some of the soldiers for whom Whitman wrote letters expressly asked him to write that their relatives should *not* try to come visit them.

25. To his enduring gratification, a number of the men he tended wrote to him later as did their families to whom he had written on their behalf (see below). They would refer to him as "dear friend," "dear comrade," "dear uncle,"

"dear father," and "dear Walt." Some of this correspondence continued for decades as survivors kept him up to date on their doings, often sending along photographs of children, of their farms, and so forth (Morris, 2000, pp. 235–36).

26. The tender human touches in the vignettes that follow reflect, in part, the cultural ethos of the time, when public affection between men (for example, handholding and kissing) was a familiar sight in everyday life, as was public affection between women (it was decades later that such conduct was deemed "deviant" by some that merited punishment, cf. Morris, 2000, p. 133; Coviello, pp. xxxvi–xxxvii; Reynolds, 1995, pp. 198–99; Zweig, 1984, p. 299). Whitman's loving attentiveness occurred in full view of other wounded soldiers and the hospital staff, who expressed no objections to it. Quite on the contrary, his warm, physical presence was respected. He remarks in a letter home: "I have long discarded all stiff conventions [with the wounded men]; they & I are too near to each other, there is no time to lose, & death & anguish dissipate ceremony here between my lads & me—I pet them, some of them it does so much good, they are so faint & lonesome—at parting at night sometimes I kiss them right & left—The doctors tell me I supply the patients with a medicine which all their drugs & bottles & powders are helpless to yield" (in Zweig, 1984, p. 338). (The scholarship on Whitman remains conflicted about the question of his overall gender and sexual orientation, and its relationship with his life and work. See, inter alia, Erkkila, 2020; Pollok, 2020; and Reynolds, 1995).

27. Before describing another comparable situation, Whitman writes: "I wonder if I could ever convey to another—to you, for instance, Reader dear—the tender and terrible realities of such cases, (many, many happen'd)" (p. 56). Alcott (1960, pp. 51–58) echoes the heartbreak Whitman often felt in her moving account of a stoic, undemanding soldier whom she came to love and lost when he finally died of his terrible wounds: "The first red streak of dawn was warming the grey east, a herald of the coming sun; John saw it, and with the love of light which lingers in us to the end, seemed to read in it a sign of hope of help, for, over his whole face there broke that mysterious expression, brighter than any smile, which often comes to eyes that look their last" (p. 57). These poignant moments the two writers record mirror what might be called a poesis of care.

28. Not once in the *Memoranda* does Whitman refer to clergymen, though we know they had a presence in the wards and on the battlefields. (Alcott mentions several ministers who attended the men with varying degrees of sensitivity.) Whitman does describe reading to soldiers, on request, from the Bible and discussing questions about its meaning with them. As we have seen, he deploys biblical motifs in his writing. But he was known to his family and friends as atheistic if not also antireligion in its institutionalized form (cf. Zweig, 1984, pp. 13, 294), a point he acknowledges indirectly while also illuminating further the nature of his witness.

> In these Wards, or on the field, as I thus continue to go round, I have come to adapt myself to each emergency, after its kind or call, however trivial, however solemn—every one justified and made real under its circumstances—not only visits and cheering talk and little gifts—not [only] washing and dressing wounds, (I have some cases where the patient is unwilling any one should do this but me)—but passages from the Bible, expounding them, prayer at the bedside, explanations of doctrine, &c. (I think I see my friends smiling at this confession, but I was never more in earnest in my life.) (p. 54)

At another point, he describes how a badly wounded soldier begged him to read at length from the Bible. "I read very slowly," writes Whitman,

> for Oscar was feeble. It peas'd him very much, yet the tears were in his eyes. He ask'd me if I enjoy'd religion. I said: "Perhaps not, my dear, in the way you mean, and yet, may-be, it is the same thing." He said: "It is my chief reliance." He talk'd of death, and said he did not fear it. . . . He spoke calmly of his condition. The wound was very bad; it discharg'd much. Then the diarrhoea had prostrated him, and I felt that he was even then the same as dying. (p. 36)

29. In one of his many wartime letters to his mother, Whitman writes of a young soldier who died of his wounds while being carried from an ambulance van through the hospital entrance. For Whitman, a terrible aspect of the event was "that he is entirely unknown—there was nothing on his clothes, or any one with him to identify him. . . . Very likely his folks will never know in the world what has become of him" (in Morris, 2000, p. 172). The historian Drew Gilpin Faust estimates that more than 40 percent of Union dead, and an even larger proportion of Confederate dead, were buried during the war with names unknown (see Buinicki, 2010, p. 134).

30. Given these somber realities, it comes as no surprise that when Louisa May Alcott's letters from her hospital sojourn were published in 1863, they became instantly popular among a readership hungry for knowledge of the front lines.

31. We saw how Sebald, in his witness to events, raises this same question including through the voice of Austerlitz's history teacher, André Hilary (see above, p. 39).

32. Consider also Zweig's (1984) perspective: "In the hospitals, Whitman set aside his metaphors, in order to live them. . . . [H]is poet's world had been an 'open road,' and the poet had opened his mind to embrace whatever came his way. Now the hospitals were his open road. As he went up and down the wards,

it seemed to him that all of America was at his feet, represented by this gathering of the sick and the dying . . . from all over the country" (pp. 340).

33. Morris (2000, pp. 17, 238–39), among other critics, reminds us of how intensely bitter Whitman could become about the failures of the nation, as seen in pessimistic, almost nihilistic works such as the poem "Respondez!" and several postwar essays. At times he does sound nationalistic, even jingoistic, but elsewhere he strongly counters that impression. His eventual international reputation seems to confirm the point, given how many persons the world over saw him as a seer of democracy, to recall Dewey's appellation (cf. Allen and Folsom, 1995, p. 8).

## Chapter 5

1. Incidentally, Borges published (in 1941) a translation—titled "Canto a mi Mismo"—of Whitman's *Song of Myself.*

2. I first heard this affecting question in a presentation by Cathy Bi, a student in the program where I teach, in the context of one of my courses on bearing witness.

3. As mentioned previously, for a fuller account of the question of trustworthiness, see Hansen and Sullivan (2022).

4. Dori Laub (1992, pp. 59–60) provides a particularly moving instance in which a Holocaust survivor misremembered, and consequently exaggerated, the number of crematoria that were destroyed during a rebellion by the Jewish inmates of a concentration camp. But her very error, Laub shows, attests to the astounding truth that the inmates rose up in the first place, an extremely rare occurrence in the grim history of the Nazi concentration camps. For commentary, see Simon (2005, pp. 55–58).

5. This paragraph derives from Hansen (2021, p. 150).

6. Can children be witnesses? This wonderful question, which has come up in my teaching, contrasts with the fraught question I have also heard, namely, whether a Nazi can bear witness. The argument in this book, as indicated previously, suggests that the answer to the latter question is an emphatic no. There is no moral justification, much less moral fruitfulness, that I can conceive that pertains to the murderous racism embedded in Nazism. In a general way, it is difficult to imagine, for me, any person being capable of bearing witness who is inclined to harm others or to be indifferent to others' suffering.

The case of children is radically different. The openness and wonder so characteristic of their way of being is ground, on their part, for highly affecting and insightful first-order testimony about the world. But the challenging demands in taking on the orientation of a second- or third-order witness require a more mature, critical life experience. In the preface, I referred to listening to my father's and his friends' accounts of their experience of war. Though highly absorbed by all this at the time, I was not equipped at that young age to formulate its meaning and significance, nor its possible long-term effect on my own consciousness.

7. As we saw with Sebald, Césaire, and Whitman, moral witnesses themselves can feel keenly the weight of suffering and perceived injustice. Teachers can draw this fact to students' attention as part of helping them become both more ready and more receptive.

# References

Agamben, G. (2002). *Remnants of Auschwitz: The witness and the archive*. Zone Books.
Alcott, L. M. (1960). *Hospital sketches*, ed. B. Z. Jones. Belknap Press of Harvard University Press. (Original work published 1863).
Alexievich, S. (2018). *The unwomanly face of war*, trans. R. Pevear & L. Volokhonsky. Random House.
Allen, G. W., & Folsom, E. (Eds.). (1995). *Walt Whitman and the world*. University of Iowa Press.
Allen, Jason. (2017). Aimé Césaire and *The divine comedy*: Self-enlightenment and the dialectic of relation in *And the dogs were silent*. *Journal of Postcolonial Writing 53*(4), 482–494.
Allen-Paisant, J. (2022). Thinking with spirits, or dwelling and knowing in the work of Aimé Césaire. *French Studies 76*(4), 576–590.
Anderson, M. (2003). The edge of darkness. *October 106*(1), 102–121.
Angier, C. (2007). Who is W. G. Sebald? In L. S. Schwartz (Ed.), *The emergence of memory: Conversations with W. G. Sebald*, pp. 63–76. Seven Stories Press.
Angier, C. (2021). *Speak, Silence: In search of W. G. Sebald*. Bloomsbury Circus.
Arnold, A. James. (1981). *Modernism and negritude: The poetry and poetics of Aimé Césaire*. Harvard University Press.
Arnold, A. James. (2004). Césaire's notebook as palimpsest: The text before, during, and after World War II." *Research in African Literatures 35*(3): 133–140.
Arnold, A. James. (2008). Beyond postcolonial Césaire: Reading *Cahier d'un retour au pays natal* historically. *Forum for Modern Language Studies 44*(3), 258–275.
Baldwin, J. (1964). James Baldwin, Television narrative about his life, WNEW-TV, New York City, June 1, 1964, produced by Arthur Barron.
Barone, T., & Eisner, E. (2011). *Arts-based research*. Sage.
Barry, S. (2017). *Days without end*. Penguin.
Barzilai, M. (2006). On exposure: Photography and uncanny memory in W. G. Sebald's *Die Ausgewandereten* and *Austerlitz*. In M. Denham & M. McCulloh (Eds.). *W. G. Sebald: History, memory, trauma* (pp. 205–218). De Gruyter.

Baxter, J., Henitiuk, V., & Hutchinson, B. (Eds.). (2015). *A literature of restitution: Critical essays on W. G. Sebald*. Manchester University Press.
Benfry, C. (2010). The real critter. *New York Review of Books* June 24, 2010, n.p.
Blackler, D. (2007). *Reading W. G. Sebald: Adventure and disobedience*. Camden House.
Boler, M. (1999). *Feeling power: Emotions and education*. Routledge.
Borges, J. L. (1968). *A Personal Anthology*, trans. A. Kerrigan. Grove Atlantic.
Breton, A. (1978). *Andre Breton: What is Surrealism? Selected Writings*, ed. F. Rosemont. Pathfinder.
Buinicki, M. T. (2011). *Walt Whitman's reconstruction: Poetry and publishing between memory and history*. University of Iowa Press.
Burch, K. (2020). *Jefferson's revolutionary theory and the reconstruction of educational purpose*. Palgrave Macmillan.
Césaire, A. (1983). Notebook of a Return to the native land. In *The collected poetry of Aimé Césaire*, trans. C. Eshleman and A. Smith (pp. 32–85). University of California Press.
Césaire, A. (1990). Poetry and knowledge. In *Aimé Césaire: Lyric and dramatic poetry 1946–82*, trans. C. Eshleman and A. Smith (pp. xlii–lvi). University Press of Virginia. (Original work published 1944–1945).
Césaire, A. (1995). *Notebook of a Return to my native land*, trans. M. Rosello with A. Pritchard. Bloodaxe Books.
Césaire, A. (2000a). *Discourse on colonialism*, trans. J. Pinkham, intro. R. D. G. Kelley. Monthly Review Press. (Original work published 1955).
Césaire, A. (2000b). *Toussaint Louverture: La révolution Française et le problème colonial*. Presence Africaine. (Original work published 1961).
Césaire, A. (2013). *The original 1939 Notebook of a return to the native land*, ed. A. J. Arnold and C. Eshleman. Wesleyan University Press.
Césaire, A. (2014). *Return to my native land*, trans. J. Berger & A. Bostock. Archipelago Books. (Original work published 1969).
Césaire, A. (2017). *Cahier d'un retour au pays natal (Journal of a Homecoming)*, trans. N. G. Davis. Duke University Press. (Original work published 1939 and revised 1947, 1956).
Chinnery, A. (2010). "What good does all this remembering do, anyway?" On historical consciousness and the responsibility of memory. In Gert Biesta (Ed.). *Philosophy of education* (pp. 397–405). Philosophy of Education Society.
Chinnery, A. (2013). Caring for the past: On relationality and historical consciousness. *Ethics and Education* 8(3), 253–262.
Comber, P. (2014). *Ariadne's thread: In memory of W. G. Sebald*. Propolis.
Condé, M. (1978). *Cahier d'un retour au pays natal. Profil d'une oeuvre*. Hatier.
Cooper, A. J. (2016). *A voice from the South*. Dover Publications. (Original work published in 1892).
Cooper, J. M. (2012). *Pursuits of wisdom: Six ways of life in ancient philosophy from Socrates to Plotinus*. Princeton University Press.

Coviello, P. (2004). Introduction: Whitman at war. In *W. Whitman, Memoranda during the War* (pp. ix–liv). Oxford University Press.
Cowley, M. (1986). Introduction. In *W. Whitman, leaves of grass: The First (1855) edition*, ed. M. Cowley (pp. vii–xxxvii). Penguin Classics.
Crary, A. (2012). W. G. Sebald and the ethics of narrative. *Constellations 19*(3), 494–508.
Crichlow, W., Strong-Wilson, T., Castro, R. L., & Yoder, A. (Eds.). (2023). *Curricular and architectural encounters with W. G. Sebald: Unsettling complacency, reconstructing subjectivity*. Routledge.
Davis, G. (1997). *Aimé Césaire*. Cambridge University Press.
Davis, G. (2007). 'Homecomings without home': Representations of (post)colonial nostos (homecoming) in the lyric of Aimé Césaire and Derek Walcott. In B. Graziosi & E. Greenwood (Eds.), *Homer in the twentieth century: between world literature and the Western canon* (pp. 191–209). Oxford University Press.
Davis, G. (2016). Forging a Caribbean literary style: 'Vulgar eloquence' and the language of Césaire's *Cahier d'un retour au pays natal*. *South Atlantic Quarterly 115*(3), 457–467.
Dease, B. C. (1980). Césaire's concept of negritude in 'Cahier d'un Retour au Pays Natal.' *Journal of Caribbean Studies 1*(1), 35–61.
Dewey, J. (1984). *The public and its problems. John Dewey: The later works 1925–1953, Volume 2: 1925–1927*, ed. J. A. Boydston (pp. 235–372). Southern Illinois University Press.
Dewey, J. (1985). *Democracy and education. John Dewey: The middle works 1899–1924, Volume 9: 1916*, ed. J. A. Boydston. Southern Illinois University Press.
Dewey, J. (1988). *Experience and nature. John Dewey: The later works 1925–1953, Volume 1: 1925*, ed. J. A. Boydston. Southern Illinois University Press.
Dewey, J. (1989). *Art as experience. John Dewey: The later works 1925–1953, Volume 10:1934*, ed. J. A. Boydston. Southern Illinois University Press.
Diagne, S. B. (2010). In praise of the post-racial: Négritude beyond négritude. *Third Text 24*(2), 241–248.
Diagne, S. B. (2011). *African Art as Philosophy: Senghor, Bergson and the Idea of Negritude*, trans. C. Jeffers. Seagull.
Diagne, S. B. (2023). Négritude. *Stanford encyclopedia of philosophy*. Stanford University Press.
Diawara, M. (1998). *In Search of Africa*. Harvard University Press.
Di Paolantonio, M. (2009). Guarding and transmitting the vulnerability of the historical referent. In D. Kerdeman (Ed.), *Philosophy of Education*, 129–137. Philosophy of Education Society.
Di Paolantonio, M. (2015). Roger Simon as a thinker of the remnants: An overview of a way of thinking the present, our present. *Studies in Philosophy of Education 34*(3), 263–277.
Di Paolantonio, M. (2018). Wonder, guarding against thoughtlessness in education. *Studies in Philosophy and Education 38* (3), 213–228.

Doig, I. (2006). *The Whistling Season*. Harcourt.
Dustin, C. A., & Ziegler, J. E. (2007). *Practicing mortality: Art, philosophy, and contemplative seeing*. Palgrave Macmillan.
Duttlinger, C. (2004). Traumatic photographs: Remembrance and the technical media in W. G. Sebald's *Austerlitz*. In J. J. Long & A. Whitehead (Eds.). *W. G. Sebald: A critical companion* (pp. 155–171). University of Washington Press.
Dutro, E. (2011). Writing wounded: Trauma, testimony, and critical witness in literacy classrooms. *English Education 43*(2), 193–211.
Dutro, E. (2013). Towards a pedagogy of the incomprehensible: Trauma and the imperative of critical witness in literacy classrooms. *Pedagogies: An International Journal, 8*(4), 301–315.
Edmondson, M. (2019). Walt Whitman's guide to a thriving democracy. *Atlantic Monthly*, May issue, 100–110.
Edwards, B. H. (2003). *The practice of diaspora: Literature, translation, and the rise of Black internationalism*. Harvard University Press.
Edwards, B. H. (2005). Aimé Césaire and the syntax of influence. *Research in African Literatures 36*(2), 1–18.
K. Egan, A. Cant, & G. Judson (Eds.). (2013). *Wonder-full education: The centrality of wonder in teaching and learning across the curriculum*. Routledge.
Eliot, G. (1985). *Middlemarch*. Penguin. (Original work published 1871–72).
Elon, A. (2002). *The pity of it all: A portrait of the German-Jewish epoch 1743–1933*. Picador.
Erkkila, B. (2020). *The Whitman revolution: sex, poetry, and politics*. University of Iowa Press.
Eshleman, C., & Smith, A. (1983). Introduction. In *The Collected Poetry of Aimé Césaire*, trans. C. Eshleman and A. Smith (pp. 1–31). University of California Press.
Etherington, B. (2018). *Literary primitivism*. Stanford University Press.
Felman, S., & Laub, D. (1992). *Testimony: Crises of witnessing in literature, psychoanalysis, and history*. Routledge.
Figueroa, V. (2009). *Not at home in one's home: Caribbean self-fashioning in the poetry of Luis Palés Matos, Aimé Césaire, and Derek Walcott*. Fairleigh Dickinson University Press.
Folsom, E. (Ed.). (1994). *Walt Whitman: The centennial essays*. University of Iowa Press.
Foucault, M. (2005). *The Hermeneutics of the Subject*, trans. G. Burchell. Macmillan.
Friedrichsmeyer, S. (2006). Sebald's elective and other affinities. In S. Denham & M. McCulloh (Eds.). *W. G. Sebald: History, memory, trauma* (pp. 77–89). Walter de Gruyter.
Garrison, J. (2011). Walt Whitman, John Dewey, and primordial artistic communication. *Transactions of the Charles S. Peirce Society 47*(3), 301–318.

Garloff, K. (2004). The Emigrant as Witness: W. G. Sebald's "Die Ausgewanderten." *The German Quarterly 77*(1), 76–93.

Garraway, D. L. (2010). "What is mine": Césairean negritude between the particular and the universal. *Research in African Literatures 41*(1), 71–86.

Gil, A. (2011). Bridging the middle passage: The textual (r)evolution of Césaire's *Cahier d'un retour au pays natal. Canadian Review of Comparative Literature 38*(1), 40–56.

Givoni, M. (2014). The ethics of witnessing and the politics of the governed. *Theory, Culture & Society 31*(1), 123–142.

Givoni, M. (2016). *The care of the witness: A contemporary history of testimony in crises*. Cambridge University Press.

Glaude, E., Jr. (2020). *Begin again: James Baldwin's America and its urgent lessons for our own*. Penguin Random House.

Goldberg, S. (2013). *Quiet testimony: A theory of witnessing from nineteenth-century American literature*. Fordham University Press.

Hadot, P. (1995). *Philosophy as a way of life: Spiritual practices from Socrates to Foucault*, trans. M. Chase. Blackwell Publishers.

Hallender, M. (2012). *The pedagogical possibilities of witnessing and testimonials: Through the lens of Agamben*. Palgrave Pivot.

Hansen, D. T. (2011). *The teacher and the world: A study of cosmopolitanism as education*. Routledge.

Hansen, D. T. (2021). *Reimagining the call to teach: A witness to teaching and teachers*. Teachers College Press.

Hansen, D. T., & Sullivan, R. (2022). What renders a witness trustworthy? Existential and curricular notes on a mode of educational inquiry. *Studies in Philosophy and Education 41*(2), 151–172.

Hansen, D. T., & Dwek, Y. (2023). The voice of poetry in cultivating cosmopolitan and democratic imagination. In J. Culp, J. Drerup, & D. Yacek, D. (Eds.). *The Cambridge handbook of democratic education* (pp. 395–415). Cambridge University Press.

Harris, S. (2001). The return of the dead: Memory and photography in W. G. Sebald's *Die Ausgewanderten. The German Quarterly 74*(4), 379–391.

Hartman, S. (2007). *Lose your mother: A journey along the Atlantic slave trade*. Farrar, Straus and Giroux.

Hartman, S. (2008). "Venus in two acts." *Small Axe 26* (June), 1–14.

Harvey, R. (2010). *Witnessness: Beckett, Dante, Levi and the foundations of responsibility*. Bloomsbury.

Hatley, J. (2000). *Suffering witness: The quandary of responsibility after the irreparable*. State University of New York Press.

Heidegger, M. (2010). *Country path conversations*, trans. B. W. Davis. Indiana University Press. (Original manuscript notes composed in 1944–1945).

Hénane, R. (2020). *Glossaire des termes rares dans l'Oeuvre d'Aimé Césaire*. Nouvelles Éditions Place.
Hiddleston, Jane. (2010). Aimé Césaire and postcolonial humanism. *The Modern Language Review 105*(1), 87–102.
Hiddleston, Jane. (2014). *Decolonising the intellectual: Politics, culture, and humanism at the end of the French Empire*. Oxford University Press.
Hillesum, E. (1996). *An interrupted life, and letters from Westerbork*. Henry Holt.
Hynes, S. (1997). *The soldiers' tale: bearing witness to modern war*. Penguin.
Irele, F. A. (2009). The poetic legacy of Aimé Césaire. *French Politics, Culture & Society 27*(3), 81–97.
Irele, F. A. (2017). Introduction. In Aimé Césaire, *Journal of a homecoming/cahier d'un retour au pays natal*, trans. N. G. Davis (pp. 1–73). Duke University Press.
Jacobs, C. (2004). What does it mean to count? W. G. Sebald's *The emigrants*. *Modern Language Notes 119*(5), 905–929.
Jahn, J. (1990). *Muntu: African culture and the Western World*. Grove Weidenfeld. (Original work published 1961).
James, C. L. R. (1989). *The Black Jacobins: Toussaint Louverture and the San Domingo revolution*, 2nd ed. Vintage. (Original work published 1963; 1st edition published 1938).
Jonas, M. (2010). When teachers must let education hurt: Rousseau and Nietzsche on compassion and the educational value of suffering. *Journal of Philosophy and Education 44*(1), 45–60.
Jones, D. V. (2010). *The racial discourses of life philosophy: Negritude, vitalism, and modernity*. Columbia University Press.
Josselson, R. (2004). The hermeneutics of faith and the hermeneutics of suspicion. *Narrative Inquiry 14*(1), 1–28.
Kerdeman, D. (2003). Pulled up short: Challenging self-understanding as a focus of teaching and learning. *Journal of Philosophy of Education 37*(2), 293–308.
Kesteloot, L. (1991). *Black writers in French: A literary history of negritude*, trans. E. C. Kennedy. Howard University Press. (Original work published 1963).
Kesteloot, L. (2008). *Comprendre le cahier d'un retour au pays natal d'Aimé Césaire*. L'Harmattan.
Kramer, S., & Weigel, S. (Eds.). (2017). *Testimony/Bearing witness: Epistemology, ethics, history and culture*. Rowman & Littlefield.
Larrier, R. (2010). A tradition of literacy: Césaire in and out of the classroom. *Research in African Literatures 41*(1), 33–45.
Lewis, C. S. (1976). *A grief observed*. Bantam. (Original work published 1963).
Lipking, L. (1981). *The life of the poet: Beginning and ending poetic careers*. University of Chicago Press.
Librett, J. S. (2015). Shoah. In P. Gratton & M.-E. Morin (Eds.), *The Nancy Dictionary* (pp. 218–220). Edinburgh University Press.
Long, J. J., & Whitehead, A. (Eds.). (2004). *W. G. Sebald: A critical companion*. Edinburgh University Press.

Long, J. J. (2007). *W. G. Sebald: Image, archive, modernity*. Columbia University Press.
McConnell, J. (2013). *Black odysseys: The Homeric Odyssey in the African Diaspora since 1939*. Oxford University Press.
McIntosh, M. (2012). The "I" as messiah in Césaire's first *Cahier*. *Research in African Literatures* 43(2), 77–94.
Margalit, A. (2002). *The ethics of memory*. Harvard University Press.
McMullen, K. (2019). "This damned act": Walt Whitman and the Fugitive Slave Law of 1850. *Walt Whitman Quarterly* 37(1–2), 1–45.
Medina, J. (2013). *The epistemology of resistance: Gender and racial oppression, epistemic injustice, and the social imagination*. Oxford University Press.
Melas, N. (2016). Poetry's circumstance and racial time: Aimé Césaire, 1935–1945. *South Atlantic Quarterly* 115(3), 469–493.
Merleau-Ponty, M. (1964). In J. M. Edie (Ed.). *The primacy of perception*. Northwestern University Press.
Miller, E. H. (1991). *Walt Whitman's "Song of myself": A mosaic of interpretations*. University of Iowa Press.
Miller, M. (2010). *Collage of myself: Walt Whitman and the making of Leaves of Grass*. University of Nebraska Press.
Mintz, A. I. (2012). The happy and suffering student? Rousseau's *Emile* and the path not taken in progressive educational thought. *Educational Theory* 62(3), 249–265.
Mintz, A. I. (2013). Helping by hurting: The paradox of suffering in social justice education. *Theory and Research in Education* 11(3), 215–230.
Mintz, A. I. (2017). Pain and education. In J. Corns (Ed.). *The Routledge handbook of philosophy of pain*. Routledge.
Monk, R. (1990). *Ludwig Wittgenstein: The duty of genius*. Free Press, 1990.
Montaigne, M. (1991). *The essays of Michel de Montaigne*, trans. M. A. Screech. Penguin. (Original work published 1595).
Morris, R, Jr. (2000). *The better angel: Walt Whitman in the Civil War*. Oxford University Press.
Nesaule, A. (1995). *A woman in amber: Healing the trauma of war and exile*. Penguin.
Nesbitt, N. (2000). Antinomies of double consciousness in Aimé Césaire's "Cahier d'un retour au pays natal. *Mosaic: An Interdisciplinary Critical Journal* 33(3), 107–128.
Nesbitt, N. (2010). The incandescent I, destroyer of worlds. *Research in African Literatures* 41(1), 121–141.
Noland, C. (2006). Red front/Black front: Aimé Césaire and the affaire Aragon. *Diacritics* 36(1), 64–85.
Noland, C. (2019). Translating Césaire. *Modernism/Modernity* 26(2), 419–426.
Nolden, T. (2015). Farcical heroism: Aimé Césaire reads Homer, Virgil, and Plautus. *Journal of Postcolonial Writing* 51(5), 531–542.

Nussbaum, M. C. (2012). *Upheavals of thought*. Cambridge University Press.
Oakeshott, M. (1989). *The voice of liberal learning*, ed. T. Fuller. Yale University Press.
O'Brien, G. (1995). Whitman's revolution. *New York Review of Books*, October 19, 1995.
Oliver, K. (2001). *Witnessing: Beyond recognition*. University of Minnesota Press.
Ormerod, B. (1985). *An introduction to the French Caribbean novel*. Heinemann.
Paton, A. (1953). *Too late the phalarope*. Charles Scribner's Sons.
Peck, R. (Director) (2016). *I am not your Negro*. Magnolia Pictures. [Film].
Peters, J. D. (2001). Witnessing. *Media, Culture & Society 23*, 707–723.
Pippin, R. (2013). Vernacular metaphysics: On Terrence Malick's *The thin red line*. *Critical Inquiry 39*(2), 247–275.
Plato. (1992). *Republic*, trans. G. M. A. Grube & C. D. C. Reeve. Hackett.
Pollak, V. R. (2000). *The erotic Whitman*. University of California Press.
Pratt, L. (Ed.). (2007). *Searching for Sebald: Photography after W. G. Sebald*. Institute for Cultural Inquiry.
Reilly, B. J. (2020). Negritude's contretemps: The coining and reception of Aime Césaire's Neologism. *Philological Quarterly 99*(4), 377–398.
Rexer, R. (2013). Black and white and re(a)d all over: *L'Étudiant noir*, communism, and the birth of négritude. *Research in African Literatures 44*(4), 1–14.
Reynolds, D. S. (1995). *Walt Whitman's America: A cultural biography*. Alfred A. Knopf.
Robertson, M. (2010). *Worshipping Walt: The Whitman disciples*. Princeton University Press.
Rorty, A. (1997). The ethics of reading. *Educational Theory 47*(1), 85–89.
Rosello, M., with Pritchard, A. (1995). *Aimé Césaire. Notebook of a return to my native land*. Bloodaxe Books.
Santí, E. M. (2005). This land of prophets: Walt Whitman in Latin America. In *Ciphers of history: Latin American readings for a cultural age* (pp. 66–83). Palgrave Macmillan.
Schama, S. (1996). Flaubert in the trenches [review of Sebastian Faulks, *Birdsong*]. *The New Yorker 72*(6), 97–98.
Scharfman, Ronnie L. (1987). *Engagement and the language of the subject in the poetry of Aimé Césaire*. University of Florida Press.
Scharfman, Ronnie L. (2010). Aimé Césaire: Poetry is/and knowledge. *Research in African Literatures 41*(1), 109–120.
Schjeldahl, P. (2005). In the mood. *The New Yorker 81*(39), 98–101.
Schwartz, L. S. (Ed.). (2007). *The emergence of memory: Conversations with W. G. Sebald*. Seven Stories Press.
Schweizer, H. (2021). *On Lingering and Literature*. Routledge.
Scott, C., & Warr, N. (Eds.). (2023). *Shadows of reality: A catalogue of W. G. Sebald's photographic materials*. MIT Press.
Sebald, W. G. (1996). *The emigrants*. New Directions.

Sebald, W. G. (1998). *The rings of saturn*. New Directions.
Sebald, W. G. (2000). *Vertigo*. New Directions.
Sebald, W. G. (2001). *Austerlitz*. Modern Library.
Sebald, W. G. (2005). *Campo santo*, trans. A. Bell. Modern Library.
Sebald, W. G. (2013). *A place in the country*, trans. J. Catling. Random House.
Sebald, W. G., & Tripp, J. P. (2004). *Unrecounted: Poems by W. G. Sebald, lithographs by Jan Peter Tripp*, trans. M. Hamburger. New Directions.
Shils, E. (1965). Charisma, order, and status. *American Sociological Review 30*(2), 199–213.
Silverblatt, M. (2001). Radio interview with Sebald, KCRW Bookworm, December 6.
Simmons, R. J. (1973). The poetic language of Aimé Césaire. [Unpublished dissertation, Harvard University].
Simon, R. I. (2005). *The touch of the past: Remembrance, learning, and ethics*. Palgrave Macmillan.
Slate, N. (2012). *Colored cosmopolitanism: The shared struggle for freedom in the United States and India*. Harvard University Press.
Smith, L. V. (2007). *The embattled self: French soldiers' testimony of the Great War*. Cornell University Press.
Snider, B. (2016). The average human. *Threepenny Review* 145 (Spring), 20.
Snyder, E. (1970). A reading of Aimé Césaire's 'Return to my native land.' *L'Esprit Créateur 10*(3), 197–212.
Sontag, S. (2000). A mind in mourning. *Times Literary Supplement*, 25 February.
Sontag, S. (2003). *Regarding the pain of others*. Picador.
Sor Juana Inés de la Cruz. (2016). *Sor Juana Inés de la Cruz: Selected works*, ed. A. More, trans. E. Grossman. W. W. Norton.
Spivak, G. C. (1990). *The postcolonial critic: Interviews, strategies, dialogues*, ed. S. Harasym. Routledge.
Strand, M. (1990). Keeping things whole. *Selected Poems*. Penguin Random House.
Sullivan, R. (2023). Bearing witness to the personal core of teaching. [Doctoral Dissertation, Columbia University].
Summers-Bremner, E. (2004). Reading, walking, mourning: W. G. Sebald's peripatetic fictions. *Journal of Narrative Theory 34*(3), 304–334.
Todd, S. (2023). *The touch of the present: Educational encounters, aesthetics, and the politics of the senses*. State University of New York Press.
Trachtenberg, A. (2000). Loving, Jerome. *Walt Whitman: The song of himself* [book review]. *Walt Whitman Quarterly Review 17*(3), 124–128.
Van der Heiden, G-J. (2022). Witnessing and testimony in hermeneutic phenomenology. *Research in Phenomenology 52*, 311–332.
Wachtel, E. (2007). Ghost hunter. In L. S. Schwartz (Ed.). *The Emergence of Memory: Conversations with W. G. Sebald* (pp. 37–61). Seven Stories Press.
Waskow, H. J. (1966). *Walt Whitman: Explorations in Form*. University of Chicago Press.

Weil, S. (1983). The Iliad or the poem of force. In *Revisions: Changing perspectives in moral philosophy*, ed. S. Hauerwas and A. MacIntyre. University of Notre Dame Press. (Original work composed 1939).

Whitman, W. (1986). *Leaves of grass: The first (1855) edition*. Penguin.

Whitman, W. (2004). *Memoranda during the war*. Oxford University Press.

Wieviorka, A. (2006). *The era of the witness*, trans. J. Stark. Cornell University Press.

Wilder, G. (2015). *Freedom time: Negritude, decolonization, and the future of the world*. Duke University Press.

Wilder, G. (2016). Here/hear now Aimé Césaire! *South Atlantic Quarterly 115*(3), 585–604.

Wilson, I. G. (Ed.). (2014). *Whitman noir: Black America and the good gray poet*. University of Iowa Press.

Wittgenstein, L. (1953). *Philosophical investigations*, trans. G. E. M. Anscombe. Macmillan.

Wittgenstein, L. (1993). *Remarks on Frazer's Golden bough*, ed. R. Rhees, trans. A. C. Miles, rev. R. Rhees. Brynmill Press.

Wolff, L. L. (2014). *W. G. Sebald's hybrid poetics: Literature as historiography*. De Gruyter.

Zerba, M. (2021). *Modern odysseys: Cavafy, Woolf, Cesaire and a poetics of indirection*. Ohio State University Press.

Zweig, P. (1984). *Walt Whitman: The making of the poet*. Basic Books.

# Name Index

Agamben, Giorgio, 184n7
Alcott, Louisa May, 199n22, 200n27, 201n30
Alexievich, Svetlana, 1, 9, 171
Allen, Gay Wilson, 111
Améry, Jean, 4, 35
Anderson, Mark, 40, 56
Angier, Carole, 186n3
Arnold, A. James, 75, 188n1

Baldwin, James, 171 172, 179
Barber, Benjamin, 170
Baudelaire, Charles, 92, 98
Berger, John, 9, 75, 76
Bernhard, Thomas, 38
Boler, Megan, 176
Borges, Juan Luis, 162–163
Buinicki, Martin, 197n14

Cease, Barbara, 93
Celan, Paul, 21
Césaire, Aimé: alienated by homeland, 79–85; critique of reason, 105–107; deep knowledge of French poetry, 190n9, 194n28; demiurge, as poet, 76; experiences second light/second sight, 93–94, 95–96, 108; as first- and second-order witness, 3, 5; humanist-cosmopolitan outlook, 97, 99, 102–103, 109; on an inner and outer odyssey, 16; and love, 104–105; as martyr, 100; on a pilgrimage, 74; as prodigal son, 76, 93; relation with French language, 106, 108, 193n27, 194n28; roles in life, 5; sojourn in Paris in 1930s, xiii, 73, 80; standing upright, 101; summoned to bear witness, 6–7, 15–16, 25, 108; surrealist style, 78–79, 107, 108; turning the soul, 85 94; writes plays, 75. *See also* bearing witness; witness
Chateaubriand, Vicomte de, 41–42, 65
Chinnery, Ann, 168
Conrad, Joseph, 65
Cooper, Anna Julia, 170
Cullen, Countee, 94

Damas, Léon, 80
Davis, F. Gregson, 75, 76, 77, 93
Descartes, René, 64
Dewey, John, 12–13, 14, 126
Douglass, Frederick, 4, 122
Du Bois, W. E. B., 116–117
Dustin, Christopher, 14
Dutro, Elizabeth, 173

Eliot, George (*née* Maryann Evans), 93
Eshleman, Clayton, 75

# 216 | Name Index

Felman, Shoshana, 29, 175, 183n2
Flaubert, Gustave, 60–61, 108
Folsom, Ed, 111

Garloff, Katja, 28
Givoni, Michal, 173
Goethe, Wolfgang von, 63, 178
Goffman, Erving, 60

Hallender, Marie, 184n7
Hamburger, Michael, 36, 189n7
Hartman, Saidiya, 189n6
Harvey, Robert, 170
Hatley, James, 169
Hillesum, Etty, 1–2, 8, 34, 77, 121–122, 151, 164, 171
Hughes, Langston, 73, 195n5

Irele, F. Abiola, 78, 188n1

Jacobs, Carol, 56–57
Jacobson, Dan, 61
Jonas, Mark, 176
Josselson, Ruthellen, 166–167

Kerdeman, Deborah, 2
Klee, Paul, vi, 40, 154

Laub, Dori, 29, 175, 183n2, 202n4
Lewis, C. S., 161
Librett, Jeffrey, 20
Lipking, Lawrence, 25, 114
Lincoln, Abraham, xix
L'Ouverture, Toussaint, 87, 190n15

Malick, Terrence, 15–16
Marchand, André, 14
Margalit, Avishai, 183n4, 187n13
Marx, Karl, 172
Medina, José, 168–169
Miller, Matt, 25, 28
Mintz, Avi, 176

Mohr, Jean, 9
Montaigne, Michel de, 75, 110, 184n5, 196n8

Nardal, Paulette, 80
Noland, Carrie, 101

Oakeshott, Michael, 104

Paton, Alan, 41
Pestalozzi, Johan, 70
Peters, John Durham, 29
Pippin, Robert, 16
Plato, 10, 62, 76, 85, 117, 118, 170, 191n19

Reilly, Brian J., 87
Rembrandt van Rijn, 64, 93, 106
Richter, Gerhard, 71
Rilke, Rainer Maria, 1, 8, 50, 122, 153–154, 156, 161–162, 177

Schama, Simon, 69
Scharfman, Ronnie, 28, 77, 79
Schjeldahl, Peter, 71
Sebald, W. G.: caption-less photographs, 53–59; criticism of, 186n3; difficulty of bearing witness, 39, 41, 45–46, 60–62, 105; writes "essayistic semi-fiction," 36; as first- and second-order witness, 3, 5, 28–29; as moral pilgrim, 16, 36, 38, 64–65, 66; physical collapse as witness, 42, 197n13; quest for truth, 53, 59; roles in life, 5, 37; and remembrance, 60; summoned to bear witness, 6, 15–16, 24–25, 49–50; unclassifiable writer, 35, 36, 59–60. *See also* bearing witness; witness; wrongful trespass
Senghor, Léopold Sédar, 80, 191n17, 191n18

Shakespeare, William, 90, 111
Shils, Edward, 53
Simon, Roger, 36, 173, 175, 183n1
Simmons, Ruth, 82
Snider, Bruce, 154–155, 178
Socrates, 117, 124, 125, 165–166
Sontag, Susan, 49
Sor Juana Inés de la Cruz, 184n8
Strand, Mark, 156
Sullivan, Rebecca, xviii

Terence, 99, 110
Toussaint L'Ouverture, 87, 190n15
Trachtenberg, Alan, 25
Tripp, Jan Peter, 66

Van der Heiden, Gert-Jan, 166–167

Walser, Robert, 47
Whitman, Walt: like a new Adam naming things, 118, 127; against atomistic view of the world, 131; as cosmopolitan, 131; and democracy, 31, 113, 122, 125–130, 149–151; as first- and second-order witness, 3, 5, 28; and imagination, 121–123; radically inclusive, 127–128, 129, 130; interactions with ill and wounded soldiers, 136–148; on a "journey," 119, 120, 124, 130; and love, 131–132, 151; and moral perception, 130–131; on moral unity of humanity, 113, 116; poet as singer/ poetry as song, 115–118, 121, 132, 150; poetry as unclassifiable, 114; questions about being an American, xiv, 113; roles in life, 5, 112; self-cultivation and self-examination, 112, 140; sense of wonder, 126, 129, 131; on sexuality, 111, 200n26; versus skepticism, 125–126; spiritual exhaustion from bearing witness, 135–136, 142–143, 197n13, 198n21; summoned to bear witness, 7–8, 15–16, 127, 143; as wanderer, 16, 195n7. *See also* bearing witness; witness
Wittgenstein, Ludwig, 38, 46, 50, 51, 57–58, 64, 66, 69, 70
Wolff, Lynn, 29
Wordsworth, William, 122

Ziegler, Joanna, 14
Zweig, Paul, 20

# Subject Index

"The Albatross" (Baudelaire), 92, 98
*Anatomy Lesson* (Rembrandt), 64, 106
*Angelus Novus* (Klee), 40–41
*Austerlitz* (Sebald), 37, 38–39, 40, 50, 52–53, 65–66

bearing witness: analogy with a walker in a forest, 14–15; association with "lingering," "loitering," and "idleness," 15–16, 20, 184n5; as attesting to beauty, 8–9; Biblical root, 4; and children, 202n6; as demanding, 3, 39, 68–69, 105, 197n13, 198n21; difficulty of writing it, 5, 17, 20, 45–46, 60–62, 161; not an "identity," 24–27; as a moral orientation, 10–11, 158–159; motivated by wonder and concern, 30, 160; necessity of ethical self-cultivation, 9–11, 31–32, 98, 159–160; necessity of waiting and patience, 13–16; as an "orientation" rather than "method," 10, 158–159, 169; origins of framework in the book, xx, 27–28, 183n3; as personal summons, xiii, 6–9, 12, 16, 19, 21, 34, 148, 170; and proximity, 11; and re-inhabiting the world, 33, 160; and solidarity, 168; undertaken from a standpoint of the self-in-transition rather than of autobiography, 13, 22, 23–27; teaching of, 164–165, 174–177; temporal aspects of, 19–20, 135; and war, 134. *See also* Aimé Césaire; ethics; historical consciousness; remembrance; W. G. Sebald; trust; Walt Whitman; witness
*Bildungsroman*, 78, 188n20
"Black Orpheus" (Sartrc), 191n17

*Campo Santo* (Sebald), 186n6
Civil War (American), xix, 7–8, 133, 135, 146–147

*De l'égalité des races humaines* (On the Equality of Human Races, Firmin), as contrast with *Essai sur l'inégalité des races humaines* (Essay on the Inequality of Human Races, Gobineau), 99
Democracy: xix, 113, 116, 122, 125, 129; democratic faith, ix, 113; democratic person, 31, 113, 149–150, 194n1
Doctors Without Borders, 173–174

education: 35; as self-formation, 31–32, 159–160; as developing

220 | Subject Index

education *(continued)*
historical consciousness, 32, 154–156; as cultivating remembrance, 32–33, 148–151, 154–157; vs. "presentism," 156; as (re)inhabiting the world, 33, 160
*The Emigrants* (Sebald), 37, 42, 50, 60, 124. *See also* W. G. Sebald
ethics: fused with the aesthetic, moral, and intellectual, 9–11; and feeling, 10; as a mode of heeding, 2; and responsibility, xix, 166, 177; as self-cultivation, 9–10, 11, 135. *See also* truth

*A Fortunate Man: The Story of a Country Doctor* (Berger and Mohr), 9

*Hamlet* (Shakespeare), 90
heed, 2, 11, 156–157, 159, 179
hermeneutics of suspicion and of trust, 167
historical consciousness, 32, 154–156, 168
Holocaust (and Shoah), xix, 20, 35, 39–40
"*Homo sum; humani nil a me alienum puto* (I am a human being, therefore nothing that is human is foreign to me, Terence), 99

*I Am Not Your Negro* (film, Peck), 171
"immediate quality" of "primary experience" (Dewey), 14
instrumental thinking, problem of: xi–xii, 169
"intelligent sympathy" (Dewey), 12–13

*Journal of a Homecoming* (*Cahier d'un retour au pays natal*, Césaire):
as nature poem, 192n24; related to other poetic epics, 76, 188n1, 188n4; structure of, 74–79; textual history of, 188n2, 189n5; translations of, 75–76. *See also* Aimé Césaire

*Leaves of Grass* (Whitman), 25, 111, 112. *See also* Walt Whitman
Litzmannstadt ghetto (Poland), 66–67
martyr (root of witness), 4, 83, 99

*Melancholia* (Dürer), 62
*Memoranda During the War* (Whitman): 8, 31, 112, 133–148; meaning of title, 133. *See also* Walt Whitman

Naming, ethics of: 44, 46–51, 162, 187n; witness as a new Adam, 118, 162
negritude, 74, 87–88, 92, 96, 100–104, 107. *See also* Aimé Césaire
Nuremberg Laws of 1935, 43, 44, 45

*Patience des signes* (Patience of signs, Césaire), 79
"perspicuous representation" (Wittgenstein), 57
*Phaedo* (Plato), 117
"Preface to Lyrical Ballads" (Wordsworth), 122
"pulled up short" (Kerdeman), 2

"quiet testimony" (Goldberg), 8

*Remarks on Frazer's* Golden Bough (Wittgenstein), 69
remembrance, 32–33, 133–134, 148–151, 154–157, 162–164, 168, 177–178
*Republic* (Plato), 118, 165–166

*Rings of Saturn* (Sebald), 37–38, 57, 60, 65. *See also* W. G. Sebald
Roche limit, 63
Rose of Jericho, 63

"shaped entities of language" (Zweig), 20
*Song of Myself* (Whitman): 25, 28, 31, 112, 113, 124, 128, 133, 140; textual aspects, 114–115, 195n3. *See also* Walt Whitman
*The Souls of Black Folk* (Du Bois), 116–117
Surrealism, 107, 108, 189n8

teachers, xvii–xviii, 70–71
teaching, 13, 70
*The Thin Red Line* (Malick), 15–16
*Too Late the Phalarope* (Paton), 41
"touch of the past" (Simon), 36
*Tractatus* (Wittgenstein), 46
trust: in the summons rather than in oneself as witness, 27; and trustworthiness of the witness, 18–19, 23, 30, 165–167
truth, xiv, 11–13, 52
"turbulent puzzles of experience" (Zweig), 20

war: its barbarism, 9; learning about as child, xv–xvi
"What is Africa to me?" (Cullen), 94
witness: as a "contemporary," 32; different from a journalist or historian, 11–12, 16–17, 19; pair with historians' work, 23, 33, 166, 167–169; as educator, xiv, 3, 31–34, 164–167; first-order, 2–3, 4–5, 20; closer to a novelist or poet, 17–18; and representation, 20–21, 44; second-order, 3, 20, 159–160, 167; problem of self-doubt, 21–22; third-order, 29–30; vulnerability of, 21–22. *See also* bearing witness
witness, reading a: challenging to read, xv, 27, 29; how to read: xiv–xv, 29–30; a philosophical and poetical approach, xiv, 30; relationship with recipient, 22–23
"witness as obligation" and "witness as study" (Simon), 173
"The Witness" (*El Testigo*, Borges), 162–163
"wrongful trespass" (Sebald): xiii, 21, 36, 53, 54, 67, 68–69; vs. "rightful trespass," 36, 40, 45, 60

www.ingramcontent.com/pod-product-compliance
Lightning Source LLC
Chambersburg PA
CBHW021839220426
43663CB00005B/321